# The Public Intellectual

# The Public Intellectual

Edited by Helen Small

**Blackwell**
Publishing

Copyright © 2002 by Blackwell Publishers Ltd
a Blackwell Publishing company

Editorial matter copyright © Helen Small 2002
All chapters copyright © 2002 their named authors.

Editorial Offices:
108 Cowley Road, Oxford OX4 1JF, UK
 Tel: +44 (0)1865 791100
350 Main Street, Malden, MA 02148-5018, USA
 Tel: +1 781 388 8250

First published 2002 by Blackwell Publishers Ltd

Library of Congress Cataloging-in-Publication Data has been applied for.

ISBN 0-631-23197-8 (hbk); ISBN 0-631-23198-6 (pbk)

A catalogue record for this title is available from the British Library

Set in 10 on 12.5 pt Meridien
by SNP Best-set Typesetter Ltd., Hong Kong
Printed and bound in Great Britain by MPG Books Ltd, Bodmin, Cornwall

For further information on Blackwell Publishers, visit our website:
www.blackwellpublishers.com

# Contents

# Contents

# Contributors

**Stefan Collini** is Professor of Intellectual History and English Literature in the Faculty of English at Cambridge University. He has held visiting posts in Canberra, Caracas, Paris, and Princeton, and is a Fellow of the British Academy. His books include *Public Moralists: Political Thought and Intellectual Life in Britain 1850–1930* (1991) and *English Pasts: Essays in History and Culture* (1999); he is currently writing a book about the question of intellectuals in twentieth-century Britain.

**Rita Copeland** is Professor in Comparative Literature and Classical Studies at the University of Pennsylvania. Her most recent book is *Pedagogy, Intellectuals, and Dissent in the Later Middle Ages* (2001). She is currently working on the intersection between the history of rhetoric and the history of the premodern intellectual.

**Margreta de Grazia** is Clara M. Clendenen Term Professor in English at the University of Pennsylvania. She is the author of *Shakespeare Verbatim* (1991) and co-editor (with Maureen Quilligan and Peter Stallybrass) of *Subject and Object in Renaissance Culture* (1996), and (with Stanley Wells) *The Cambridge Companion to Shakespeare* (2001). She is presently completing a book entitled *Hamlet's Delay*.

**Jeremy Jennings** is Professor of Political Theory at the University of Birmingham. He has written extensively on the history of political thought and is editor of *Intellectuals in Politics: From the Dreyfus Affair to Salman Rushdie* (1997).

**Linda S. Kauffman** is Professor of English at the University of Maryland. She is the author of three books: *Bad Girls and Sick Boys: Fantasies in Contemporary Art and Culture* (1998), *Special Delivery: Epistolary Modes in Modern Fiction* (1992), and *Discourses of Desire: Gender, Genre,* *and Epistolary Fictions* (1986). She has edited three collections of essays on feminist theory, including *American Feminist Thought at Century's End* (1993), and has published numerous articles on contemporary fiction, film, and performance art.

**Bruce Robbins** is currently Visiting Professor in the English Department at Columbia University. His latest book is *Feeling Global: Internationalism in Distress* (1999).

**Jacqueline Rose** teaches literature at Queen Mary College, University of London. Her publications include *The Haunting of Sylvia Plath* (1991), *States of Fantasy* (1996, the 1994 Oxford Clarendon lectures), and *Albertine*, a novel.

**Edward W. Said** is University Professor of English and Comparative Literature at Columbia University. He is the author of more than 20 books including *Orientalism* (1978), *Culture and Imperialism* (1993), *Out of Place: A Memoir* (1999), and *The End of the Peace Process: Oslo and After* (2000). His most recent publications include *Reflections on Exile and Other Essays* (2001), and *Power, Politics and Culture* (2001).

**Helen Small** is Lecturer in English Literature at the University of Oxford and a Fellow of Pembroke College, Oxford. Her publications include *Love's Madness: Medicine, the Novel, and Female Insanity, 1800–1865*, and (co-edited with James Raven and Naomi Tadmor) *The Practice and Representation of Reading in England*. She is currently the holder of a Leverhulme Major Research Fellowship (2001–4), and is a Visiting Scholar at New York University, where she is writing a book on old age.

**David Wallace** is Judith Rodin Professor and Chair of English, University of Pennsylvania. His most recent book is *Chaucerian Polity* (1997) and he has edited *The Cambridge History of Medieval English Literature* (1999). He is currently completing a new book, entitled *Premodern Places*.

# Acknowledgments

I would like to acknowledge the financial support of the Oxford University Faculty of English and the News International Fund in bringing together the participants in this volume for a conference on "The Public Role of Writers and Intellectuals," held at St Catherine's College, Oxford, in September 2000.

I am also grateful to Andrew McNeillie, an exemplary editor, and to Lucy Newlyn, Tom Paulin, Isabel Rivers, and Paul Strohm, without whom neither the conference nor the book could have happened.

Helen Small

# Introduction

## Helen Small

The word "Clercs," which occurs throughout the book, is defined by M. Benda as "all those who speak to the world in a transcendental manner." I do not know the English for "all those who speak to the world in a transcendental manner." (Translator's note to Julien Benda, *The Treason of the Intellectuals* [1928])[1]

The terms "public intellectual" is a fairly recent addition to the vocabulary of cultural debate. It is a not unproblematic one, as both Edward Said and Stefan Collini point out in their essays for this volume: close to, if not quite, a pleonasm. (What kind of intellectual would not merit the adjective "public" – even if only by dint of being published, or of speaking to others?) Having first gained currency in the United States a little over a decade ago, the phrase caught on in Britain comparatively slowly and has only really entered common usage within the last two or three years. It has signally failed to make an equivalent impression to date on the French and other European participants in what is, in most respects, an increasingly transnational conversation. It reflects, in other words, a new and predominantly American anxiety about the viability of what is still sometimes called "the profession of thought" – a concern that, in a society often thought of as peculiarly hostile to the intellectual life, most of those who might be expected to take responsibility for its cultivation seem, in the late twentieth century, to have withdrawn altogether from the public arena. As Joyce Carol Oates puts it, in a recent interview on the subject, "The term 'intellectual' is a very self-conscious one in the United States. To speak of oneself as an 'intellectual' is equivalent to arrogance and egotism, for it suggests that there is a category of persons who are 'not-intellectual'."[2] To speak of the "*public* intellectual," then, would appear

1

to be a defensive manifestation of that self-consciousness: a deliberate decision to assert, in the face of perceived opposition, not just the continuing serviceability of the word "intellectual," but to protest (too much?) that those to whom it is applicable, including perhaps oneself, have a role to play in public life.

But if the term "public intellectual" is the product of a specifically American cultural and historical context, the concerns it formalizes are in no way confined to the United States. Among the numerous clichés which have taken hold in writing about intellectuals in the West during the past several decades, two seem more persistent than any other: that public intellectuals are in serious decline, if not absolutely extinct, and (as contentiously) that we are at a point in history where the need for their re-emergence is particularly acute. The level of alarm differs, of course, as does the sense of what, if anything, needs to be done, but there is some agreement that an explanation is to be found in a series of structural changes across the course of the twentieth century which have fundamentally affected the ways in which we conceive of the public domain and the kinds of influence that the public intellectual can therefore wield. The increased power of the media and development of new information technologies; the expansion of higher education; greater state regulation of the universities and, simultaneously, their penetration by commercial and corporate interests; a widening gap between the fragmented and complexly interrelated nature of the public realms we inhabit and the simplified ways in which "being a public" still tends to be thought of[3] – all these appear to have contributed to a diminution in the perceived legitimacy and felt responsibility of those few writers and academics still willing to define themselves as intellectuals.

They have also led to more evident tensions between the terms "intellectual," "writer," and, especially, "academic." A much higher proportion of the individuals who attract the label "intellectuals" now are tenured academics rather than the freelance writers or journalists who were prominent a generation or so back (though the shift is nowhere near as pronounced as some writing on the subject would lead one to believe). Given the changes outlined above, many have doubted whether the academic can plausibly be an intellectual, especially when the institution providing him or her with financial support seeks in some measure to define the kinds of work undertaken.

Michael Ignatieff's 1997 lament for an older, better, public life of the mind can stand as representative of one familiar strain of response. For Ignatieff, the prestige of an earlier generation of writers (he instances Sartre, Beauvoir, Camus, and, in the British context, Priestley, Berlin, Ayer, Gombrich) "depended on habits of deference which have rightly had their day. . . . But however deferential it might have been, it was a *public* culture." What we have lost is not merely intelligence disinterestedly and visibly at work within public life (and therefore a good in itself), but a more active custodianship of our cultural values:

> The information revolution has made the intellectual's translation function more important than ever. [. . .] We know too much, understand too little, and when we turn to the humanities and social sciences for help, what do we get? The tenured radicals who went into academe after 1968 were supposed to free the university from the conformist functionalism of American social science. Instead, they set to work erecting new stockades of conformism: neo-Marxist scholasticism, deconstruction, critical theory – the language games people play when they have given up on contributing to public debate.[4]

Among the several points of incoherence which emerge in the course of this jeremiad, and others of its genre,[5] is a high degree of uncertainty about where exactly today's defaulting intellectuals have gone wrong in their interaction with the public sphere. Ignatieff's most serious accusation is that the humanities and social sciences have reneged on their responsibilities toward "liberal and social democracy," epitomized for him in the post-war Britain of the Reithian BBC, the Third Programme, and (to augment the list) Penguin Books. "Ashamed of their élitism," the "tenured radicals" are cowards in the face of "a populist loathing of high culture itself." But it is far from clear whether this "sullen populism which holds most forms of genuine intellectual expertise and authority in contempt" is a consequence of the failure of the intellectuals, as the apparent retributiveness of "sullen" would imply, or a persistent trait of the masses, against which intellectuals have always had to struggle: "From Zola's 'J'accuse' to Havel's 'Letter of Husak,' intellectuals used the power of the word to fight intimidation and prejudice." In Ignatieff's characterization of populism it is difficult not to suspect nostalgia for deference; in his characterization of true intellectuals, it is difficult not to suspect a more dubious nostalgia for the glory of persecution ("Now Havel's voice is fading, and with it the myth he embodied risks being forgotten.").[6]

One of the much remarked oddities of such declinist narratives is that they are as readily the reflex of those on the political left as those on the political right (or, indeed, pretty much any position in between). So, Ignatieff's defense of liberalism produces an almost exact replica of Pierre Bourdieu's *attack* on a "neo-liberal consensus" among French intellectuals only too happy to play up to the media and subordinate their critical function to "the demand of economic and political powers."[7] Moreover Ignatieff, for all his identification with the liberal tradition of Isaiah Berlin, is ready enough to endorse the title of Roger Kimball's paranoically conservative *Tenured Radicals* (1990), which claimed to uncover an organized conspiracy of left-wing university professors attempting to defraud the American public of its cultural inheritance. This concertinaing of the politics of intellectual debate has most often been observed in the American context, where it was particularly highlighted by the almost simultaneous publication in 1987 of Russell Jacoby's leftish dirge *The Last Intellectuals: American Culture in the Age of Academe* and its conservative twin, Allan Bloom's *The Closing of the American Mind*.[8] Whether the critic in question takes his or her critical bearings from Antonio Gramsci and Michel Foucault,[9] or from Leo Strauss and T.S. Eliot, the narrative tends to run along uncannily similar lines: intellectual life has become increasingly specialized and academized since the post-war expansion of higher education, and individual intellectuals now derive what compromised authority remains to them from the deployment of a specific or merely technical expertise in place of any general moral authority to speak on matters of cultural and social moment.

In keeping with the political sympathies and interests represented in this volume, this introduction focuses primarily on the ways in which certain strands of American writing about the public intellectual in recent years have encouraged (rightly in my view) a rethinking of the nature of professionalism, redefining the intellectual and the public sphere so as to allow for responsiveness to new, as well as older, forms of culture and for the intellectual as an active, rather than remotely adjudicatory, presence in political and cultural life. A particular emphasis will therefore emerge in what follows on how "action" itself might have to be reconceived in its relation to thought. This involves playing down – indeed resisting – another version of what might be called the public intellectual: those who influence public policy more directly by acting as advisers to governments and members of think tanks, government commissions, and policy committees. The introduction will also have relatively little to say about new information technologies and new forms of media, primarily because it is as yet far from clear what their effect has been on the role of the intellectual. "New media" such as the Net, electronic news, and e-mail have dramatically increased the speed with which information can be dispersed, and the quantity of information available to users, but they have not supplanted older modes of communication (official reports, government papers, radio, television, speeches). The choice offered by much recent writing on politics and technological change, between an entirely dispersed public (whether good or bad in its implications) and utopian new publics coming together irrespective of nationality and ethnicity, is surely a false one.[10] It is more plausible (to take a lead from post-modernist writing about social spaces) that technologies such as the Web and e-mail increasingly permit people to move in and out of different "knowledge situations" in which they have widely varying degrees of expertise and influence. In short, they may operate as public intellectuals in some public contexts, while in others they will have no claim to intellectual authority at all. New technologies have not been the cause of this multiplying of roles and spaces, but they have served to make it much more evident.

It is certainly the case, as Edward Said points out, that new media require those who accept the title of public intellectual to be more than ever resourceful in their selection of different locations for speech and writing. But it is also the case (particularly with the Web) that the choice of forum is less than ever entirely theirs, since an article or speech given in one context will be quickly filleted and networked into any number of sites. And, as with the continuing presence of those who, even as they bemoan the loss of the public intellectuals of the past, seem to others amply to fulfill that role, there is no straightforward narrative to be found here of new modes of address taking over from and ousting old ones, new heterogenous versions of audiences taking over from the old concept of the public sphere. Looked at from one angle, the question of the definition and viability or otherwise of the public intellectual is one way of examining the nature and consequences of social change much more broadly.

*　　*　　*

For those who take seriously the diagnosis that public life in Western democracies is no longer of a kind that permits claims to general intellectual authority, declinism, of whatever political coloring, is too plainly a posture rather than an answer. Much of the writing which came out of France on this subject in the 1990s, and which found a prominent venue in *Le Monde*, has taken the view that resistance is possible so long as one looks not to other people or to external social structures for authentication, but within, to one's own sense of a fundamental ethical obligation entailed in thinking and writing. The danger, of course, is that writing in this vein quickly generates a new set of pieties, not so different from the old ones, about the duties one exercises when one no longer possesses powers or rights. As Zygmunt Bauman puts it (summarizing Lyotard), the "duty" of intellectuals to make themselves heard now becomes "a duty without authority": "in our post-legitimation era whatever we do cannot count on the comfort of supra-human truth which would release us from the responsibility for doing what we do and convince us and everyone else that we have the right to do it and that what we do is right."[11] Here a more discreet form of declinism, but declinism nonetheless, gets incorporated into a heroic individualist narrative which is, at base, remarkably little different from the stance taken by Julien Benda in *La Trahison des clercs*, his classic protest against the decline of the priestly intellectual in 1920s Europe (or, for that matter, from the implicit self-representation of Ignatieff). In the process, any force the word "public" might possess effectively disappears. The only notion of community allowed for is the purely notional community of writers and readers willing to be persuaded by such a concept of duty – though, to discriminate between Lyotard and Bauman, that community is more readily discernible in Bauman's emphasis on the possibilities for thought facing "the intellectuals" (plural, out there somewhere) than in Lyotard's references to "the writer" (singular) struggling to recognize what it is that "the Other demands."[12]

For anyone seeking a definition of intellectual labor as more than a private "taking of thought" about one's relations to the world, this is plainly not enough. One of the most persistent anxiety reflexes that Stefan Collini identifies, in his analysis of the literature on intellectuals, is a desire for intellectuals to be somehow clearer and more effective than (putative) non-intellectuals in their translation of thought into politically effective action – even as a counterwish is expressed for them to remain somehow untainted by politics and economics. That conflict of impulses lies at the heart of most, if not all, of the ambivalences and confusions that writing about intellectuals seems peculiarly prone to generate. Writers about intellectuals typically expect more from their subjects than from themselves, and expect it specifically in the gray zone (whose grayness is resented) where thought either does or doesn't issue into deeds. To urge that the intellectual go forth and act is, implicitly or explicitly, to want to espouse a notion of action informed and justified by thought (or the intellectual would degenerate into a mere politician or pundit). To urge, on the other hand, that the intellectual remain aloof from action, is to recognize, or perhaps to fear, that thought cannot possibly maintain its purity, its moral credibility, or – less romantically – a sufficient complexity when it "descends" to the marketplace or the television studio.

Pressure has come from several quarters in recent years to move the terms of debate on past the modes of elegy and vituperation (from the outside), melancholy renunciation or equally melancholy heroism (from the inside), and toward a definition of the intellectual which includes the possibility of meaningful action. One of the more helpful forms it has taken involves resisting the assumption that affiliation of intellectuals to universities necessitates a diminution of their claim to *be* intellectuals or to remain politically credible. Significantly, that impulse has come from within the American academy, where writers on intellectual and cultural life (particularly those on the political left) have been conscious of a higher degree of separation from their national public life than academics in other countries, and have had to find their audience in a transnational rather than a transoccupational community. Bruce Robbins's Introduction to the 1990 collection of essays, *Intellectuals: Aesthetics, Politics, Academics*, anticipated the fuller statement of his defense of the academic profession (as opposed to its administration), in *Secular Vocations* (1993):

> the conceptual relocation of intellectuals *within* rather than outside occupations, which is an essential step in their grounding, is also an ethical demand to achieve vocationally "contented lives" without sacrificing political consistency. . . . If the intellectual is a figure of the political imagination, a character who cannot be separated from the various political narratives in which he or she appears, grounded in the emergences and declines of successive oppositional forces and institutions, then we must not call for a return of intellectuals to an illusory state of prior autonomy, but must reconsider the political narratives whose peripeteias and dénouements have left the intellectual hanging or unraveling. That is, we must consider the intellectual as a character in search of a narrative.[13]

Any such narrative would involve (as Andrew Ross argues in the same volume) an end to the commonplace post-1968 equation of professionalization with political apostasy, and of an expanded definition of culture with loss of cultural values. It might also involve letting go the characteristic conviction of academics on the political left that the job of the intellectual is always and necessarily to be a voice of opposition:

New intellectuals . . . are likely to belong to different social groups and have loyalties to different social movements. . . . In the face of today's uneven plurality of often conflicting radical interests it is quite possible that they will be leading spokespersons, diffident supporters and reactionaries at one and the same time – that is, legitimists in some areas of political discourse and action, and contesters in others.[14]

This helps, but it still leaves unanswered the question of whether the intellectual has a role to play in defining those groups and movements and interests, or whether those groups and movements and interests take on their own existence, without help or patronage from outside. Much recent writing has been rightly skeptical of an idealization of "the people" implicit in assuming the latter position – as if "[r]eality just happens in factories, asylums, and prison houses; and the expressions that emanate from those sites are not 'about' . . . experiences; they *are* those unmediated meaning-events."[15] But it is not so easy to decide what can or should be done if writers' public interventions are not simply to be confined to the professions and institutions in which they work. For Cornel West what is required is an active redefinition of the publics to whom we speak (as well as redefinition of ourselves) through a "prophetic pragmatism" which owes something to Gramsci's notion of the organic intellectual, but which also moves beyond it. In order to fulfill (what West takes to be) the intellectual's task of trying "to preserve a sense of the whole," he or she must be alert to the multiple constituencies of today's public:

What I actually mean by organic is a much more fluid and constructed notion of participating in the organizations of people. So when I think of my own organic link with the black community, it's not that I am somehow thoroughly immersed in the black community, in some pantheistic way. Rather, I'm simply contesting among ourselves how we can best generate visions, analysis, and forms of political action. I want to say "be organized," rather than "be organic."[16]

This kind of organized, and organizing, intellectual does not just speak to or for these constituencies, but gets involved in struggles between different interests and alliances which will, inevitably, be divisive at times as well as co-operative. He or she turns thought to action, but modestly (or not immodestly) seeks to let both thought and action be responsive to pressure from others.

If other intellectuals have not rushed to embrace these "micropolitical" and "multicontextual" versions of who and what they should be, either in America or elsewhere – and Bernard-Henri Lévy's recent collection of interviews with prominent writers, *What Good Are Intellectuals?* (2001), provides ample evidence that they have not[17] – it may be because thinking in such strategic and dispersed terms makes it difficult to articulate recognizably coherent statements of allegiance and purpose, let alone general propositions of theory.[18] The nature of that contradiction, or at the very least that competition of needs, has been perhaps most fully analyzed and politicized in the course of post-colonial criticism's engagement with Foucault, and with post-structuralism more generally. There, the impulse to reject the possibility of political (and symbolic) representation altogether and to declare the obsolescence of the whole category of "the intellectual" – as Foucault and Gilles Deleuze did in their much cited conversation "Intellectuals and Power"[19] – all too evidently closes the door on those many political movements for whom representation is, or would be, a new, hard-won, historically overdue means to a better life, not the tainted residue of imperial or class or masculinist power.[20]

But, having diagnosed the failure of post-structuralism sufficiently to take account of who is announcing the death of the intellectual (and on whose behalf), post-colonial theory has often found itself struggling for a vocabulary which will give expression to a concept of intellectual commitment that can be more than a merely context-led and hectic shuttling between the specific and the general, the local and the global, the active and the renunciative. "Praxis" is, by tacit consent, too theory-led a term, too static, and associated too closely with forms of Marxism which have, themselves, fallen foul of the "no imperialistic generalizations" rule. But some of the most conceptually promising metaphors for rethinking the public sphere so that intellectuals might more viably engage with it have proved pretty remotely utopian to date, even when selected with the explicit intention that they be more than just prophetic or idealizing.[21]

The importance of multiculturalism as a spur to the redefinition of the intellectual as political agent, or would-be political agent, is – like the term "public intellectual" – a recognizably American emphasis (though one which is becoming stronger in other Western contexts). It has the effect of pressing the terms of the debate in a significantly different direction from the forms it currently takes in France – even as France remains, for many commentators, the natural starting point for any analysis of the public intellectual. France's significance in the history of intellectuals – its exemplarity and, at the same time, its exceptionality – are themselves in need of more skeptical analysis than they generally receive, as both Jeremy Jennings and Stefan Collini argue here. But in so far as French accounts of the decline of the intellectual, and his (almost always "his") potential for re-emergence, are different in tenor and explanatory framework from their American and British counterparts, it may be, as Jennings argues, because French intellectual culture has so far been reluctant to come to terms with the implications of multiculturalism – and even, more fundamentally, to endorse the "reality" of social groupings.

Here, to take a provocative example, is Jean Baudrillard in a 1985 essay announcing the illusory function of the intellectual in a world where "the real" has been entirely absorbed into "its statistical, simulative projection in the media." In such a context,

> . . . the masses are deeply aware that they do not have to make a decision about themselves and the world; that they do not have to wish; that they do not have to know; that they do not have to desire.
>
> The deepest desire is perhaps to give the responsibility for one's desire to someone else. A strategy of ironic investment in the other . . . Clerks are there for that, so are professionals . . . Publicity, information, technics, the whole intellectual and political class are there to tell us what we want, to tell the masses what they want – and basically we thoroughly enjoy this massive transfer of responsibility because perhaps, very simply, it is not easy to know what we want; because perhaps, very simply, it is not very interesting to know what we want to decide, to desire. Who has imposed all this on us, even the need to desire, unless it be the philosophers?[22]

Here the intellectuals play a double role. On the one hand they are merely fictive authorities: psychological projections of the masses who thereby get rid of the burden of choosing what may or may not matter out of the welter of information in the world – a burden the masses know it is not in fact necessary to accept (hence the "ironic" nature of their investment). On the other hand, the intellectuals' authority is more than just a fiction, in so far as they have been historically responsible for exerting upon the masses the pressure to desire. In all this, they are (in a characteristically Baudrillardian twist to more conventionally left-wing narratives) merely part of a much larger system: aligned with the politicians and the bureaucratic functionaries, the media, and the opinion polls, and all the other means by which the public is invited to see itself, illusorily, as a public. In this account of the masses, there is no place for an articulation of social groupings, let alone ethnicities (which get no mention at all) which will not be just as "unreal" as any other version of the public. The only source of power imagined for "the people" is one of attitude, not action: the "radically" silent antagonism of the ironist.[23]

At the other end of the spectrum of debate, and far more influential within France at present, is Pierre Bourdieu's defiant defense of universalism. His concept of "a corporatism of the universal," a collective "*Internationale des intellectuels*," reasserts the political and moral importance of a transnational community of autonomous intellectuals as defenders of universal cognitive, aesthetic, and ethical values in the face of post-modernist "irrationalism" and "nihilism."[24] Unsurprisingly, even his most sympathetic critics have found it difficult to defend this stance against charges of political and cultural high-handedness. As a recent commentator puts it, a little wanly: despite Bourdieu's defense of France's immigrant populations against racism and his "exemplary sensitivity" to issues of sexuality, his universalism "remains in the final instance strangely exclusive," vulnerable to charges that it is, at heart, yet "another example of the 'false universalism of the West'."[25]

If differences in openness to multiculturalism and in the perception of "the people" are in part responsible for current disparities between French and other Western accounts of the intellectual, there is nevertheless an evident desire in both contexts for a language of political and cultural life that can be in some measure holistic or at least coherently generalizing. That desire may, I am suggesting, be one reason for the curious persistence of the old narratives of decline and/or imminent revitalization of the intellectual – and the difficulty for the critic of that literature in getting beyond the merely diagnostic. Another, and simpler, may be that even some of those most articulate about the need for better ways of conceiving of "the public intellectual" at some level prefer the old ones. Talk of the decline of intellectuals or (its rhetorical counterpart) assertions that the time is ripe for a re-emergence of the intellectual, in however compromised or qualified a form, have in common a desire to raise an ideal standard over what we do (or think we once did). Put bluntly, they make us feel good about ourselves. Speaking about intellectuals has, in other words, been a way of posing the perennially troubling question of how much what we say matters.[26] To which the answer will always, inevitably, be "not as much as we might wish" – but perhaps also, in most cases, as much as we ought to wish.

\*     \*     \*

The essays in this volume attempt – of course – to identify, and avoid repeating, the clichés. Taken together, they shift the focus of writing about intellectuals in several ways. The geographical reach of the collection is broad, though by no means inclusive. All its contributors are American or British (or both), though several have other national affiliations as well. Most of their essays are geographically comparative, none more so than Edward Said's opening essay, which returns to the topic of his 1993 Reith lectures in order to consider what the effect of the major political and economic transformations of the last eight years has been on the definition of the writer and intellectual. In his widely comparative analysis, it is now no longer possible, if it ever was, to avoid politicization of the intellectual's work, but it is also more than ever difficult for intellectuals to define their own audiences. The urgent tasks of today's public intellectual are, he argues, to keep the past visible, and to construct fields of political and cultural co-existence as the outcome of intellectual labor. In order to do so, he or she will have to be unprecedentedly resourceful in taking advantage of the range of platforms available for speech, and, perhaps, unprecedentedly alert to the dangers of "depoliticized or aestheticized submission." Taking a cue from Adorno's account of modern music as unassimilable to its social setting, Said's version of the intellectual is, finally, at home only in an equivalently "exilic" mode of art: painfully aware of the impossibility of finding an adequate solution to political and cultural conflicts such as that between Palestine and Israel, but nonetheless committed to the labor of trying.

Perhaps a more striking difference between this volume and most other writing about intellectuals (and one also exemplified by Said's article) is that it elasticates by several centuries the historical time span usually felt to be pertinent to the debate. Rather than taking their bearings from the Dreyfus Affair, the essays by Said, Rita Copeland, David Wallace, and Margreta de Grazia seek to uncover much deeper roots to our ways of thinking about how intellectuals have historically been defined and redefined in public consciousness. Copeland's account of the centrality to that process of intellectual biography, from Hellenistic late antiquity, through the university culture of thirteenth-century Europe, to the heresy trials of fifteenth-century Oxford and Prague, provides an important corrective to any assumption that the "grounding" of intellectuals is a late nineteenth-century phenomenon. Her analysis of the shifting nature of individual intellectuals' relationship to their institutions, and, especially, to the concept of the *techne*, or systematization of education, is also a vital reminder that the terms and effects of that grounding are anything but uniform: in one context the collective "profession of thought" will depend upon (and even promote) the charismatic presence of the individual intellectual, in another it will carefully conceal it. David Wallace's rereading of the history of early modern humanism insists upon an equally potent form of grounding – one which has, he suggests, been all but ignored until now: namely, the commercial and political underpinning of the cultural achievements of Florentine Republican humanism in a system of slavery and despotism. Genoa, he argues pithily, played the historically under-acknowledged role of id to the Florentine ego. His recovery of humanism's commercial and political base is a potent reminder that intellectual history, even now, can be extraordinarily blind to its immersion in not just local but much wider structures of exploitation.

Karl Mannheim's ideal of the *freischwebende Intelligenz* (the free-floating intelligence or, as it is more commonly translated, the free-floating intellectual) as subsequently applied to specific historical and class contexts could not prove anything other than illusory, but to recover forgotten dimensions to the history of the public intellectual is not necessarily to find cause for retrospective chagrin. Margreta de Grazia's essay critically re-examines a version of the intellectual which found its paradigmatic expression in Shakespeare's Hamlet and, scarcely less famously, in Rodin's *Le Penseur*: the man of thought as man of staged inaction. But as de Grazia shows, in Hamlet's case that staging is the product of a Romantic and post-Romantic rereading of Shakespeare which has concealed from us both the activeness of the early modern theaters' Hamlets and – in a nice link with several other essays in this volume – has concealed also a pointedly Republican politics to the prince's antic delays. Once recognized as a theatrical descendent of the two Brutuses of Roman antiquity, Hamlet the king-slayer is not "just" a thinker, but a thinker whose active delays declare a need for a particular and decisive form of political intervention.

Several of the essays in the volume press at the same fundamental question here about how we give public expression to thought, and how we are to understand the not always obvious relation thought bears to action. Jacqueline Rose and Bruce Robbins both focus specifically on the psychological and political dynamics of apathy – perhaps the most commonly diagnosed, and self-diagnosed, failing of the intellectual. For Rose, reading the official report of South Africa's Truth and Reconciliation Committee alongside J.M. Coetzee's novel *Disgrace* (1999), the issue is – pressingly – not just how we measure and, more fundamentally, how we *think* our own and others' accountability for the actions we failed to take and which might have made a difference within a context of historically prolonged injustice, but how we move beyond thinking towards something that might start to resemble justice. Coetzee's novel brings that difficulty home for the white liberal intellectual by placing it in the context of the university, the one institution which escaped the Commission's investigations; but in his account of the psychic circularity of indifference (indifference as its own cause), apathy can be seen to contain, potentially, "the germ of its own undoing."

Bruce Robbins's essay, "The Sweatshop Sublime" also takes as its subject the seeming impossibility of action for the intellectual – here the threat of political paralysis for the individual who confronts at the level of thought the overwhelming scale and complexity of the global division of labor, and his or her own inevitable immersion in it. Robbins argues that a danger of gross self-aggrandisement haunts all discussions of the responsibility of writers and intellectuals, and the more acutely when those responsibilities are imagined, as they now must be, on a global rather than a national scale. His essay seeks to define a proper sense of those responsibilities by exploring an analogy between the Kantian sublime and the anti-sweatshop movement's positioning of its intended reader or target in the international division of labor. Connecting this version of sublimity to Raymond Williams's "Culture and Society" tradition (probably the single most influential paradigm of responsibility for literary critics in the past 50 years), Robbins explores how, with revisions, it might continue to guide our sense of necessary action, within and outside the university.

As Jeremy Jennings points out in his "Comparative Autopsy" of American, British, and French "deaths of the intellectual" over the past several decades, France has, to some degree, remained more willing than either America or Britain to countenance the view that the "universal intellectual" is not in terminal decline. Analyzing the forms taken by declinism in all three national contexts, Jennings identifies the determining influence of four factors in the French context: the relative structural and economic weaknesses of the French university system, which permit French writers still to conceive of themselves as autonomous intellectuals rather than academic professionals; the continued strength of a "radical left," which plays a much more visible role in public debate than it does in Britain and, certainly, the United States; relatedly, a widely held public antipathy towards liberalism and globalization; and – perhaps most importantly – a comparatively strong sense of national identity and a "relatively homogenous republican political culture that eschews multiculturalism."

If public intellectuals are still openly able to defend their existence on the French cultural and political scene, in other contexts their role can only be conceived of as much more indirect and embattled. In Linda S. Kauffman's account of contemporary artists, filmmakers, and novelists, artists earn the title of intellectuals, and deserve our support in the increasingly conservative cultural climate of America especially, because they are the first to describe "what is really happening in our culture, at a moment when we are moving toward a radically different understanding of what 'culture' might be." Warning against a recent increase of censorship in the United States, Kauffman argues that the artist as (unacknowledged) intellectual must, now, read culture "symptomatically," not least because art's function is to remind us of the deep irrationality of psychic life – including (as in Jacqueline Rose's account of apathy) those non-rational dimensions of what intellectuals do or claim to have done.

Stefan Collini's paper is the last in this volume, but should perhaps be read first, as a warning against the temptations not just to what Bruce Robbins calls "self-aggrandisement" but to various equally absurd postures which have attained formulaic status in the recent literature on intellectuals. Taking his title, "Every Fruit-juice Drinker, Nudist, Sandal-wearer . . ." from George Orwell's notorious attack on the more embarrassing adherents of socialism, Collini offers a witty exposé of the cliché-ridden state of current, and historical, writing about intellectuals and intellectualism. There is, he argues, something wrong with a tradition which habitually sets the standard for intellectuals heroically high and, unsurprisingly, finds them impossible to meet in the here and now. Resistance to the clichés, then, is a necessary first step toward accepting that, if the name "intellectual" is to have any value, those who make thinking their profession, and whose thoughts impinge on our various public spheres, must be willing to accept it as their own.

## Notes

1  Julien Benda, *The Treason of the Intellectuals (La trahison des clercs)*, R. Aldington, trans. (New York: W.W. Norton, [1928] 1969).
2  Joyce Carol Oates, in Bernard-Henri Lévy (ed.), *What Good Are Intellectuals?: 44 Writers Share Their Thoughts* (New York: Algora Publishing, 2000), pp. 238–9 (quotation p. 238).

3   For a fuller critical summary of these issues see Peter Osborne (ed.), *A Critical Sense: Interviews with Intellectuals* (London: Routledge, 1996), pp. xviii–xxviii. On the gap between the structures of public life and the representation of public life, see also Cornel West's reflections in the same volume, pp. 134–7.

4   Michael Ignatieff, "The Decline and Fall of the Public Intellectual," *Queen's Quarterly*, 104/3 (1997): 395–403 (extracts pp. 398–9).

5   For a more recent example, see Andrew Anthony, "What Are We Thinking Of?," *The Observer*, 8 July 2001, Review section, pp. 1–2.

6   Ignatieff, "Decline and Fall," pp. 399–400.

7   Pierre Bourdieu, *Free Exchange* (Cambridge, UK: Polity Press, 1995), p. 52. Bourdieu's most extended statement of this position can be found in *La Misère du monde*, trans. P.P. Ferguson, *The Weight of the World: Social Suffering in Contemporary Society* (Cambridge, UK: Polity Press, 2000). For discussion of Bourdieu's long-standing opposition to the perceived erosion of intellectual autonomy by market forces, see Jeremy F. Lane, *Pierre Bourdieu: A Critical Introduction* (London: Pluto Press, 2000), pp. 184–91.

8   Roger Kimball, *Tenured Radicals* (New York: Harper Row, 1990); Russell Jacoby, *The Last Intellectuals: American Culture in the Age of Academe* (New York: Basic Books, 1987); Allan Bloom, *The Closing of the American Mind* (New York: Simon and Schuster, 1987).

9   The similarities between their positions, despite the obvious differences, have been much remarked. See, for example, R. Radhakrishnan, "Toward an Effective Intellectual: Foucault or Gramsci?," in Bruce Robbins (ed.), *Intellectuals: Aesthetics, Politics, Academics* (Minneapolis: University of Minnesota Press, 1990), pp. 57–99.

10  These issues are helpfully reviewed in Barrie Axford, "The Transformation of Politics or Anti-Politics?," in Barrie Axford and Richard Huggins (eds.), *New Media and Politics* (London: Sage Publications, 2001), pp. 1–29 (esp. p. 5). See also Paul T. Durbin, "Philosophy of Technology: Retrospective and Prospective Views," in Eric Higgs, Andrew Light, and David Strong, *Technology and the Good Life?* (Chicago: University of Chicago Press, 2000), pp. 38–49 (esp. pp. 44–7), for an example of the declinist narrative about intellectuals invoked within the context of the debate about new media and technologies.

11  Zygmunt Bauman, *Life in Fragments: Essays in Postmodern Morality* (Oxford: Blackwell, 1995), pp. 242, 241.

12  Jean-François Lyotard, "La Ligne de résistance," *Le Monde*, 22 October 1993, quoted in Bauman, *Life in Fragments*, p. 241.

13  Robbins, *Intellectuals*, pp. xxiv–v. See also *Secular Vocations: Intellectuals, Professionalism, Culture* (London: Verso, 1993).

14  Andrew Ross, "Defenders of the Faith and the New Class," in Robbins (ed.), *Intellectuals*, pp. 101–32 (extract pp. 126–7).

15  Radhakrishnan, "Toward an Effective Intellectual," p. 72.

16  Cornel West, interviewed by Peter Osborne in 1994, in Osborne (ed.), *A Critical Sense*, p. 136.
17  Those interviewed include Susan Sontag, Salman Rushdie, Nadine Gordimer, Mario Vargas Losa, and Joyce Carol Oates.
18  On the latter point, see Gayatri Spivak, "Interview with Ellen Rooney," in Spivak, *Outside in the Teaching Machine* (New York: Routledge, 1993), pp. 1–23 (esp. pp. 3–4).
19  In Michel Foucault, *Language, Counter-Memory, Practice: Selected Essays and Interviews* (Ithaca, NY: Cornell University Press, 1980), pp. 205–17.
20  See particularly Edward W. Said, "Foucault and the Imagination of Power," in David Couzens Hoy (ed.), *Foucault: A Critical Reader* (Oxford: Blackwell, 1986), pp. 149–55; Gayatri Chakravorty Spivak, "Can the Subaltern Speak?," in Cary Nelson and Lawrence Grossberg (eds.), *Marxism and the Interpretation of Culture* (Urbana: University of Illinois Press, 1988), pp. 271–83; Radhakrishnan, "Toward an Effective Intellectual," p. 66.
21  To take a now dated, but for that very reason, telling example: Jesse Jackson's assertion of the need for a new social and political "equation" between different races and ethnicities, taken up by R. Radhakrishnan in 1990 as a potentially useful tool for intellectuals, indubitably sounds good:

> The term . . . covers a lot of significant ground. With its connotations of equality, it carries the moral urgency of affirmative action and the need to redress existing imbalances and asymmetries. As an algebraic trope, it establishes the valence of any given variable within the equation as a function of a collectively negotiable reality. In other words, given the operational logic of the equation, no variable within it can remain aloof, isolated, and unaffected by the equational process. (Radhakrishnan, "Toward an Effective Intellectual," p. 59)

The trouble is, as the outcome of Jackson's 1988 presidential bid demonstrated all too clearly, good metaphors are not enough. In the absence of a social base for political change, they remain no more than rhetorical – indicative primarily of the very great deal of structural organization still to be done.
22  "The Masses: The Implosion of the Social in the Media," in Jean Baudrillard, *Selected Writings*, 2nd edn., revised and expanded, ed. and introduced by Mark Poster (Cambridge: Polity Press, 2001), pp. 210–22, quotation pp. 218–9.
23  Interviewed much more recently, in the wake of the Balkans conflict (which seemed to him to demonstrate an aggressive singularity irrecoverably taking over from the universal), Baudrillard was still more dismissive of the intellectual. He declared himself now no longer an *intellectuel engagé* but, avowedly, an *intellectuel dégagé*, eschewing even the Foucault-

ian role of diagnostician – though (at the risk of truism) it is hard to see what Baudrillard's account of the demise of Western universalism is if not diagnostic. See *Paroxysm: Interviews with Philippe Petit* (London: Verso, 1998), pp. 7–25 (esp. pp. 12–15).

24  Pierre Bourdieu, "The Corporatism of the Universal: The Role of Intellectuals in the Modern World," *Telos*, 81 (1989): 108. For a fuller account see Jeremy Jennings's essay in this volume, and Lane, *Pierre Bourdieu*, pp. 199–200.

25  Lane, *Pierre Bourdieu*, p. 201.

26  See Stefan Collini's essay in this volume.

# Chapter 1

# The Public Role of Writers and Intellectuals

## Edward W. Said

Almost exactly 20 years ago, *The Nation* magazine convened a congress of writers in New York by putting out notices for the event and, as I understood the tactic, leaving open the question of who was a writer and why he or she qualified to attend. The result was that literally hundreds of people showed up, crowding the main ballroom of a midtown Manhattan hotel almost to the ceiling. The occasion itself was intended as a response by the intellectual and artistic communities to the immediate onset of the Reagan era. As I recall the proceedings, a debate raged for a long time over the definition of a writer in the hope that some of the people there would be selected out or, in plain English, forced to leave. The reason for that was twofold: first of all, to decide who had a vote and who didn't, and second, to form a writer's union. Not much occurred in the way of reduced and manageable numbers; the hearteningly large mass of people simply remained immense and unwieldy since it was quite clear that everyone who came as a writer who opposed Reaganism stayed on as a writer who opposed Reaganism. I remember clearly that at one point someone sensibly suggested that we should adopt what was said to be the Soviet position on defining a writer, that is, a writer is someone who says that he or she is a writer. And, I think that is where matters seem to have rested, even though a National Writer's Union was formed but restricted its functions to technical professional matters like fairer standardized contracts between publishers and writers. An American Writers' Congress to deal with expressly political issues was also formed, but was derailed by people who in effect wanted it for one or another specific political agenda that could not get a consensus.

Since that time, an immense amount of change has taken place in the world of writers and intellectuals and, if anything, the definition of who or what a writer and intellectual is has become more confusing and difficult to pin down. I tried my hand at it in my 1993 Reith Lectures, but there have been major political and economic transformations since that time, and in planning this paper, I have found myself revising a great deal and adding to some of my earlier views. Central to the changes has been the deepening of an unresolved tension as to whether writers and intellectuals can ever be what is called non-political or not, and if so, obviously, how and in what measure. The difficulty of the tension for the individual writer and intellectual has been paradoxically that the realm of the political and public has expanded so much as to be virtually without borders. We might well ask whether a non-political writer or intellectual is a notion that has much content to it. Consider that the bipolar world of the Cold War has been reconfigured and dissolved in several different ways, all of them first of all providing what seems to be an infinite number of variations on the location or position, physical and metaphorical, of the writer, and second of all, opening up the possibility of divergent roles for him or her to play if, that is, the notion of writer or intellectual itself can be said to have any coherent and definably separate meaning or existence at all.

Yet, despite the spate of books and articles saying that intellectuals no longer exist and that the end of the Cold War, the opening up of the mainly American university to legions of writers and intellectuals, the age of specialization, and the commercialization and commodification of everything in the newly globalized economy, have simply done away with the old somewhat romantic-heroic notion of the solitary writer-intellectual (I shall provisionally connect the two terms for purposes of convenience here, then go on to explain my reasons for doing so in a moment), there still seems to be a great deal of life in the ideas and the practices of writer-intellectuals that touch on, and are very much a part of, the public realm. There wouldn't be discussions like the present one if that weren't the case.

In the three or four quite distinct contemporary language cultures that I know something about, that is eminently – indeed overwhelmingly – true, in part because many people still feel the need to look at the writer-intellectual as someone who ought to be listened to as a guide to the confusing present, and also as a leader of a faction, tendency, or group vying for more power and influence. The Gramscian provenance of both these ideas about the role of an intellectual is evident.

Now in the Arab-Islamic world, the two words used for intellectual are *muthaqqaf*, or *mufakir*, the first derived from *thaqafa* or culture (hence, a man of culture), the second from *fikr* or thought (hence, a man of thought). In both instances the prestige of those meanings is enhanced and amplified by implied comparison with government, which is now universally regarded as without credibility and popularity, or culture and thought. So in the moral vacancy created, for example, by dynastic republican governments like those of Egypt, Iraq, Libya, or Syria, many people turn either to religious or secular intellectuals for the leadership no longer provided by political authority, even though governments have been adept at co-opting intellectuals as mouthpieces for them. But the search for authentic intellectuals goes on, as does the struggle.

In the French-speaking domains the word *intellectuel* unfailingly carries with it some residue of the public realm in which recently deceased figures like Sartre, Foucault, and Aron debated and put forward their views for very large audiences indeed. By the early 1980s when most of the *maîtres penseurs* had disappeared, a certain gloating and relief accompanied their absence, as if the new redundancy gave a lot of little people a chance to have their say for the first time since Zola. Today, with what seems like a Sartre revival in evidence and (until his untimely death in January 2002) with Pierre Bourdieu or his ideas appearing in every other issue of *Le Monde* and *Libération*, a considerably aroused taste for public intellectuals has gripped many people, I think. From a great distance, debate about social and economic policy seems pretty lively, and isn't quite as one-sided as it is in the USA.

Raymond Williams's succinct presentation in *Keywords* of the force field of mostly negative connotations for the word "intellectual" is about as good a starting point as we have for understanding the historical semantics of the word in England. Excellent subsequent work by Stefan Collini, John Carey, and others has considerably deepened and refined the field of practice where intellectuals and writers have been located. Williams himself has gone on to indicate that, after the mid-twentieth century, the word takes on a new, somewhat wider, set of associations, many of them having to do with ideology, cultural production, and the capacity for organized thought and learning. This suggests that English usage has expanded to take in some of the meanings and uses that have been quite common in the French, and generally European, contexts. But as in the French instance, intellectuals of Williams's generation have passed from the scene (the almost miraculously articulate and brilliant Eric Hobsbawm being a rare exception) and, to judge from some of his successors on the *New Left Review*, a new period of Left quietism may be setting in, especially since New Labour has so thoroughly renounced its own past. Neo-liberal and Thatcherite intellectuals are pretty much where they have been (in the ascendancy), and have the advantage of many more pulpits in the press from which to speak.

In the American setting, however, the word "intellectual" is less used than in the three other arenas of discourse and discussion that I've mentioned. One can only speculate as to why this is so. One reason is that professionalism and specialization provide the norm for intellectual work much more than they do in Arabic, French, or British English. The cult of expertise has never ruled the world of discourse as much as it now does in the USA. Another reason is that even though the USA is actually full of intellectuals hard at work filling the airwaves, print, and cyberspace with their effusions, the public realm is so taken up with questions of policy and government, as well as with considerations of power and authority, that even the idea of an intellectual who is driven neither by a passion for office, nor by the ambition to get the ear of someone in power, is difficult to sustain for more than a second or two. Profit and celebrity are powerful stimulants. In far too many years of appearing on television or being interviewed by journalists, I have never *not* been asked the question "What do you think the USA should do about such and such an issue?" I take this to be an index of how the notion of rule has been lodged at the very heart of intellectual practice outside the university. And may I add that it has been a point of principle for me *not ever* to reply to the question.

Yet it is also overwhelmingly true that in America there is no shortage in the public realm of partisan policy intellectuals who are organically linked to one or another political party, lobby, special interest, or foreign power. The world of the Washington think tanks, the various television talk shows, innumerable radio programs, to say nothing of literally thousands of occasional papers, journals, and magazines – all this testifies amply to how densely saturated public discourse is with interests, authorities, and powers whose extent in the aggregate is literally unimaginable in scope and variety, except as that whole bears centrally on the acceptance of a neo-liberal post-welfare state responsive neither to the citizenry nor to the natural environment, but to a vast structure of global corporations unrestricted by traditional barriers or sovereignties. (A telling detail of the resultant shift in power is provided by information – *NY Times*, Sept. 5, 2000 – saying that the US foreign service is steadily losing employees to the international corporations.) With the various specialized systems and practices of the new economic situation, only very gradually and partially being disclosed, we are beginning to discern an immense panorama of how these systems and practices (many of them new, many of them refashioned holdovers from the classical imperial system) assembled together to provide a geography whose purpose is slowly to crowd out and override human agency. (See, as an instance of what I have in mind, Yves Dezelay and Bryant G. Garth, *Dealing in Virtue: International Commercial Arbitration and the Construction of a Transnational Legal Order*, Chicago, 1996.) We must not be misled by the effusions of Thomas Friedman, Daniel Yergin, Joseph Stanislas, and the legions who have celebrated globalization into believing that the system itself is the best outcome for human history, nor in reaction should we fail to note what, in a far less glamorous way, globalization from below, as Richard Falk has called the post-Westphalian world-system, can provide by way of human potential and innovation. There is now a fairly extensive network of NGOs created to address minority and human rights, women's and environmental issues, movements for democratic and cultural change, and while none of these can be a substitute for political action or mobilization, many of them do embody resistance to the advancing global status quo.

Yet, as Dezelay and Garth have more recently argued (*Le Monde diplomatique*, May 2000), given the funding of many of these international NGOs, they are co-optable as targets for what the two researchers have called the imperialism of virtue, functioning as annexes to the multinationals and great foundations like Ford, centers of civic virtue that forestall deeper kinds of change or critiques of long-standing assumptions.

In the meantime, it is sobering and almost terrifying to contrast the world of academic intellectual discourse (mainly the humanities, but not the natural sciences or even the social sciences) in its generally hermetic, jargon-ridden, unthreatening combativeness, with what the public realm all around has been doing. Masao Miyoshi has pioneered the study of this contrast, especially in its marginalization of the humanities. The separation between the two realms, academic and public, is, I think, greater in the United States than anywhere else, although in Perry Anderson's dirge for the Left with which he announced his editorship of *New Left Review* it is all too plain that in his opinion the British, American, and Continental pantheon of remaining heroes is, with one exception, resolutely, exclusively academic and almost entirely male and Eurocentric. I found it extraordinary that he takes no account of non-academic intellectuals like John Pilger and Alexander Cockburn, or major academic and political figures such as Chomsky, Zinn, the late Eqbal Ahmad, Germaine Greer, or such diverse figures as Mohammed Sid Ahmad, bell hooks, Angela Davis, Cornel West, Henry Louis Gates, Miyoshi, Ranajit Guha, Partha Chatterjee, to say nothing of an impressive battery of Irish intellectuals that would include Seamus Deane, Luke Gibbons, and Declan Kiberd, plus many others, all of whom would certainly not accept the solemn lament intoned for what he calls the "the neo-liberal grand slam."

The great novelty alone of Ralph Nader's candidacy in the American presidential campaign was that a genuine adversarial intellectual was running for the most powerful elected office in the world using the rhetoric and tactics of demystification and disenchantment, in the process supplying a mostly disaffected electorate with alternative information buttressed with precise facts and figures. This went completely against the prevailing modes of vagueness, vapid slogans, mystification, and religious fervor sponsored by the two major party candidates, underwritten by the media, and paradoxically by virtue of its inaction, the humanistic academy. Nader's competitive stance was a sure sign of how far from over and defeated the oppositional tendencies in global society are; witness also the upsurge of reformism in Iran, the consolidation of democratic anti-racism in various parts of Africa, and so on, leaving aside the November 1999 protests in Seattle against the WTO, the liberation of South Lebanon, and so forth. The list would be a long one, and very different in tone (were it to be interpreted fully) from the consolatory accomodationism recommended by Anderson. In intention, Nader's campaign was also different from those of his opponents in that he aimed to arouse the citizenry's democratic awareness of the untapped potential for participation in the country's resources, not just greed or simple assent to what passes for politics.

Having earlier summarily assimilated the words "intellectual" and "writer" to each other, it is best for me now to show why and how they belong together, despite the writer's separate origin and history. In the language of everyday use, a writer in the languages and cultures that I am familiar with is a person who produces literature, that is, a novelist, a poet, a dramatist. I think it is generally true that in all cultures writers have a separate, perhaps even more honorific, place than do intellectuals; the aura of creativity and an almost sanctified capacity for originality (often vatic in its scope and quality) accrues to them as it doesn't at all to intellectuals, who with regard to literature belong to the slightly debased and parasitic class of critics. (There is a long history of attacks on critics as nasty niggling beasts capable of little more than carping and pedantic word-mongering.) Yet during the last years of the twentieth century the writer has taken on more and more of the intellectual's adversarial attributes in such activities as speaking the truth to power, being a witness to persecution and suffering, supplying a dissenting voice in conflicts with authority. Signs of the amalgamation of one to the other would have to include the Salman Rushdie case in all its ramifications, the formation of numerous writers' parliaments and congresses devoted to such issues as intolerance, the dialogue of cultures, civil strife (as in Bosnia and Algeria), freedom of speech and censorship, truth and reconciliation (as in South Africa, Argentina, Ireland, and elsewhere), and the special symbolic role of the writer as an intellectual testifying to a country's or region's experience, thereby giving that experience a public identity forever inscribed in the global discursive agenda. The easiest way of demonstrating that is simply to list the names of some (but by no means all) recent Nobel Prize winners, then to allow each name to trigger in the mind an emblematized region, which in turn can be seen as a sort of platform or jumping-off point for that writer's subsequent activity as an intervention in debates taking place very far from the world of literature. Thus, Nadine Gordimer, Kenzaburo Oë, Derek Walcott, Wole Soyinka, Gabriel García Márquez, Octavio Paz, Elie Wiesel, Bertrand Russell, Günter Grass, Rigoberta Menchú, among several others.

Now it is also true, as Pascal Casanova has brilliantly shown in her synoptic book *La République mondiale des lettres*, that, fashioned over the past 150 years, there now seems to be a global system of literature in place, complete with its own order of literariness (*litérarité*), tempo, canon, internationalism, and market values. The efficiency of the system is that it seems to have generated the types of writers that she discusses as belonging to such different categories as assimilated, dissident, translated figures, all of them both individualized and classified in what she clearly shows is a highly efficient, globalized quasi-market system. The drift of her argument is in effect to show how this powerful and all-pervasive system can even go as far as to stimulate a kind of independence from it, in cases like those of Joyce and Beckett, writers whose language and orthography do not submit to the laws either of state or of system.

Much as I admire it, however, the overall achievement of Casanova's book is nevertheless contradictory. She seems to be saying that literature as globalized system has a kind of integral autonomy to it that places it in large measure just beyond the gross realities of political institutions and discourse, a notion that has a certain theoretical plausibility to it when she puts it in the form of *"un espace littéraire internationale,"* with its own laws of interpretation, its own dialectic of individual work and ensemble, its own problematics of nationalism and national languages. But she doesn't go as far as Adorno in saying, as I would too (and plan to return to briefly at the end of my paper), that one of the hallmarks of modernity is how at a very deep level, the aesthetic and the social need to be kept in a state of irreconcilable tension. Nor does she spend enough time discussing the ways in which the literary, or the writer, is still implicated, indeed frequently mobilized for use, in the great post-Cold War cultural contests provided by the altered political configurations I spoke of earlier.

Looked at from that perspective, for example, the debate about Salman Rushdie was never really about the literary attributes of *The Satanic Verses*, but rather about whether there could be a literary treatment of a religious topic that did not also touch on religious passions in a very, indeed in an exacerbated, public way. (See the excellent analysis of this in Mohammed Hassanein Heykal's, " 'ala atraf al adab, al din, wal siyassah," *Wijhat Nazar*, July, 2000.) I don't think that such a possibility existed, since from the very moment the fatwa was released to the world, the novel, its author, and its readers were all deposited squarely inside an environment that allowed no room at all for anything but politicized intellectual debate about such socio-religious issues as blasphemy, secular dissent, and extra-territorial threats of assassination. Even to assert that Rushdie's freedom of expression as a novelist could not be abridged – as many of us from the Islamic world actually did assert – was in fact to debate the issue of the literary freedom to write within a discourse that had already swallowed up and totally occupied (in the geographical sense) literature's apartness.

In that wider setting then, the basic distinction between writers and intellectuals need not therefore be made since, insofar as they both act in the new public sphere dominated by globalization (and assumed to exist even by adherents of the Khomeini fatwa), their public role as writers and intellectuals can be discussed and analyzed together. Another way of putting it is to say that I shall be concentrating on what writers and intellectuals have in common as they intervene in the public sphere. I don't at all want to give up the possibility that there remains an area outside and untouched by the globalized one that I shall be discussing here, but as I have said, I don't really want to discuss that until the end, since my main concern is with what the writer's role is squarely within the actually existing system.

Let me say something about the technical characteristics of intellectual intervention today. To get a dramatically vivid grasp of the speed with which communication has accelerated during the past decade I'd like to contrast Jonathan Swift's awareness of effective public intervention in the early eighteenth century with ours. Swift was surely the most devastating pamphleteer of his time, and during his campaign against the Duke of Marlborough in 1711, he was able to get 15,000 copies of his pamphlet "The Conduct of the Allies" onto the streets in a few days. This brought down the Duke from his high eminence but nevertheless did not change Swift's pessimistic impression (dating back to *A Tale of a Tub*, 1704) that his writing was basically temporary, good only for the short time that it circulated. He had in mind of course the running quarrel between ancients and moderns in which venerable writers like Homer and Horace had the advantage of great longevity, even permanence, over modern figures like Dryden by virtue of their age and the authenticity of their views. In the age of electronic media, such considerations are mostly irrelevant, since anyone with a computer and decent Internet access is capable of reaching numbers of people quantum times more than Swift did, and can also look forward to the preservation of what is written beyond any conceivable measure. Our ideas today of archive and discourse must be radically modified, and can no longer be defined as Foucault painstakingly tried to describe them a mere two decades ago. Even if one writes for a newspaper or journal, the chances of multiplying reproduction and, notionally at least, an unlimited time of preservation have wreaked havoc on even the idea of an actual, as opposed to a virtual, audience. These things have certainly limited the powers that regimes have to censor or ban writing that is considered dangerous, although, as I shall note presently, there are fairly crude means for stopping or curtailing the libertarian function of online print. Until only very recently, Saudi Arabia and Syria, for example, successfully banned the Internet and even satellite television. Both countries now tolerate limited access to the Internet, although both have also installed sophisticated and, in the long run, prohibitively interdictory, processes to maintain their control.

As things stand an article I might write in New York for a British paper has a good chance of reappearing on individual websites or via e-mail on screens in the USA, in Japan, Pakistan, the Middle East, and South Africa as well as Australia. Authors and publishers have very little control over what is reprinted and recirculated. I am constantly surprised (and don't know whether to be angry or flattered) when something that I wrote or said in one place turns up with scarcely a delay halfway across the world. For whom then does one write, if it is difficult to specify the audience with any sort of precision? Most people, I think, focus on the actual outlet that has commissioned the piece, or for the putative readers we would like to address. The idea of an imagined community has suddenly acquired a very literal, if virtual, dimension. Certainly, as I experienced when I began 10 years ago to write in an Arabic publication for an audience of Arabs, one attempts to create, shape, refer to a constituency, now much more than during Swift's time, when he could quite naturally assume that the persona he called a Church of England man was in fact his real, very stable, and quite small audience.

All of us should therefore operate today with some notion of very probably reaching much larger audiences than any we could have conceived of even a decade ago, although the chances of retaining that audience are by the same token quite chancy. This is not simply a matter of optimism of the will; it is in the very nature of writing today. This makes it very difficult for writers to take common assumptions between them and their audiences for granted, or to assume that references and allusions are going to be understood immediately. When assumptions can be assumed, they are usually the wrong ones, that is, they tend to be those prevailing *idées reçues* which one's whole effort as an intellectual is to dislodge, dismantle, and change completely. But, writing in this expanded new space strangely does have a further unusually risky consequence, which is to be encouraged to say things that are either completely opaque or completely transparent, and if one has any sense of the intellectual and political vocation (which I shall get to later), it should of course be the latter rather than the former. But then, transparent, simple, clear prose presents its own challenges, since the ever-present danger is that one can fall into the misleadingly simple neutrality of a journalistic World-English idiom that is indistinguishable from CNN or USA-Today prose. The quandary is a real one, whether in the end to repel readers (and more dangerous, meddling editors), or to attempt to win readers over in a style that perhaps too closely resembles the mind-set one is trying to expose and dismiss. The thing to remember, I keep telling myself, is that there isn't another language at hand, that the language I use must be the same used by the State Department or the President when they say that they are for human rights, and I must be able to use that very same language to recapture the subject, reclaim it, and reconnect it to the tremendously complicated realities these vastly over-privileged antagonists of mine have simplified, betrayed, and either diminished or dissolved. It should be obvious by now that for an intellectual who is not there simply to advance someone else's interest, there have to be opponents that are held responsible for the present state of affairs, antagonists with whom one must directly engage.

While it is true and even discouraging that all the main outlets are, however, controlled by the most powerful interests, and consequently by the very antagonists one resists or attacks, it is also true that a relatively mobile intellectual energy can take advantage of and, in effect, multiply the kinds of platforms available for use. On one side, therefore, six enormous multinationals presided over by six men control most of the world's supply of images and news. On the other, there are the independent intellectuals who actually form an incipient community, physically separated from each other but connected variously to a great number of activist communities shunned by the main media, but who have at their actual disposal other kinds of what Swift sarcastically called "oratorical machines." Think of the impressive range of opportunities offered by the lecture platform, the pamphlet, radio, alternative journals, the interview form, the rally, church pulpit, and the Internet to name only a few. True, it is a considerable disadvantage to realize that one is unlikely to get asked on to PBS's *Newshour* or ABC's *Nightline*, or if one is in fact asked, only an isolated fugitive minute will be offered. But then, other occasions present themselves not in the sound-bite format, but rather in more extended stretches of time. So rapidity is a double-edged weapon. There is the rapidity of the sloganeeringly reductive style that is the main feature of expert discourse – to-the-point, fast, formulaic, pragmatic in appearance – and there is the rapidity of response and format that intellectuals and indeed most citizens can exploit in order to present fuller, more complete expressions of an alternative point of view. I am suggesting that by taking advantage of what is available in the form of numerous platforms (or "stages-itinerant," another Swiftian term) and an alert and creative willingness to exploit them by an intellectual (that is, platforms that either aren't available to or are shunned by the television personality, expert, or political candidate), it is possible to initiate wider discussion.

The emancipatory potential – and the threats to it – of this new situation mustn't be under-estimated. Let me give a very powerful recent example of what I mean. There are about four million Palestinian refugees scattered all over the world, a significant number of whom live in large refugee camps in Lebanon (where the 1982 Sabra and Shatila massacres took place), Jordan, Syria, and in Gaza and the West Bank. In 1999 an enterprising group of young and educated refugees living in Deheisheh Camp, near Bethlehem on the West Bank, established the Ibdaa Center whose main feature was the Across Borders project; this was a revolutionary way through computer terminals of connecting refugees in most of the main camps – separated geographically and politically by impassable barriers – to each other. For the first time since their parents were dispersed in 1948, second-generation Palestinian refugees in Beirut or Amman could communicate with their counterparts inside Palestine. Some of what the participants in the project did was quite remarkable. Thus the Deheisheh residents went on visits to their former villages in Palestine, and then described their emotions and what they saw for the benefit of other refugees who had heard of, but could not have access to, these places. In a matter of weeks, a remarkable solidarity emerged at a time, it turned out, when the so-called final status negotiations between the PLO and Israel were beginning to take up the question of refugees and return, which along with the question of Jerusalem made up the intransigent core of the stalemated peace process. For some Palestinian refugees, therefore, their presence and political will were actualized for the first time, giving them a new status qualitatively different from the passive objecthood that had been their fate for half a century. On August 26, 2000, all the computers in Deheisheh were destroyed in an act of political vandalism that left no one in doubt that refugees were meant to remain as refugees, which is to say that they were not meant to disturb the status quo that had assumed their silence for so long. It wouldn't be hard to list the possible suspects, but it is equally hard to imagine that anyone will either be named or apprehended. In any case, the Deheisheh camp-dwellers immediately set about trying to restore the Ibdaa Center, and seem to some degree to have succeeded in so doing.

To answer the question why, in this and other similar contexts, individuals and groups prefer writing and speaking to silence, is equivalent to specifying what in fact the intellectual and writer confront in the public sphere. What I mean is that the existence of individuals or groups seeking social justice and economic equality, and who understand (in Amartya Sen's formulation) that freedom must include the right to a whole range of choices affording cultural, political, intellectual, and economic development, ipso facto will lead one to a desire for articulation as opposed to silence. This is the functional idiom of the intellectual vocation. The intellectual therefore stands in a position to make possible and to further the formulation of these expectations and wishes.

Now every discursive intervention is, of course, specific to a particular occasion and assumes an existing consensus, paradigm, episteme, or praxis (we can all pick our favorite concept that denotes the prevailing accepted discursive norm), say, during the NATO war against Kosovo, during national elections in Egypt and the United States, about immigration practices in one or another country, or about the ecology of West Africa. In each of these and so many other situations, the hallmark of the era we live in is that there tends to be a mainstream-media-government orthodoxy against which it is very difficult indeed to go, even though the intellectual must assume that alternatives can clearly be shown to exist. Thus, I would begin by restating the obvious, that very situation should be interpreted according to its own givens, but (and I would argue that this is almost always the case) that every situation also contains a contest between a powerful system of interests on the one hand and, on the other, less powerful interests threatened with frustration, silence, incorporation, or extinction by the powerful. It almost goes without saying that for the American intellectual the responsibility is greater, the openings numerous, the challenge very difficult. The USA after all is the only global power; it intervenes nearly everywhere, and its resources for domination are very great, although very far from infinite.

The intellectual's role generally is dialectically, oppositionally, to uncover and elucidate the contest I referred to earlier, to challenge and defeat both an imposed silence and the normalized quiet of unseen power wherever and whenever possible. For there is a social and intellectual equivalence between this mass of overbearing collective interests and the discourse used to justify, disguise, or mystify its workings while also preventing objections or challenges to it. In our time, and almost universally, phrases like "the free market," privatization, less (as opposed to more) government, and others like them, which have become the orthodoxy of globalization and counterfeit universals, are the staples of dominant discourse, designed to create consent and tacit approval. From that nexus emanate such ideological confections as "the West," the clash of civilizations, and traditional values and identity (perhaps the most over-used phrases in the global lexicon today). All these are deployed not as they sometimes seem to be, as instigations for debate, but quite the opposite; they are used to exploit the deep bellicosity and fundamentalism that work to stifle, preempt, and crush dissent whenever the false universals face resistance or questioning.

The main goal of this dominant discourse is to fashion the merciless logic of corporate profit-making and political power into a normal state of affairs, "that is the way things are," in the process rendering rational resistance to these notions into something altogether and practically unrealistic, irrational, and utopian. Behind the Punch-and-Judy show of energetic debate concerning the West and Islam, for example, all sort of anti-democratic, sanctimonious, and alienating devices (the theory of the Great Satan or of the rogue state and terrorism) are in place as diversions from the social and economic disentitlements occurring in reality. In one place, Rafsanjani exhorts Parliament to greater degrees of Islamization as a defense against America; in the other, Bush, Blair, and their feeble partners prepare their citizens for an indeterminate war against Islamic terrorism, rogue states, and the rest. Realism and its close associate pragmatism are mobilized from their real philosophical context in the work of Peirce, Dewey, and James, and put to forced labor in the boardroom where, as Gore Vidal recently put it, the real decisions about government and presidential candidates are made. Much as one is for elections, it is also a bitter truth that elections do not automatically produce democracy or democratic results.

As against the abuse of identity-defense mechanisms which has become so endemic to nationalist thought from its origins in education to its expression in public discourse, the intellectual offers instead a dispassionate account of how identity, tradition, and the nation are constructed things, most often in the insidious form of binary oppositions that are inevitably expressed as hostile attitudes to the Other. Every public domain today is infected with this type of thinking. Certainly one cannot deny that some identities are indeed threatened with destruction and attack, but such actual dangers to identity and self-determination can be and are used cynically to justify unjustified political repression. This is particularly true in Palestine, where the Palestinian Authority is encouraged by the Israeli and US governments to maintain the notorious State Security Court, which has, among many other abuses, permitted the jailing and torture of any kind of dissenter; the across-the-board censorship of books, newspapers, and magazines; and has routinely shut down television and radio channels for broadcasting even a whiff of criticism of the peace process or the Authority itself. All of this is done in the name of a dispossessed, long-suffering, and largely disenfranchised people. The unfortunate tendency is to say, as government apologists elsewhere have always said during times of war or national emergencies, that we must stick together, show unity in the face of threats to the commonwealth, and so on. I think it is doubly important in such difficult situations, as well as in the West generally and the USA particularly, to dismiss patriotism and loyalty as the covers for human and civil rights abuses that they usually are.

The late Pierre Bourdieu and his associates have very interestingly suggested that political ideology such as the Clinton–Blair neo-liberalism of the 1990s, or Bush's current "compassionate conservatism," which, though seemingly different, in fact have both been built on the conservative dismantling of the great social achievements (in health, education, labor, social security) of the welfare state during the Thatcher–Reagan period, has constructed a paradoxical doxa, a symbolic counterrevolution which obviously includes the kind of national self-glorification I've just mentioned. Such ideology, he says, is

> conservative but presents itself as progressive; it seeks the restoration of the past order in some of its most archaic aspects (especially as regards economic relations), yet it passes regressions, reversals, surrenders, as forward-looking reforms or revolutions leading to a whole new age of abundance and liberty (as with the language of the so-called "new economy" and the celebratory discourse around "network firms" and the internet).

As a reminder of the damage this reversal has already done, Bourdieu and his colleagues produced a collective work in 1993 entitled *La Misère du monde* (translated in 1999 as *The Weight of the World: Social Suffering in Contemporary Society*) whose aim was thereby to compel the politicians' attention to what, in French society, the misleading optimism of public discourse had hidden. This kind of book, therefore, plays a sort of negative intellectual role, whose aim is, to quote Bourdieu again, "to produce and disseminate instruments of defense against symbolic domination which increasingly relies on the authority of science," or expertise or appeals to national unity, pride, history, and tradition, to bludgeon people into submission. Obviously India and Brazil are different from Britain and the USA, but those often striking disparities in cultures and economies shouldn't at all obscure the even more startling similarities that can be seen in some of the techniques and, very often, the aim of deprivation and repression that compel people to follow along meekly. I should also like to add that one needn't always present an abstruse and detailed theory of justice to go to war intellectually against injustice, since there is now a well-stocked internationalist storehouse of conventions, protocols, resolutions, and charters for national authorities to comply with, if they are so inclined. And, in the same context, I would have thought it almost moronic to take an ultra-post-modern position (like Richard Rorty while shadowboxing with some vague thing he refers to contemptuously as "the academic Left") and say when confronting ethnic cleansing, or genocide as it is occurring today in Iraq, or any of the evils of torture, censorship, famine, ignorance (most of them constructed by humans, not by acts of God), that human rights are cultural things, and when they are violated they do not really have the status accorded them by crude foundationalists, such as myself, for whom they are as real as anything we can encounter.

I think it is correct to say that depoliticized or aestheticized submission, along with all of the different forms of in some cases triumphalism and xenophobia, in others of apathy and defeat, has been principally required since the 1960s to allay whatever residual feelings of desire for democratic participation (also known as "a danger to stability") still existed. One can read this plainly enough in *The Crisis of Democracy*, co-authored at the behest of the Trilateral Commission a decade before the end of the Cold War. There the argument is that too much democracy is bad for governability, that supply of passivity which makes it easier for oligarchies of technical or policy experts to push people into line. So if one is endlessly lectured by certified experts who explain that the freedom we all want demands deregulation and privatization and that the new world order is nothing less than the end of history, there is very little inclination to address this order with anything like individual or even collective demands. Chomsky has relentlessly addressed this paralyzing syndrome for several years.

Let me give an example from personal experience in the United States today of how formidable the challenges are to the individual, and how easy it is to slip into inaction. If you are seriously ill, you are suddenly plunged into the world of outrageously expensive pharmaceutical products, many of which are still experimental and require FDA approval. Even those that aren't experimental and aren't particularly new (like steroids and antibiotics) are life-savers, but their

exorbitant expense is thought to be a small price to pay for their effi-
cacy. The more one looks into the matter, the more one encounters
the corporate rationale, which is that while the cost of manufacturing
the drug may be small (it usually is tiny), the cost of research is enormous and must be recovered in subsequent sales. Then you discover
that most of the research cost came to the corporation in the form of
government grants, which in turn came from the taxes paid by every
citizen. When you address the abuse of public money in the form of
questions put to a promising, progressively minded candidate (e.g.,
Bill Bradley), you then quickly understand why such candidates never
raise the question. They receive enormous campaign contributions
from Merck and Bristol-Myers, and are most unlikely to challenge
their supporters. So you go on paying and living, on the assumption that if you are lucky enough to have an insurance policy, the
insurance company will pay out. Then you discover that insurance
company accountants make the decisions on who gets a costly medi-
cation or test, what is allowed or disallowed, for how long and in what
circumstances, and only then do you understand that such rudimen-
tary protections as a patient's genuine bill of rights still cannot be
passed in Congress, given that immensely profitable insurance corporations lobby there indefatigably.

In short, I find myself saying that even heroic attempts (such as
Fredric Jameson's) to understand the system on a theoretical level or
to formulate what Samir Amin has called "delinking alternatives," are
fatally undermined by their relative neglect of actual political intervention in the existential situations in which as citizens we find ourselves – intervention that isn't just personal but is a significant part of
a broad adversarial or oppositional movement. Obviously, as intellectuals, we all carry around some working understanding or sketch of
the global system (in large measure thanks to world and regional
historians like Immanuel Wallerstein, Anwar Abdel Malek, J.M. Blaut,
Janet Abu-Lughod, Peter Gran, Ali Mazrui, William McNeil), but it is
during the direct encounters with it in one or another specific geography, configuration, or problematic that the contests are waged and
perhaps even winnable. There is an admirable chronicle of the kind of
thing I mean in the various essays of Bruce Robbins's *Feeling Global:
Internationalism in Distress* (1999), Timothy Brennan's *At Home in the
World: Cosmopolitanism Now* (1997), and Neil Lazarus's *Nationalism and
Cultural Practice in the Postcolonial World* (1999), books whose self-
consciously territorial and highly interwoven textures are in fact an
adumbration of the critical (and combative) intellectual's sense of the

35

world we live in today, taken as episodes or even fragments of a broader picture which their work as well as the work of others like them is in the process of compiling. What they suggest is a map of experiences that would have been indiscernible, perhaps invisible, two decades ago, but which in the aftermath of the classical empires, the end of the Cold War, the crumbling of the socialist and non-aligned blocks, the emergent dialectics between North and South in the era of globalization, cannot be excluded either from cultural study or from the somewhat protected precincts of the humanistic disciplines.

I've mentioned a few names, not just to indicate how significant I think their contributions have been, but also to use them in order to leapfrog directly into some concrete areas of collective concern where, to quote Bourdieu for the last time, there is the possibility of "collective invention." He continues by saying that

> the whole edifice of critical thought is thus in need of critical reconstruction. This work of reconstruction cannot be done, as some thought in the past, by a single great intellectual, a master-thinker endowed with the sole resources of his singular thought, or by the authorized spokesperson for a group or an institution presumed to speak in the name of those without voice, union, party, and so on. This is where the collective intellectual [Bourdieu's name for individuals the sum of whose research and participation on common subjects constitutes a sort of ad hoc collective] can play its irreplaceable role, by helping to create the social conditions for the collective production of realist utopias.

My reading of this is to stress the absence of any master-plan or blueprint or grand theory for what intellectuals can do, and the absence now of any utopian teleology toward which human history can be described as moving. Therefore one invents – in the literal use of the Latin word *inventio* employed by rhetoricians to stress finding again, or reassembling from past performances, as opposed to the romantic use of invention as something you create from scratch – goals abductively, that is, hypothesizing a better situation from the known historical and social facts. So, in effect, this enables intellectual performances on many fronts, in many places, many styles that keep in play both the sense of opposition and the sense of engaged participation that I mentioned a moment ago. Hence, film, photography, and even music, along with all the arts of writing, can be aspects of this activity. Part of what we do as intellectuals is not only to define the situation, but also to discern the possibilities for active intervention, whether we then perform them ourselves or acknowledge them in others who have either gone before or are already at work – the intellectual as lookout. Provincialism of the old kind – for example, I am a literary specialist whose field is early seventeenth-century England – rules itself out and, quite frankly, seems uninteresting and needlessly neutered. The assumption has to be that even though one can't do or know about everything, it must always be possible not only to discern the elements of a struggle or tension or problem near at hand that can be elucidated dialectically, but also to sense that other people have a similar stake and work in a common project. I have found a brilliantly inspiring parallel for what I mean in Adam Phillips's recent book *Darwin's Worms* in which Darwin's lifelong attention to the lowly earthworm revealed its capacity for expressing nature's variability and design without necessarily seeing the whole of either one or the other, thereby, in his work on earthworms, replacing "a creation myth with a secular maintenance myth" (p. 46).

Is there some non-trivial way of generalizing about where and in what form such struggles are taking place now? I shall limit myself to saying a little about only three, all of which are profoundly amenable to intellectual intervention and elaboration. The first is to protect against and forestall the disappearance of the past, which in the rapidity of change, the reformulation of tradition, and the construction of simplified bowdlerizations of history, is at the very heart of the contest described by Benjamin Barber rather too sweepingly as Jihad versus McWorld. The intellectual's role is first to present alternative narratives and other perspectives on history than those provided by combatants on behalf of official memory and national identity, who tend to work in terms of falsified unities, the manipulation of demonized or distorted representations of undesirable and/or excluded populations, and the propagation of heroic anthems sung in order to sweep all before them. At least since Nietzsche, the writing of history and the accumulations of memory have been regarded in many ways as one of the essential foundations of power, guiding its strategies, charting its progress. Look, for example, at the appalling exploitation of past suffering described in their accounts of the uses of the Holocaust by Tom Segev, Peter Novick, and Norman Finkelstein or, just to stay within the area of historical restitution and reparation, the invidious disfiguring, dismembering, and disremembering of significant historical experiences that do not have powerful enough lobbies in the present and therefore merit dismissal or belittlement. The need now is for de-intoxicated, sober histories that make evident the multiplicity and complexity of history without allowing one to conclude that it moves forward impersonally according to laws determined either by the divine or by the powerful.

The second is to construct fields of coexistence rather than fields of battle as the outcome of intellectual labour. There are great lessons to be learned from decolonization which are first that, noble as its liberatory aims were, it did not often enough prevent the emergence of repressive nationalist replacements for colonial regimes; and second, that the process itself was almost immediately captured by the Cold War, despite the non-aligned movement's rhetorical efforts; and third, that it has been miniaturized and even trivialized by a small academic industry that has simply turned it into an ambiguous contest between ambivalent opponents. Benita Parry has magnificently addressed this matter in a recent paper. In the various contests over justice and human rights that so many of us feel we have joined, there needs to be a component to our engagement that stresses the need for the redistribution of resources, and that advocates the theoretical imperative against the huge accumulations of power and capital that so distort human life. Peace cannot exist without equality; this is an intellectual value desperately in need of reiteration, demonstration, and reinforcement. The seduction of the word itself – peace – is that it is surrounded by, indeed drenched in, the blandishments of approval, uncontroversial eulogizing, sentimental endorsement. The international media (as has been the case recently of the sanctioned wars in Iraq and Kosovo) uncritically amplifies, ornaments, and unquestioningly transmits all this to vast audiences for whom peace and war are spectacles for delectation and immediate consumption. It takes a good deal more courage, work, and knowledge to dissolve words like "war" and "peace" into their elements, recovering what has been left out of peace processes that have been determined by the powerful, and then placing that missing actuality back in the center of things, than it does to write prescriptive articles for "liberals" à la Michael Ignatieff that urge more destruction and death for distant civilians. The intellectual is perhaps a kind of countermemory with its own counterdiscourse that will not allow conscience to look away or fall asleep. The best corrective, as Dr. Johnson said, is to imagine the person whom you are discussing – in this case the person on whom the bombs will fall – reading you in your presence.

Still, just as history is never over or complete, it is also the case that some dialectical oppositions are not reconcilable, not transcendable, not really capable of being folded into a sort of higher, undoubtedly nobler, synthesis. The example closest to home for me is the struggle over Palestine which, I have always believed, cannot really be simply resolved by a technical and ultimately janitorial re-arrangement of geography allowing dispossessed Palestinians the right (such as it is) to live in about 20 percent of their land that would be encircled and totally dependent on Israel. Nor on the other hand would it be morally acceptable to demand that Israelis should retreat from the whole of former Palestine, now Israel, becoming refugees like Palestinians all over again. No matter how I have searched for a resolution to this impasse, I cannot find one, for this is not a facile case of right versus right. It cannot be right ever to deprive an entire people of their land and heritage. But the Jews too are what I have called a community of suffering and have brought with them a heritage of great tragedy. But unlike Zeev Sternhell, I cannot agree that the conquest of Palestine was a necessary conquest. The notion offends the sense of real Palestinian pain, in its own way also tragic especially since the onset of Israel's collective punishments that have continued throughout the most recent intifada.

Overlapping yet irreconcilable experiences demand from the intellectual the courage to say that *that* is what is before us, in almost exactly the way Adorno has throughout his work on music insisted that modern music can never be reconciled with the society that produced it, but in its intensely and often despairingly crafted form and content, music can act as a silent witness to the inhumanity all around. Any assimilation of individual musical work to its social setting is, says Adorno, false. I conclude with the thought that the intellectual's provisional home is the domain of an exigent, resistant, intransigent art into which, alas, one can neither retreat nor search for solutions. But only in that precarious exilic realm can one first truly grasp the difficulty of what cannot be grasped, and then go forth to try anyway.

# Chapter 2

# Pre-modern Intellectual Biography[1]

## Rita Copeland

Antiquity had no word for intellectuals; neither had the Middle Ages. When historians of antiquity or the Middle Ages approach the question of intellectuals, it is always in terms of the formation of the social concept in modernity, and often with the (guilty) sense of importing a term that – while elusive itself – has come to define modernity and its modes of social relations, political change, and even discourse about itself. Here, however, I will not be interested in any competition between the modern and the pre-modern over claims to the notion of the "intellectual." I do not seek to define or justify the historical grounds in antiquity and the Middle Ages for speaking of the "intellectual" as a type or "intellectuals" as a class.[2] Instead I want to foreground a dialogue within the pre-modern itself, between antiquity and the Middle Ages, about how intellectual lives are produced as literary artifacts, turning individual lives to public, historical account.

Although modernity is not in the picture I describe here, it is, of course, in the frame: without the modern conceptual vocabulary (from the turn of the nineteenth century to the present) of the "intellectual," and without the modern political, sociological, and even literary debate about intellectuals and their roles and functions, we would have no debate about earlier avatars of intellectuals and intellectual lives.[3] But comparison between modern uses of the noun "intellectual" and pre-modern examples of intellectual work or intellectual types are usually undertaken for enabling purposes, to legitimize applications of the word to pre-modern conditions or, more rarely, to restrict importation of the term to historiographies of the pre-modern.[4] I begin here by accepting the term, with any of its possible anachronisms and other imperfections, and focus on a relationship *within* the pre-modern, between antiquity and the Middle Ages.

Interestingly, European classicists began talking about ancient intellectuals partly in response to a landmark study of medieval intellectuals, Jacques Le Goff's 1957 book *Intellectuels au moyen âge*; the second edition of Le Goff's book appeared in Italian translation in 1979, the same year that an exemplary colloquium on the "Role of the Intellectual in Ancient Society" was held at the University of Genoa, over whose published proceedings Le Goff's medieval study presides in a kind of historiographical alliance with classical scholarship. It is in this spirit that I want to explore what antiquity and the Middle Ages might have to say to each other within the parameters of a literary genre, the intellectual biography.

In naming such a genre for antiquity and the Middle Ages we can ask how intellectuals could indeed be envisioned as individual and collective *lives* to be narrated. I want to consider how a pre-modern category of intellectuals comes into being, not simply as a phenomenon unto itself, but rather as a kind of career and life trajectory that can be – must be – *narrativized*. I am interested in the point at which, and the conditions under which, intellectual careers themselves take on literary form and claim a place in a literary-historical narrative. How does intellectual biography – as a particular kind of literary genre – actually serve to invent and articulate ideas of an intellectual class and intellectual careers? Writing intellectual lives – a form distinct from other kinds of biography – is a surprisingly unusual literary genre in early periods (and perhaps even now too). The conditions under which it emerges and under which it disappears, as well as the imperatives which such narrative seems to answer, are worth considering closely. How does this vein of biographical narrative pass from antiquity to the Middle Ages?

Walter Benjamin famously connected the work of narration with the authority of death;[5] and even the memorial narratives of historical epochs require the authorizing presence of individuated actors, exemplary lives and deaths. But while we can discover the prototype of a familiar modern genre, intellectual biography, in pre-modern literary history, we should not expect to recognize in its early forms the struggles of our own modern "professional narratives" to introject meaningful private lives into a public domain.[6] In the pre-modern intellectual scene, it is not the "private life" – as we would render it – that matters, but rather the outlines of a public, professional career defined through individual pedagogical contact. Where pre-modern professional biographies are recorded (and we will see that they are not always narrativized), they found their authority on a particular kind of death, the passing of a charismatic pedagogy embodied in the living presence of teachers, and by extension, their schools. It is in the expectation of this particular kind of commemorative work that we must turn to pre-modern narratives of intellectual lives.

This essay will move across a large temporal frame to focus on three moments of such narrative possibility in pre-modern Europe: first, Hellenistic late antiquity, where the biographer Philostratus wrote his *Lives of the Sophists* sometime in the middle of the third century AD; Philostratus looked back to the first sophistic movement of Athens in the fifth century BC and then brought his story forward to his own contemporary scene of the Second Sophistic in the Greek cities of the later Roman empire; second, the university culture of thirteenth-century Europe, an institutional environment which – it is often argued – sees the emergence of the "modern" intellectual as a figure who claims a connection between the vocational calling and the profession of intellectual work; and third, fifteenth-century Oxford and Prague, where the intellectual leaders of late medieval heresies can become the subjects of a newly impassioned kind of intellectual life narrative.

\* \* \*

Philostratus is not the only ancient biographer of eminent lives lived according to certain intellectual regimes. Plutarch and Suetonius had earlier written accounts of literary, philosophical, and educational figures, as did Philostratus' own near-contemporary, Diogenes Laertius, who produced a compendium on the lives and doctrines of the ancient philosophers. Among other individual biographies are lives of the philosophers Plotinus and Proclus. All of these writings could, in the broadest sense, constitute intellectual biographies. But Philostratus' *Lives of the Sophists* has a character that distinguishes it from these other texts: it gives an account of what it defines as a coherent professional school. Philostratus is writing, not just individualized *lives* of the 57 figures whose careers as sophists he traces, but the life of an entire movement and especially what he sees as the renaissance of a certain intellectual culture tied to the urban centers of the imperial Greek east. In the Greek cities of the later Roman empire – especially Athens, but also Pergamum, Smyrna, and Ephesus – the old prestige of rhetorical education found its spectacular niche in the declamatory performances of professional speakers who invested themselves both in large imperial interests and in intensely local municipal projects.[7] So much is sophistic, from its earliest to its latest manifestations, tied to the city and to urban and interurban metropolitanisms, that to write its history, as Philostratus does for the first time, is also to construct an image of a public, urban intellectual phenomenon, that is, to write an account of intellectual life as city life. The contemporaries of whom Philostratus writes, orators who made their way to urban centers from their native places throughout Asia Minor, founded their reputations on the prestige of an imperial, urban, epideictic practice. The sophists were a privileged intellectual class, recognized by governors and emperors, earning official salaries and occupying chairs, exploiting the decline of judicial and political rhetoric (under the conditions of imperial absolutism) by magnifying the power of declamatory rhetoric, and participating enthusiastically in the imperial apparatus. Philostratus himself is positioned between the power structures of the municipality and the emperor; his *Lives of the Sophists* can be read as a surrogate for a history of Greek politics and culture from the Athenian and Hellenistic periods to the domination of Achaia by Rome.[8]

Philostratus *invented* the "Second Sophistic" by giving it its name, and so characterizing it as a coherent intellectual movement with a discernible historical trajectory, more than the assembled practice of some prestigious and well-remunerated public orators. In *Lives of the Sophists* he is trying to write the history of contemporary rhetoric as philosophy, trying to forge a historical identification of those whom he calls sophists with those he would also represent as professing philosophy. To achieve this Philostratus links the present practice of rhetoric, and its professional examplars, with the ancient schools of the sophists of Athens nearly eight hundred years earlier, in the fifth century BC. The present practitioners of epideictic rhetoric are a "second" sophistic: not *new*, he proclaims (because if new, surely, they would have no pedigree for their representation as an intellectual cadre), but *later*, following on a tangible and traceable ancient precedent in which rhetoric and philosophy were linked. Of the earliest sophistic, Philostratus declares: "We must regard the ancient sophistic art as philosophic rhetoric. . . . The men of former days applied the name 'sophist,' not only to orators whose surpassing eloquence won them a brilliant reputation, but also to philosophers who expounded their theories with ease and fluency."[9]

But Philostratus does more than invent the Second Sophistic: he *reinvents* the "first" sophistic as an age of philosophy.[10] The word "sophist," in his use, is now elevated and enlarged to comprehend both rhetoric and philosophy, or more precisely, he describes the improvement of philosophy when it is attached to the disciplinary power of rhetoric. In his apotheosis of the first sophistic, Philostratus revises tradition. From the time of Plato, the reputation of the early sophists (of whom Gorgias is probably the most famous) had been much debased, their contributions to philosophy either ignored or suppressed. But it is in his unconventional approach to the early sophists that Philostratus finds a framework and language for writing a certain kind of intellectual life narrative. He makes individual and collective sophistic lives stand for something beyond themselves: he makes the whole historical phenomenon of sophistic stand for the profession of thought. The sophists, who had already regarded themselves as "professionals of the intelligence," were indeed the ideal subject (the only possible subject, perhaps) for such a new kind of narrative.[11]

What aspects of the self-making of the early (the "first") sophistic of fifth-century Athens would lend themselves to such a coherent narrative model of intellectual professionalism? First, there is the external, social, operative character of their teaching. They offered a radical and practical pedagogy which promised sure success to the eager students who wanted a leg up in the skills necessary for major roles in Athenian public life. Unlike traditional education in arts, trades, or even philosophy, sophistic *paideia* offered a systematic induction into intellectual skills which could produce orators and other civic professionals, that is, citizens competent to undertake public affairs. Its educational outlook put a new premium on intellectual preparation, over the old emphasis on physical or athletic pursuits: like Abelard fifteen hundred years later, the early sophists displaced athletic "chivalry" with intellectual competition. For their innovative, professionalized teaching, the sophists exacted fees. They were surely not the first teachers to earn a living by charging students, but they were apparently the first purveyors of an intellectual system – grounded in philosophical, dialectical, and especially rhetorical training – to accept *any* fee-paying pupil, and for this they were famously derided by Socrates and his disciple, Plato. In sum, they offered an intellectual and educational *techne*.[12]

I want to pause over the dynamics of this. Their *techne* – a curriculum and a practical apparatus for reasoning (exercises, model speeches, or arguments) – set them apart as professionals of thought. For example, in the dialogue *Protagoras*, Plato has the sophist Protagoras promising his *techne* to a young man with an assurance that it will work. But the *techne* that passes from teacher to pupil has a peculiar characteristic in which the fee charged for it plays some part: it requires the presence of the sophist-teacher to pass it on, and yet, because the *techne* is just that, an infinitely reproducible system, it does not require the sophist's presence to be effective. Much of the sophists' power to attract students depended on their personal presence as radical, innovative teachers. The magic of their teaching success, which relied on their own power to exemplify their oratorical teaching, gave them a kind of charisma as a new class of pedagogical leaders, "charisma," that is, in the Weberian sense: the "charisma" is centered in the person and works apart from traditional orders.[13] We might describe them, indeed, as "pedagogical virtuosi," a term which recalls Weber's "religious virtuoso."[14]

Yet the success of the sophists' methods also depended on the effectiveness of their system in their absence. Thus, notably, they were criticized for producing written handbooks which their pupils (and many others) could take away, thus allowing their system to be learned and used without their immediate supervision. We do not know very much about what these handbooks might have looked like, since only fragments of sophistic writings remain today. But the historical significance of the handbooks is still clear. The sophists offered an education that was so systematized that it did not depend on personal ethos; yet it derived its radical magic (here we might think of Gorgias and his magical rhetoric) from the kind of discipleship that has a charismatic focus. It is as if the whole Weberian dynamics of charisma, where the charismatic broadens out into routinization, is married in sophistic in one piece: the personal ethos of the teacher and his absence, in one package.

The ancient sophists, like their late antique successors, were creatures of the city. They were foreigners to Athens, described often as ambulant teachers and lecturers, attractive and useful in diplomacy, but also alienated from local civic affairs. Most importantly, their identification with cities made them both visible and vulnerable, key factors in their success and in the persecutions they sometimes suffered. It was also their visibility in cities that played into the personal ethos of their teaching: their success was a balance of public visibility and more intimate pedagogical presence.

In his *Lives of the Sophists*, Philostratus wants to rehabilitate the image of the first sophistic and link the rhetorical culture of his own day with a historical tradition of public intellectuals. Thus Socrates, Plato, Aristotle, and other philosophical figures play no role in his narrative formation of a tradition. Rather, he looks to recapture the charismatic character of early sophistic, and secure it as an integral feature of his Second Sophistic through an emphasis on public visibility, personal ethos, and the professionalization of thought. He is aware that the public visibility of the early sophists opened them to a persecution which is not suffered by the state-sponsored sophists of his own day; but he finds in public visibility and individual ethos the defining traits of a professional intellectual class. Thus the lives he is narrating only matter for their public, professional faces, and for the declamatory style exemplified by each figure: he is not interested in whole biographies, but in professional biographies.[15] And it is here that ethos matters the most. For example, in the account of Damianus of Ephesus, an older contemporary of Philostratus himself, the representation of personal presence is inseparable from the public visibility of stylistic example. Damianus, generous with his expertise, wealthy enough to forgive the fees from poor students coming from remote areas, had a style, says Philostratus, "more sophistic than is usual in a legal orator, and more judicial than is usual in a sophist"; and in his old age, he still allowed visits from younger orators attracted by his renown, Philostratus himself among them.[16] Philostratus invents a new genre of intellectual biography: the lives narrated constitute an institutional truth and thus create an institutional discourse. It is in the collectivity of the lives narrated that the notion of a profession of thought is brought into being. This is biography as institutional *prosopopoeia*: the individual human figure embodies a cultural condition, the ambitions and possibilities of a professional class. And the very possibility of narrating them is the transmission of their collective *techne*.

*     *     *

Antiquity thus beats both the Middle Ages and modernity to the principle of defining intellectual careers in narrative. Philostratus' model is not, however, passed on into the Middle Ages in any recognizable form. The Augustinian model of spiritual-intellectual autobiography is not the same thing as Philostratus' genre of lives defined by their intellectual, institutional, visibility; moreover, of course, the Augustinian autobiographical genre of intellectual-spiritual theodicy was not resumed during the early and central Middle Ages. It is a fair generalization that what might potentially have been forms of intellectual biography were absorbed into hagiography and similar genres related to *acta sanctorum* (notably, for example, canonization documents), or more broadly, into the genres of ecclesiastical and dynastic chronicles. In other words, the early, central, and high Middle Ages has biographies, but not substantial intellectual biographies in the form that late antiquity sees. Abelard's extraordinary self-professionalizing autobiography is the exception that proves the rule, and I will deal here with his work in light of this.

However, it is not a simple case of there being no intellectual biographies in the Latin academic cultures of the twelfth and thirteenth centuries. For in fact, there are various nascent forms of intellectual biography in the academic cultures of the twelfth-century cathedral schools in western Europe. Abelard's autobiography is the most remarkable and developed of them, although it remains the exception. Throughout the twelfth century there are various biographical and autobiographical eruptions that give limited accounts of individual careers, or schools, or groups of masters. Some of these are directed to specific personal or communal-sacral purposes. In 1125 Rupert of Deutz defended his theological career in an *Apologia* attached to his commentary on the Benedictine rule.[17] Also early in the twelfth century, the monk Guibert de Nogent, writing a history of the administrative and political crises that beset his monastery, included what is now a very famous account of his childhood education and his entrance into monastic orders.[18] In the latter half of the century, Gerald of Wales, indefatigable in his struggles to secure the Bishopric of St. David's, constructed an elaborately self-serving account of his administrative career and some of his literary successes.[19] Perhaps most interesting of these biographical narratives that serve other kinds of purposes is the hostile account of Abelard and his teaching included in the life of St. Goswin, which provided an occasion to depict Goswin in his youth as a courageous challenger to Abelard in the dialectical combats on the Mont Ste. Geneviève, a young David taking on the intellectual arrogance of the Parisian Philistine giant, Abelard, vanquishing him in a disputative encounter in Abelard's own school. Most of the account is given over to recording Goswin's success, and indeed, this is an example of the absorption of intellectual biography into the genre of saint's life.[20]

More relevant to a history of intellectual biography are certain broadly institutional gestures, catalogues of masters or surveys of schools. Baudri of Bourgeuil (mid-twelfth century) has a poem in which he lists the famous schools of France in order to praise the cathedral school at Rheims above all others.[21] An anonymous satirical poem of the mid-twelfth century, the "Metamorphosis Goliae," produces a catalogue of the masters of Parisian and other important schools in order to target monastic attempts to suppress certain adventurous strains of philosophical speculation.[22] The most notable of these are the accounts offered in John of Salisbury's *Metalogicon* (mid twelfth-century). John's reminiscences of his teacher Bernard of Chartres concern the master's pedagogical method, rather than his career, but his short survey of all the best known masters in northern France of the first half of the twelfth century comes somewhat closer to the making of the genre of intellectual biography on the model of Philostratus, that is, the life of a school as well as of individual careers.[23] This section of the *Metalogicon*, with its attention to pedagogical ethos, is on the cusp between anecdote and biographical narrative. With this embryonic form of intellectual biography, we might see the institutional conditions of northern France in the twelfth century, with the emergence of truly urban schools in the major cathedral centers, as ideal for the full expression of the genre in the centuries to follow. But curiously, these narrative gestures do not eventuate in a fuller institutional manifestation of the genre.

In has often been argued that post-classical Europe did not see the "profession" of thought until the beginning of the thirteenth century, with the rise of the universities. "In the beginning there were the towns," says Jacques Le Goff of the "birth" of a medieval intellectual class along with the commercial, industrial division of labor in the cities and towns of western Europe in the twelfth century and after.[24] This may be a significant link with the two sophistic movements of antiquity: as the sophists were urban internationalists on the scale of the ancient world, so the urban communities of medieval universities attracted scholars from far afield. E.R. Dodds' description of sophistic schools as "kingdoms of the intelligence" for an ambulant, deracinated class of professionals might also serve – with little modification – to describe the sensibility of medieval university communities.[25] So we could say that the later Middle Ages did not "invent" the modern intellectual (contrary to what Le Goff and others have argued), but rather that it reinvented the "modern" intellectual of the two ancient sophistics.

Thus it might be surprising that university culture, between the thirteenth and fifteenth centuries, produced no form of intellectual biography. After all, there were hundreds of *magistri* living lives of hard-won privilege and no doubt great professional memorability across the universities of western and central Europe, products of environments that were at once oral and richly textual.[26] But we seem to have no narrative account, by an admiring student, or indeed colleague, of how those lives were lived professionally – and this in an age not otherwise innocent of biography. My interest here is to wonder why it did not emerge.

The structures of teaching in the medieval university reprise the success of the urban sophists of antiquity: their key features are also curriculum, professionalism, the taking of fees, and most of all, the transmission of a *techne*. Perhaps, however, the university is so successful in its transmission of a *techne* that the master needs only to be part of the system which absorbs the particularity of his career.

Thus we might ask what is the place of the individual pedagogical ethos in representations of intellectual work in the university. First, university discourse about intellectual process tends to emphasize work, assiduous labor in the attainment of knowledge. It is continual labor that most defines this intellectual life, not the celebrated and individuated product (this the university has in common with the earliest ongoing tradition of monasticism). Another factor that might obviate the individuation of professional life narratives is that induction into the university structure entails a kind of (symbolic) wiping clean of one's former life (this is somewhat comparable to the Cistercian monastic principle of "blanching" the memory of one's former life before taking the vows of the order). From this moment on, one's progress through the institutional life of the university is expressed in broadly communal bureaucratic terms, through curricular statutes, and the processes of determination or inception and the conferring of degrees. In this respect, then, it is the system, the routinized transmission of a *techne*, that becomes the life narrative, represented in the systematic documentary culture of university statutes, legal proceedings (and wranglings), decrees, and infinitely repeatable ceremonial paradigms laid down by statute.

The most important magisterial expressions are the methods of their work – lectures, preaching, disputations – to which are tied the written genres by which we know the masters – biblical commentaries, sermons, and especially the disputative genres of *summa*, *quaestio*, and *quodlibet*.[27] These last genres, the *summa*, the *quaestio*, and the *quodlibet* of the theology faculties, are the characteristic forms in which the magisterial "what I think/what I am" is recorded. I want to pause here over the *quodlibet*, to consider how this, the quintessential genre of theology masters, registers a meeting of two contradictory imperatives: the personal ethos, indeed, the charisma of the master in oral performance, and the necessary distribution or dissipation of charismatic contact into a formulaic written document. Herein we must look for the residue of a magisterial prosopography.

A *quodlibet* is a set of questions posed by any questioner "on any topic" (as the name implies), entertained by a master of theology (most typically) and held in two sessions. In the first session the questions would be heard and there would be preliminary answers (perhaps by a bachelor assisting the regent master); in the following session (which followed as soon as possible after the first) the master would present his final determinations on the questions.[28] The records of quodlibetal sessions, in which the question and the master's responses are written up and published after the event, are the closest we may come to envisioning something of the personal ethos of a university teaching situation. Moreover, the records are prepared not only by the master but by his assistants, his juniors, so these records are the closest we will come to an observer's "narration" of the career of a master.

The very success of a disputation such as the *quodlibet* depends on the immediacy and the tangibility of the master's ethos: in the intensely public and oral culture of university disputation and intellectual exchange, it is the gesture, the tone of voice, the magisterial performance that would ensure that the complex resolution of a question is properly understood by the audience. While this is the case with any public disputation, it is especially important with the *quodlibet*, because the master does not prepare the agenda in advance, but must respond to unexpected questions from any quarter. It is precisely this ephemeral ethical relationship with an academic audience that a biographical narrative would seek to capture. But the form that captures this instead is that of the magisterial signatures incorporated in the written records of the *quodlibetales*: the formulas *"Respondeo dicendum,"* or sometimes *"circa primum dico/circa secundum dico,"* or just *"Respondeo,"* which indicate the precise point at which the master is introducing his own resolution or determination of a given question. Other magisterial formulas might indicate that the master did not see his proposed resolution as definitive, for example: *"sed nihil circa hoc determinando sed probabiliter coniecturando."*[29] These textual magisterial signatures are in place to ensure, long after the public, oral event, that the arguments are read properly; this is an environment in which magisterial ethos and pedagogical charisma can be replaced by the signatures in the text, and in which the conventions of reading the text and spotting the appropriate clues are just as important as the public event itself.

The telling contrast with this advanced stage of textual conventionality is the earlier career of Abelard, which spans the late eleventh to the mid-twelfth centuries, the period of the urban cathedral schools before the formation of the universities, a period that leaves us (as we have seen) some nascent intellectual narratives. Abelard, by contrast, leaves us a remarkable autobiographical record of his own restless character and his charismatic draw as a teacher.[30] The attention he gives to the charismatic power of his teaching marks him as an ideological product of the eleventh century whose intellectual outook Stephen Jaeger has characterized as a true culture of personality, of the personal authority of the teacher, in which orality (of a highly literate kind) produced what he calls 'charismatic learning."[31] (Thus, considering the reputed grandeur of its intellectual achievements, the eleventh century has left behind rather little artifactual record – written or otherwise – of its intellectual culture.) As is clear from Abelard's narrative, the success and effect of his teaching was tied to his personal presence, as he formed and disbanded school after school, trailing disciples from place to place, even where he sought eremitic solitude in his oratory of the Paraclete. But he was, of course, also formed by the academic ideology of the twelfth century in that he wrote prolifically, and it was his writings that brought him professional disaster and two condemnations. For in his writings he has a tendency to absent himself, conspicuously and sometimes even contemptuously, from any determinative magisterial presence: it is as if he is saying to his readers: it's not *my* responsibility to ensure that *you* don't misread the arguments I lay out for you – here are the arguments, they speak for themselves. Thus at the end of his *Ethics* (written about 1125) he says: "It is sufficient for me in everything I write to expound my opinion rather than put forward a definition of the truth."[32] Perhaps this was a contemptuous glance backward at the Council of Soissons of 1121, where he had endured the condemnation of one of his first theological tracts, by readers who failed precisely (perhaps willfully so) to get the point.

Abelard was terribly persecuted in his lifetime partly because he *did not* record his own teacherly ethos in his writings, because he disdained the magisterial signature, because he offered little guidance, in the absence of his person, to how his conclusions ought to be read. It is a deep irony that someone of such powerful charisma was ruined professionally because he did not leave the character mark in his writings. One hundred years after Abelard's death, the university masters of the thirteenth century took Abelard's revolutionary methods of disputation fully on board, and of course used their own classroom presence to make their reasoning understood: but they were also working in a world where the textual conventions of understanding were clear, and where the personal ethos of the teacher was translated into and distributed throughout routinized magisterial formulas: "*Respondeo.*"

\*     \*     \*

In a sense, then, the masters wrote their own "narratives", inscribing themselves in a conventionalized, routinized documentary system that made them both less visible individually and less vulnerable. Unlike the sophists of early and later antiquity, the medieval masters were not legible on the terms of collective or individual biographical narrative. Where the ancient sophists successfully inhabited the paradox of personal presence and impersonal, written *techne*, the medieval university masters seem to have disappeared into the overwhelming success of their technical, documentary effects. With the university masters we have the return of the written *techne* itself, that material effect which marked the earliest sophistic teaching as a kind of heterodoxy, as a form of teaching that could potentially make teacherly presence redundant (ironically even as the near-magical force of sophistic teaching depended on intimate contact). But it is another paradox of history that the university masters' written *techne*, the published records of their disputations, was fully incorporated into an institutional orthodoxy, and that it was the rhetorical information conserved in their documentary effects that protected them from suspicion. As embodiments of a public professionalism, the masters were completely enveloped – shrouded – in a documentary orthodoxy which rendered their individual careers invisible to narrative and even supererogatory to narrate.

The return of narrative representation of intellectual lives, the genre through which Philostratus could imagine a profession of thought and make individual lives into a historical and cultural phenomenon, instead has to await the eruptive moment of heresy in the late Middle Ages. The fact of heresy alone might produce martyrology; but heresy that grows out of an academic core produces narratives of intellectual work and identity. The medieval heresy narratives to which I will now turn do not, in appearance, resemble Philostratus' expansive collection of professional lives of sophists, but they constitute a late premodern avatar of Philostratus' genre. Academic heretics stand outside the sanctions of the intellectual system that produced them, but the narratives that commemorate their charismatic presence also make the heretics visible through and against conventional professional discourses. Heretical intellectuals are all ethos, but the narratives make them visible members of a professional class and keepers of a *techne*.

Both the Wycliffite heresy in England, which began in the later fourteenth century, and its younger sibling, the Hussite reformist movement in Bohemia, which took shape in the first decade of the fifteenth century, originated in academic circles: the circle of the Oxford theologian John Wyclif, and the circle of the Prague arts master and preacher Jan Hus. I want to begin by looking at a commemoration of Wyclif and his university followers, in a text that offers a rather embryonic form of intellectual biography. From its beginnings in Oxford in the 1370s, the English Wycliffite (or Lollard) movement reached out to a substantial and receptive popular audience. By the 1380s its popular pedagogical missions were already seen as a threat to church and state; by the 1390s both the original Oxford inner circle of Wyclif's acolytes and the popular lay reception of the heterodoxy had come under vigorous suppression; and in 1401 the heresy was declared a capital offense.

In 1407, William Thorpe, who had been a younger member of Wyclif's circle at Oxford, was arrested in Shrewsbury for preaching Lollard doctrine; he then wrote an account of his interrogation at the hands of Thomas Arundel, the Archbishop of Canterbury. The historical facticity of Thorpe's experience and the veracity of his account have long posed a problem, because there are no further documentary records of Thorpe's arrest and interrogation; but the less we can confirm about Thorpe himself, the more it frees us to look at the rhetorical character of the narrative left to us under his name. Most of Thorpe's narrative recounts the details of his day-long examination by the Archbishop, but in one section, in answer to a question from the Archbishop about how Thorpe first became a Lollard, the narrative veers into autobiography and an account of Wyclif and his circle of academic disciples at Oxford. Thorpe recounts that in his youth he disappointed his parents and friends who had paid for him to study for the priesthood, because he had no desire to be a priest; finally he found a group of reformist priests and began to study with them. When asked by the Archbishop who these men were he describes Wyclif and his circle:

Ser, in his tyme maister Ioon Wiclef was holden of ful many men the grettist clerk that they knewen lyvynge upon erthe. And therwith he was named, as I gesse worthili, a passing reuli man and an innocent in al his lyvynge. And herfore grete men of kunnynge and other also drowen myche to him, and comownede ofte with him. And thei savouriden so his loore that thei wroten it bisili and enforsiden hem to rulen hem theraftir. . . . Maistir Ion Aston taughte, and wroot acordingli and ful bisili, where and whanne and to whom he myghte, and he usid it himsilf, I gesse, right perfyghtli unto his lyves eende. Also Filip of Repintoun whilis he was a chanoun of Leycetre, Nycol Herforde, dane Geffrey of Pikeringe, monke of Biland and a maistir of dyvynyte, and Ioon Purveye, and manye other whiche weren holden rightwise men and prudent, taughten and wroten bisili this forseide lore of Wiclef, and conformeden hem therto. And with all these men I was ofte homli and I comownede with hem long tyme and fele, and so bifore all othir men I chees wilfulli to be enformed bi hem and of hem, and speciali of Wiclef himsilf, as of the moost vertuous and goodlich wise man that I herde of owhere either knew.

[Sir, in his time master John Wyclif was considered by many men the greatest living clerk they knew. And thus he was called, and I believe deservedly, a very disciplined man, of pure and wholesome living. And therefore men of great knowledge and many others were attracted to him and communed with him. And they so savored his learning that they committed it to writing, and they goverened themselves by it. . . . Master John Aston energetically taught and wrote [this learning] wherever, and whenever, and to whomever he might, and he followed it himself perfectly until the end of his life. Also Philip of Repingdon, while he was a canon of Leicester, Nicholas Hereford, Geoffrey of Pickering (monk of Byland and master of divinity), and John Purvey, and many others who were considered righteous and prudent men, taught and busily wrote down the aforesaid learning of Wyclif, and lived by it. And with all these men I was often familiar and I spent much rewarding time with them, and so over all other men I willingly chose these men as my models, and especially Wyclif himself, as the most virtuous and goodly wise man whom I knew or had heard of.][33]

It is worth nothing that, as textually prolific as Wyclif and his followers were in disseminating their thought, this seems to be the only narrative account, by a witness or an associate, of Wyclif's actual circle. As intellectual biography it does not go very far, but it gives us a flavor of how the creation of an intellectual movement might be narrated. This is indeed an intellectual movement, although it is also presented as spiritual discipleship; it is important that the Thorpe narrative stresses the work of copying, writing, and teaching by those men who seem to have clustered around Wyclif at Oxford (it is almost certain that the scene described is an Oxford one, since most of the associates named here were connected with Oxford, where such textual work would also have been most easily carried out). What is crucial to the narrative is the ethos of the master, Wyclif, and the distribution of that ethos among the inner circle. The institutional world presented here is the medieval university, which as we have seen normally resists narrative, but here the members' work as professionals transmitting a *techne* is also what makes their heretical identity most legible and memorable. Their heresy is rendered as a different but still recognizable version of the technical work of universities: teaching, writing, copying, distributing. Moreover, the long after-effects of the *techne* produced by Wyclif's academic associates were precisely of the sort that orthodoxy (whether religious or civic) most fears when pedagogical presence is separated from pedagogical system. The Wycliffites produced what were, in essence, "handbooks," systematic guides to biblical study for lay people without professional exegetical training. What these have in common with the handbooks of the earliest sophists (and there is much that they do not have in common with the sophistic handbooks) is that the master's charismatic presence could survive into and be seen to inhabit the routinized, widely distributed, textual expression of his teaching. The medieval heretics could marry charismatic affect and quasi-impersonal technical system in one package.

Jan Hus, the Prague reformer, comes into narrative view in much more spectacular terms. Hus became a regent master in the arts faculty at the University of Prague in 1398, and was rector of the University in 1409.[34] In 1402 he had also become rector and preacher of the Bethlehem Chapel in Prague. In his student years he had been an admirer of John Wyclif's philosophical writings; but during the first decade of the fifteenth century, as he became more involved in pastoral duties, he was at the center of the growing church reform movement in Bohemia, which owed some of its tenets to Wycliffite theology, and its dissenting outlook to the English heretical movement. Among Hus's reformist associates in Prague was the nobleman John of Chlum, who appointed as his own secretary a young man named Peter of Mladoňovice. Peter had been a student of Hus at the University of Prague, and had fallen under his intellectual and spiritual leadership. In late 1414, Hus was summoned to the Council of Constance to answer questions about his supposed heretical beliefs. The nobleman John of Chlum accompanied Hus, as did the young secretary, Peter of Mladoňovice. Peter's role, during the long detainment of Hus at Constance, became that of recording the proceedings against Hus, proceedings that led to Hus's condemnation and execution in July, 1415.

Peter had access to all the written documents that were flying around the conciliar proceedings, which he duly incorporated into his account. But he was also an eyewitness to Hus's two hearings by the Council, and like a good secretary, he put his ear to the ground to collect all the intrigue and whispers among the prosecuting parties at the Council.

Thus we have a record of the last year of Hus's life as observed by a former student, a sympathetic member of Hus's own professional class. Peter's account is certainly part martyrology, and part legal-documentary transcript. But it is also intellectual prosopography, a representation of an intellectual persona under interrogation. The account of Hus's two hearings before the Council in early June, 1415, erupts into the drama of high-stakes academic encounter. Peter's narrative of the legal-institutional discourse of an international church council hearing a celebrated heresy case is suddenly interrupted by another genre, intellectual *prosopopoeia*, an individuated intellectual trajectory. At the same time, the institutional setting of the Council of Constance is also like that of a university: it consists of documents, clerical crowds, magisterial hierarchies, judgements and determinations, deliberations, and the issuing of decrees. Thus Peter's account of Hus's two hearings functions generically like the *reportatio* of a quodlibetal session, with rapid-fire questions posed, resolutions offered, new questions issued from other quarters. But this *reportatio* has a plot, a hero, a life and ethical presence beyond the magisterial signature.

It is not surprising that the account of the hearings between Hus and his conciliar prosecutors reads like scholastic sparring: they were all academics, and the questions under issue were familiar from academic theology (although in this case, a man's life depended on the outcome of the disputation). I will give two examples from the hearings. In the middle of the first hearing the discussion revolves around the very familiar questions of universals and particulars, and substance and accident, for Hus was accused of holding the heretical Wycliffite position against transubstantiation, that is, denying the annihilation of the substance of the bread after the consecration of the eucharist. Pierre d'Ailly, one of the major intellectual figures at the University of Paris, rises to ask Hus a question about universals in order to entrap Hus into denying transubstantiation. Hus delicately evades the trap, at which point the secretary, Peter of Mladoňovice, reports, "a certain Englishman wished to prove by an exposition of the subject that the material bread remained there. The Master [Hus] said: 'That is a puerile argument that schoolboys study' – and acquitted himself thereby."[35] The questions being raised are in fact more appropriate to academic disputation than to theological examination, but it is Hus's dispatching of logical objections that is more memorable and persuasive, narratively, than his various and repeated heartfelt professions of faith on central theological matters. In a moment like this, with the contemptuous squelching of a too-elementary line of argument, the snuffing of a weak opponent, the master's career in classroom and lecture hall is etched in bold. This is the schoolmaster as hero, doomed to be sacrificed in the war of ecclesiastical politics, but triumphant as disputative opponent.

At the end of the second hearing, on June 8, Hus is asked to abjure the heretical beliefs wrongly attributed to him. This is a crucial moment, and in Peter's narrative it is shown to hang on Hus's philological rigor: the meaning of the word "abjure." Peter reports Hus's words:

> "But that I should abjure all the articles laid against me, of which many are – God knows – falsely ascribed to me, I should by lying prepare for myself a snare of damnation. For 'to abjure,' as I recall having read in the *Catholicon*, is to renounce a formerly held error. But since many articles that I have never held are ascribed to me, nor have they entered my heart, it appears to me, therefore, contrary to conscience to abjure them and to lie." And they [the Council] said: "No! no! that is not the meaning of 'to abjure'." And the Master [Hus] said: "Thus have I read: that is 'to abjure'."[36]

At this liminal moment, when he is minutes away from condemnation and death sentence by the Council, Hus's invocation of John of Balbus's *Catholicon*, the ubiquitous scholastic lexicon and encyclopedic dictionary, the late medieval equivalent of the *Larousse*, is an act of heroic pedantry. At least it is heroism in Peter's account, and that is what matters. This moment traces the trajectory from classroom to conciliar courtroom, and it is Hus as professional intellectual, not simply as reformist martyr, who emerges into stark legibility.

So in the example of the Hus narrative, and more weakly in the case of the Thorpe account of the circle of Wyclif, we have the ethos of the master projected beyond the *techne* of which he is the keeper. It was the possibility of that ethical impression that Philostratus sought to rescue from the scattered detritus of the first sophistic and implant in his representation of the Second Sophistic as an intellectual movement; and it was precisely this ethical presence that medieval university masters translated into the formulaic signatures which point to, but do not embody, their professional lives.

Our contemporary arguments about what is, what *makes* an intellectual – about how intellectuals can be defined against other "classes" of people, or from what position intellectual discourse enters the social frame, whether universal or specific, organic or traditional interests – revolve around how we go about representing intellectual lives. Their historical presence is always mediated to us through the representational mechanics of the literary genre of intellectual biography. And in this respect it is always the question of representation as literary artifact, as *Darstellung*, that haunts our analysis and conversation. It haunts it precisely where we are unresolved about how we would want to have ourselves represented: would we want to have our own work as intellectuals – or indeed our own careers as academics and teachers – represented in terms of personal presence or of impersonal (and reproduceable) *techne*?[37] Through which form do our own afterlives, our own after-effects, make a better intervention? If we have come to privilege the narratives of ethos or personal presence beyond *techne*, we might ponder that it was in the oppositional cultures and charismatic teaching of ancient sophistic and of late-medieval heresy that our narrative preferences have their pre-modern roots. Where we acknowledge that our arguments always return to conflicts of representation, to what can or cannot be represented in intellectual life narratives, we can also look to what the pre-modern can teach us about the fitful, difficult history of the invention of the genre itself.

## Notes

1   I am grateful to Ralph Rosen, Ian Wei, and Nicolette Zeeman for advice, information, and insight at various stages of this project.
2   This issue is discussed in R. Copeland, *Pedagogy, Intellectuals, and Dissent in the Later Middle Ages* (Cambridge, UK: Cambridge University Press, 2001), pp. 24–49.
3   The best recent survey of these issues is J. Jennings and A. Kemp-Welch, "The Century of the Intellectual: From the Dreyfus Affair to Salman Rushdie," in J. Jennings and A. Kemp-Welch (eds.), *Intellectuals in Politics: From the Dreyfus Affair to Salman Rushdie* (London: Routledge, 1997), pp. 1–21.
4   Both purposes are evident in C. Leonardi, "L'intellettuale nell'altomedioevo," in Università di Genova, *Il comportamento dell'intellettuale nella società*

*antica* (Genoa: Istituto di Filologica Classica e Medievale, 1980), pp. 119–39. More skeptical about the transference of the concept is H. Bardon, "La notion d'intellectuel à Rome," *Studii clasice* (Bucharest), 13 (1971): 95–107.

5   Walter Benjamin, "The Storyteller," in H. Arendt (ed.) and H. Zohn (trans.) *Illuminations* (New York: Schocken, [1955] 1969), pp. 83–109.

6   The "professional narrative" as "vocational discourse" is the subject of important studies by B. Robbins, "Death and Vocation: Narrativizing Narrative Theory," *PMLA*, 107 (1992): 38–50; and "The Insistence of the Public in Postmodern Criticism," in *Secular Vocations: Intellectuals, Professionalism, Culture* (London: Verso, 1993), pp. 84–117.

7   See M. Mazza, "L'intellettuale come ideologo: Flavio Filostrato ed uno *speculum principis* del III secolo d.C.", in Università di Genova, *Il comportamento dell'intellettuale*, pp. 33–66 (esp. pp. 44–55) and G. Anderson, *Philostratus: Biography and Belles Lettres in the Third Century A.D.* (London, Sydney: Croom Helm, 1986), pp. 17–24.

8   On state dependence see Mazza, "L'intellettuale come ideologo," and also A.B. Breebaart, "The Freedom of the Intellectual in the Roman World," *Talanta*, 7 (1976): 55–75 (esp. 70–3).

9   Philostratus, *Lives of the Sophists*, W.C. Wright, trans. (Cambridge, MA.: Loeb Classical Library, Harvard University Press, 1998), book 1, prologue.

10  See C.P. Jones, "The Reliability of Philostratus," in G.W. Bowersock (ed.), *Approaches to the Second Sophistic* (University Park, PA: American Philological Association, 1974), pp. 11–16 (esp. p. 14).

11  For the early sophists as "professionals of the intelligence" see J. de Romilly, *The Great Sophists in Periclean Athens*, J. Lloyd, trans. (Oxford: Clarendon, [1988] 1992), p. 1.

12  de Romilly, *The Great Sophists*, pp. 6–7, 33–50. A helpful introduction to the sophists' professionalism is in W.K.C. Guthrie, *A History of Greek Philosophy*, vol. 3, *The Fifth-Century Enlightenment* (Cambridge, UK: Cambridge University Press, 1969), pp. 35–51.

13  See *From Max Weber, Essays in Sociology*, H.H. Gerth and C. Mills, eds. and trans. (London: Routledge, 1991), pp. 248, 262, 296. The term "charisma" is problematic in this context only because the term has often been used without reference to Weber's introduction of the ideal. For example, Jaeger uses the term in a technical way to describe the personality-based teaching of high medieval schools, but he makes no reference to Weber and his model of the "religious virtuoso." C.S. Jaeger *The Envy of Angels: Cathedral Schools and Social Ideas in Medieval Europe, 950–1200*. (Philadelphia: University of Pennsylvania Press, 1994).

14  Compare the discussion in G. Roth and W. Schluchter, *Max Weber's Vision of History: Ethics and Methods* (Berkeley, Los Angeles: University of California Press, 1979), pp. 130–2, where the term "ideological virtuoso" is intro-

Rita Copeland

duced to extend the meaning of Weber's "religious virtuoso" into the sphere of countercultural political activity.

15  Jones, "The Reliability of Philostratus," pp. 11–12, points out that *Lives of the Sophists* shares this feature to some extent with Suetonius' *De Grammaticis et Rhetoribus*.

16  *Lives of the Sophists*, book 2, ch. 23.

17  See J.H. van Engen, *Rupert of Deutz* (Berkeley, Los Angeles: University of California Press, 1983), pp. 313–15, 342–52; J.-P. Migne (ed.) *Patrologia Latina*, 221 vols (Paris: J.-P. Migne, 1844–55), vol. 170, pp. 477–80.

18  Guibert de Nogent, *Autobiographie: De vita sua*, E.-R. Labarde, ed. (Paris: Les Belles Lettres, 1981); J.F. Benton, trans., *Self and Society in Medieval France: The Memoirs of Guibert of Nogent (1064?–c.1125)* (New York: Harper and Row, 1970).

19  Gerald of Wales, *The Autobiography of Giraldus Cambrensis*, H.E. Butler, ed. and trans. (London: Jonathan Cape, 1937).

20  Goswin, Extracts from *Vita Beati Gosvini Aquicinctensis Abbatis*, in M. Bouquet and M.-J.-J. Brial (eds.), *Recueil des historiens des Gaules et de la France* (Paris: Imprimerie Impériale, 1806), vol. 14, pp. 442–8.

21  Baudri of Bourgevil, *Baldricus Burgulianus Carmina*, K. Hilbert, ed. (Heidelberg: Winter, 1979), no. 99. See Jaeger, *The Envy of Angels*, p. 61.

22  "Metamorphosis Goliae," R.B.C. Huygens, ed., "Mitteilungen aus Handschriften," *Studi Medievali*, 3rd series, 3 (1962): 764–72.

23  John of Salisbury, *Metalogicon*, J.B. Hall, ed. (Turnhout, Belgium: Brepols, 1991), book 1, ch. 24; book 2, ch. 10.

24  J. Le Goff, *Intellectuals in the Middle Ages*, T.L. Fagan, trans. (Oxford: Blackwell, [1957] 1993), p. 5.

25  E.R. Dodds, *The Ancient Concept of Progress* (Oxford: Clarendon, 1973), p. 100.

26  On the place of university masters in their societies, the "regent masters" as a caste, see J. Verger, "Teachers," in H. de Ridder-Symoens (ed.), *A History of the University in Europe*, vol. 1, *Universities in the Middle Ages* (Cambridge, UK: Cambridge University Press, 1992), pp. 144–68 (esp. pp. 162–8).

27  For the connection between method and genre, see M. Asztalos, "The Faculty of Theology," in Ridder-Symoens (ed.), *A History of the University in Europe*, vol. 1, pp. 409–41 (esp. p. 420).

28  Accessible introductions to the genre of the *quodlibet* can be found in I. Wei, "The Self-image of the Masters of Theology at the University of Paris in the late Thirteenth and Early Fourteenth Centuries," *Journal of Ecclesiastical History*, 46: 398–431 (esp. p. 401), and in J.F. Wippel. "Quodlibetal Questions," in B.C. Bazàn et al. (eds.), *Les questions disputées et les questions quodlibétiques dans les facultés de théologie, de droit, et de médecine* (Turnhout, Belgium: Brepols, 1985), pp. 157–220.

29  All examples from Wippel, "Quodlibetal Questions," pp. 195–9.

30  Abelard, *Historia Calamitatum*, J. Monfrin, ed. (Paris: Vrin, 1959); English translation B. Radice, *The Letters of Abelard and Heloise* (Harmondsworth, UK: Penguin, 1974).

31  Jaeger, *The Envy of Angels*, pp. 3–4, 7–9, 36–195 (esp. pp. 76–131).

32  *Peter Abelard's Ethics*, D.E. Luscombe, ed. and trans. (Oxford: Clarendon, 1971), p. 140.

33  "Testimony of William Thorpe," in A. Hudson (ed.), *Two Wycliffite Tests: The Sermon of William Taylor (1406); The Testimony of William Thorpe (1407)*. (Oxford: Oxford University Press, 1993), pp. 40–1. (My translation).

34  The best English-language biography of Hus is M. Spinka, *John Hus: A Biography* (Princeton, NJ: Princeton University Press, 1968), on which the brief biographical account here is based.

35  Peter of Mladoňovice, *John Hus at the Council of Constance*, M. Spinka, trans. (New York: Columbia University Press, 1966), p. 168.

36  Ibid., p. 215.

37  I thank Bruce Robbins for this point.

# Chapter 3

# Humanism, Slavery, and the Republic of Letters

## David Wallace

To name that whiteness in the black imagination is often a representation of terror. One must face written histories that erase and deny, that reinvent the past to make the present vision of racial harmony and pluralism more plausible.[1]

The "humanism" of my title suggests the development of certain specific, chiefly philological, techniques that we are all more or less (in this republic of letters) heir to. Yet at the same time the term is often employed to suggest an escape from specific, locally contingent limits of history. This is especially true of the ways in which criticism has spoken of Francesco Petrarca, founding father of European humanism. Here is a typical example:

> The Renaissance discovered itself with a new, intense consciousness of rupture and loss. Antiquity was far in the past, cut off from it by all the obscurity of the *medium aevum* between them, yet far in advance of the crude barbarism which had prevailed throughout the supervening centuries. Petrarch's passionate call, at the threshold of the new age, proclaimed the vocation of the future: "This slumber of forgetfulness will not last forever: after the darkness has been dispelled, our grandsons will be able to walk back into the pure radiance of the past."

This unresistant recycling of Petrarchan terms of reference flows from the pen not of Joseph Burckhardt, but of Perry Anderson.[2] Attention to the particularities of historical process and struggle – which we might expect from a materialist criticism – flies out the window, it seems, the minute Petrarch enters the building. Remarkably, Anderson does not think to connect Petrarchan sensations of rupture, loss, and being cut off with the form of polity for and within which Petrarch worked for most of his mature life: which is to say not republicanism but despotism, its political antithesis. The Visconti, whom Petrarch served as ambassador, envoy, letter-writer and general cultural celebrity, set about the systematic destruction of local communal, decision-making, devotional, and religious traditions (including the demolition of the time-honored cathedral); local vernacular writers were neglected at Milan and Pavia, and an army of deracinated intellectuals and humanist hacks was recruited from all over to draft and promulgate princely decrees in Latin.[3] Much of this evokes comparison with developments in England under Henry VIII, including the studied cultivation of a David-like, indeed god-like, figure exercising power with studied arbitrariness.[4] Henry, famously, had six wives; Bernabò Visconti, notoriously, was at one stage credited with having 36 living children and 18 women in various stages of pregnancy.[5] Existential disorientation, coupled with an impulse to flee from the world (to imagined pasts and futures) seems an entirely appropriate response from a poet-courtier such as Petrarch in such a milieu. It is therefore hardly surprising to hear Petrarch speak so eloquently to English poets, such as Wyatt and Surrey, at the time of Henry VIII. "Their dates are different" (to rework one of Perry Anderson's more felicitous sayings), "their times are the same."[6]

My suggestion is that narration *through* greater extensions of place and time (without neglect of local, particularizing detail) might free us from some of the parochial, period-and-nation-bound limits of more recent literary-historicist method. Such an approach might prove instructive in cases where myopic engagement within traditional period markers – such as "medieval" and "Renaissance" – obscures longer and wider continuities. For example, in writing the history of women we can locate individuals on one side or another of medieval/Renaissance, Catholic/Protestant divides; or we can focus upon common, continuous, and European-wide struggles against certain perennial Pauline injunctions. Within this extended frame, we might deduce that, for women in the republic of letters, there is but one big story: that the rise of university culture equates directly to the decline of educational opportunities for women. Such an extended historical period, beginning perhaps with the cloistering of Héloïse and continuing through Virginia Woolf's trespassings on college lawns at Oxbridge, c. 1928, might be termed (to borrow from French historiography) a "long Middle Ages"; except that Hildegard of Bingen – before the rise of universities – achieved or got away with things unimaginable, for women or for anybody, for some eight hundred years.[7]

Similarly, in this essay I will be talking chiefly about texts and events located within, or just outside, the Mediterranean, the sea at the center of the world. I hope and trust that your imaginings will be pulled forward and outward to later times, more distant places.

Working on Chaucer, as I do, gets me immediately enmeshed in periodization problems the minute he leaves England. Late in 1372, for example, my man left London and traveled to Florence, where (so literary history tells us) he decisively encountered the writings of Dante, Boccaccio, and Petrarch that were to revolutionize his poetry. But before he got to Florence, in 1373, Chaucer did the king's business in Genoa.[8] And here you are faced with a more serious historiographical challenge: for in Genoa, Chaucer crosses the lines of a slave trade. To think of Chaucer and slavery in the same conceptual frame is confusing; they would seem to belong to different parts of the curricular woods. But there is no doubt that the Genoese – with whom Chaucer had daily dealings as controller of customs – were the most active agents of a flourishing, European-wide slave trade. At Genoa, as Iris Origo so memorably puts it, visitors would encounter "whole shiploads of bewildered, half-naked men, women and children, unable even to understand what was said to them . . . unloaded upon the quays and then – after being prodded and paraded like cattle at a fair . . . sold by auction to the *sensali* [brokers] who forwarded them to their clients inland, according to their requirements."[9] Chief of these inland destinations was Florence.

In this essay, then, I would like to speak first of Genoa, then of how the emergent humanisms of Boccaccio and Petrarch mesh with the practices, values, and localities of slavery; and I'll make a final, late return to English (and Irish) terrain. My contention is that western *litterati* are all (almost all) at once sons of Genoa and sons of Petrarch. The implications of "Genoa" need to be retrieved and reattached to the history of humanism. The reasons for insisting on a masculine genealogy of "sonship" will, I hope, become self-evident. And the owning up to an ongoing relationship with things Petrarchan seems imperative: for without the philological, codicological, and textual competencies pioneered by Petrarch an essay such as this could hardly have been written.

Dante, in the downward progress of his *Inferno*, has unflattering things to say about many Italian cities,[10] but his address to the Genoese is reserved for the lowest point of all. "*Ahi Genovesi,*" he says,

> *. . . uomini diversi*
> *d'ogne costume e pien d'ogne magagna,*
> *perché non siete voi del mondo spersi?*
> (33.151–3)

Ah, men of Genoa, foreign to every decency, full of every vice, why have you not been scattered from the face of the world?

The condition of being *"del mondo spersi"* that Dante wishes on Genoa is precisely chosen (from the verb *sperdere*: to disperse, scatter, or drive away): for the Genoans were indeed prone to scatter themselves throughout the known world, and beyond. "Genoans are dispersed through the world," an anonymous medieval Genoese poet writes, "and wherever they go and dwell a new Genoa takes shape."[11] The Genoese were imagined to be, literally and figuratively, all at sea: for the chief business of their tottering republic was the sea. That is, rather than relying on any large-scale manufacturing operations (such as weaponry at Milan, cloth at Florence or Ghent), the Genoese specialized in trafficking the wares (and sometimes the Crusaders, or soldiery) of other nations from place to place.[12] They thus developed instincts for seeking out and connecting pockets of scarcity and surplus; for discovering new territories and new commodities; for pushing out the limits of the known or navigable world. It was this restless, inquisitive/acquisitive spirit that induced the Genoan Vivaldi brothers in 1291 to sail westward beyond the Mediterranean into uncharted Atlantic waters: a famous episode of unfinished voyaging tracked in *Inferno* 26, where Dante's Ulysses urges *his* brothers ( *"frati"*) to sail into the sunset. Dante, of course, finds the presumption of such voyaging disastrous. It is worth noting, however, that the unknown Genoese poet cited above sounds positively Ulyssean in his navigational imagining: "all men are sailors," he says; *"ogn omo tegno marinar / chi non cessa di navigar."*[13] There is no doubt that Genoese navigational networks helped the Black Death of 1347–9 spread with unprecedented efficiency; one account of its origins (which carried off between one third and one half of the European population) traces it back to Caffa in the Crimea, where besieging Tartars catapulted plague-ridden bodies into the Genoese slave-trading compound.[14]

Boccaccio's *Decameron* (which famously opens, of course, with the Black Death) declares that Genoans are naturally and voraciously driven by their attachment to money (*"uomini naturalmente vaghi di pecunia e rapaci,"* 2.4.14); in *Decameron* 1.8 it takes a Florentine to teach a Genoese nobleman the basics of *"cortesia."*[15] "Genoa scarcely comes within the range of our task," Jacob Burckhardt argues in his land-mark *Civilization of the Renaissance*, "as before the time of Andrea Doria [early sixteenth century] it took almost no part in the Renaissance."[16] What we have here is the familiar psychosis intrinsic to "Renaissance" paradigm-making that would split the cultural from the political and economic. The study of Genoa continually confronts us with histori-cal practices (enslavement, forced conversion, colonization) upon which cultural history chooses not to dwell. But if Florence – with its glorious efflorescences of painting, building, humanism, and literature – functions as the superego of an emergent Renaissance, Genoa – always present, if out of sight – forms the id.

Passage through Genoa, in the *Decameron*, often opens out into storytelling scenarios of vast geographical compass. *Decameron* 4.3 be-gins at Marseilles (a rival seafaring and slaving city) and passes through Genoa en route to Crete and Rhodes (two islands pioneering plantation-style, slave-based colonization in the fourteenth century). *Decameron* 2.9 begins with a Genoese merchant boasting of his wife's virtue in a Parisian inn and ends in Alexandria (which was, in fact, Genoa's chief trading partner).[17] The second Day of the *Decameron* fea-tures two *novelle* in which Genoans are encountered on the high seas as agents of piracy and enslavement. The first of them, 2.4, tells how a young Amalfian pirate is himself pirated by *"due gran cocche di gen-ovesi"* (14), two great Genoese carracks (ships of the kind that were too large to sail up the Thames, hence docked at Bristol and, later, Southampton).[18] And *Decameron* 2.6 features equivalent acts of piracy, this time (most notably) the snatching of children and their nurse from a Mediterranean island, who are taken to Genoa and bought as house-hold slaves by the famous Genoese house (the only one deemed worthy of mention by Burckhardt) of Doria.[19]

The long history of medieval Genoese slaving moves from west to east to west again between c. 1150 and 1500. Saracens from Spain make up the majority of slaves at Genoa until the Genoese negotiate their way into the Black Sea and Crimea in the later thirteenth century. By the later fourteenth century there are Greek, Russian, Slav, Turkish, Bosnian, and Circassian slaves at Genoa and Florence, but the great majority are described as "Tartars." With the fall of Constantinople in 1453 and then of Caffa in 1475, the focus of trade swings back to the west (which includes the north African coastline). After about 1500 the cost of obtaining a slave becomes prohibitive to all but the richest and most powerful, popes and dukes, cardinals and *grandes dames*.[20] Portraiture from this later period is misleading, in that slave children are often deployed almost as exotic pets or (in more modern American TV currency) Websters in the houses of the great. In the earlier period, however, slaves were a serious commodity to which value – in successive stages – might be added. Plucked or sold from her family in the Crimea, a young girl might spend a period at Caffa (absorbing Christian values) before being shipped to Genoa. There she might be bought by a prosperous artisan, who would teach her a craft like silkworking, before selling her on for further transportation, say, to Aragon.

The overwhelming majority of these slaves were young teenage (and often not quite teenage) girls.[21] There have been various explanations for this: for example, that an impoverished Tartar father might be more willing to sell his daughters than his sons.[22] But it is worth noting that prices paid for pubescent girls generally exceed those paid for boys, men, or women. It is also worth noting that the famous foundling hospitals of Tuscany begin to flourish at this time.[23] One deed of sale commends the exceptional ugliness of a 12-year-old female slave (she is said to have the face of a *tavolaccio*, or badly made table) on the grounds that the master's wife "*no[n] ne pigliera gielosia.*" The presence of such young women inevitably undermined the authority of wives, who were no doubt referred to another familiar Pauline injunction: that wives should obey their husbands as slaves their masters.[24]

Many of the features we associate with full-blown European colonialism – as the slaving Mediterranean steadily evolves into the black Atlantic – are clearly forming throughout this earlier period.[25] Deeds of sale consistently attempt racial profiling. Skin color does not yet feature as an absolute criterion of worth or enslavement, but figures rather as one aesthetic criterion among many.[26] Towards the end of the period, however, "Ethiopian" begins to stand in for Africans of any provenance and "black" begins to be deployed as a racial term.[27] The marking, scarring, and tattooing of enslaved bodies is commonplace; there are complex arrangements for the recovery of runaways. There are widespread practices of *locazione* or loaning out of female slaves, often for periods of breast-feeding. There are fears in the white population of being poisoned by slaves, or of being overwhelmed by sheer numbers. There are the little-known terrors of the middle passage (insurance claims make it clear that slaves threw themselves overboard).[28] There are traces, also, of the secret language of slaves, preserved in literary fragments[29] and (a subject needing more investigation) in the palpably eastern-inflected style of certain Western paintings (slaves sometimes served artisan-painter masters).[30]

In 1396, a ship traveling between "Roumania" and Genoa contained 191 pieces of lead, 80 slaves, and 17 bales of pilgrims' robes.[31] It was an embarrassment for Christians to enslave Christians, or those who had converted, but compromises were found: for example, it was ruled that a person's fitness for enslavement might be determined not by her or his current religion, but rather by culture of origin. So it is that slaves often arrived with their names intact (at least as transcribed by semi-literate Tuscan traders) and were only given Christian names once sold and baptized: thus Cotlu, Jamanzach, Tholon, Charactas, and Sarumbieh become Maria, Caterina, and Marta. Such evolving refinements, I shall argue, were paralleled or sustained by discourses of an emergent humanism, particularly through its recuperation of classical texts and classical values. The whole mélange is neatly summarized by a transaction that took place in Genoa, in which a slave is sold for 40 pounds (*"livres"*): 25 of the pounds are paid in the form of two books, the *Office of Our Lady, the Virgin Mary* and Seneca's *Letter to Lucilius.*[32]

In *Decameron* 2.6, the *novella* which sees children snatched from a Mediterranean island and sold in Genoa, Boccaccio takes care to have the nurse snatched and sold along with the children, but the mother (his heroine, madonna Beritola) left alone on the island: for were his heroine to be enslaved, her sexual virtue could not be assured. (Boccaccio, we might note, was himself illegitimate and the father of at least five children who died in infancy; he never married and may have died as a Catholic priest.) Alone on her island, Beritola goes half-wild, breast-feeding two young roebucks as her skin color changes from white to dark (*"bruna"*, 20). The pathos of this scene recalls another Boccaccian text from this period telling of an isolated island existence: the account of what he calls the *"isole ritrovate"* (the found-again islands), what antiquity called the Insulae Fortunatae, and what we now call the Canaries. Before moving on to this text it is worth emphasizing Boccaccio's status as a figure of complexly compound, mercantile and intellectual, authority: he was the son of a merchant who trained under the Bardi as a merchant *discipulus*; and (following his decisive encounter with Petrarch) he authored works of Latin encyclopedism, literary theory, and geography that proved vastly influential for more than three centuries. He was also the lifelong servant of a historical Republic, that of Florence.

The discovery or refinding of the Canaries forms a perfect physical complement to the ongoing, recuperative work of humanist philology; for as Petrarch was discovering the missing decade of Livy, so enterprising Genoese navigators were setting foot on territory described or imagined by Strabo, Pomponius Mela, Pliny, and Horace.[33] Of course, this Western "discovery" was one (like many others) already made by Phoenicians and other Africans: Pliny's chief source for the Fortunate Islands was in fact the extensive geographical survey undertaken by, or under, King Jiuba of Mauritania, circa 7 CE.[34] Nonetheless, we would expect humanists like Boccaccio and Petrarch to hear with some excitement of the refinding of these islands beyond the sunset, beyond the pillars of Hercules. From Hesiod on, it was imagined that such islands of the extreme west would be dwelling places of the blessed, islands without season and hence beyond time. (The Canaries, situated between 90 and 300 miles west of Saharan Africa, *are* in some senses without or beyond season – hence winter trips to the island discovered by Genoan Lanzarotto Malocello: Lanzarote). In the Fortunate Islands, according to Pomponius Mela, fruits grow spontaneously and there are two fountains (the stuff of much medieval and Renaissance myth), one of which enables those who drink from it to laugh themselves to death.[35]

Boccaccio, once a pupil of the Genoan astrologer Andalò del Negro, at some point heard that an account of the 1341 expedition to the Fortunate Islands had arrived at the Florentine Bardi company for which he (and his father) had once worked. Having obtained a copy of this letter between merchants, he elaborated it into his best humanist Latin and entered it into his literary scrapbook, the volume now known as the *Zibaldone Magliabechiano*.[36] The result is a peculiar hybrid of rapacity and wonder, topography and the keeping of accounts. The expedition, financed by the King of Portugal, captained by a Genoese and crewed by Genoese, Florentines, Castilians, and other Spaniards, is clearly desperate to at least cover its costs. Boccaccio's account begins with accounting: the expedition brought back, he says, four men native to the islands, goat skins and seal skins, fish oil and fish fat, plus various materials that might work out as red dye (15–19). On the first, stoney island (clearly on the Saharan side) they find an abundance of "goats and other beasts and naked men and women, savage in appearance and demeanour" (*"capris et bestiis aliis atque nudis hominibus et mulieribus asperis cultu et ritu,"* 25); this careful making of relative or absolute degrees of nakedness continues throughout. At the next island, known now as Gran Canaria, a large number of people are spotted. Almost all are naked (*"fere nudi omnes,"* 30), but a few of the better sort wear goatskins dyed yellow and red. And now we have our first moment of cultural encounter, initiated by the islanders: the people on the island, Boccaccio says, instantly wished to communicate (*"habere commertium"*) with the people in the ship. But when the boats drew near the shore, the sailors, not understanding anything at all of what they said, did not dare to land. The natives' language, however, was polished enough and delivered Italian-fashion (*"more ytalico"*). Some of the islanders, seeing nobody descending from the boats, then swam out; four of them were taken on board and afterwards carried away. But then, seeing nothing of use there (*"nil ibi utilitatis"*), the sailors move on.

(35–41)

At the next island 25 sailors land and confront 30 men, *"nudi omnes"* (46), who run off through fear of their weaponry. The sailors, finding handsome houses, smash down the doors with stones (ignoring the cries of the householders). Nothing much of use or interest is found: just dried figs, high quality grain, and (in what appears to be an *oratorium* or temple) the stone statue of a man, naked but wearing a palm-leaf apron to shield his *"obscena,"* holding a ball in his hand; this statue is shipped off to Lisbon (51–61).

This island-by-island account includes notices of fruits, trees, and remarkable geographical features, most notably the mountain on Tenerife (Teide: the greatest volcano known to Europeans before 1778).[37] Boccaccio concludes, however, by reiterating the point that these are not rich islands[38] and that the expenses of the expedition were barely covered. It is at this precise point that the account suddenly returns us to the four native swimmers: they are young, beardless, and of graceful countenance; they go about naked. They do, however, wear aprons of rushes or palm – covering all signs of puberty and obscenity, front and rear – which cannot be raised by puffs of wind or other causes (105–10). They are, moreover, uncircumcised and have long, almost navel-length fair hair (which also covers them); they go about barefoot. Physically, they are no bigger than us; they are decently proportioned, bold and strong and of considerable intelligence; they sing sweetly, dance like Frenchmen (*"more gallico"*), smile readily, and are more domestic-minded (*"domestici,"* 119) than are many from Spain. And at this point the account blossoms into pure Golden Ageism. Once in the ship, these men ate figs and bread (which they seemed to like, tasting it for the first time): but they refused wine and drank only water. Gold and silver coins meant nothing to them; nor did spices (*"aromata"*) of any kind, golden jewels, or swords. But they were seen to be of extraordinary faithfulness and judiciousness (*"fidei et legalitiatis,"* 129): for if one were given anything to eat he would divide it into equal portions to share with everyone else. At last, it seems, we are connecting with the ancient literary canons of the Insulae Fortunatae. But we are also queasily aware of another textual tradition at work here: that of the slaving deed of sale, with its careful observation of physical virtues and identifying traits (such as circumcision); these handsome boys, so full of domestic sense and natural virtue (and so lacking in avaricious instincts) will fetch a good price.

The very end of this extraordinary Boccaccian text features a supposed transcription of the islanders' number system, from one to 16 (10, 11, 12: "*marava, vait marava, smatta marava . . .*"). This Boccaccio must have dreamed up himself: he loved such listings, and opened one of his *zibaldoni* with various alphabets. But the penultimate paragraph also features perennial preoccupations: these people marry, Boccaccio says, and the married women wear aprons like the men. Young virgins, however, go about quite naked, without any sense of shame (132–4). Elsewhere, in his vernacular fiction, Boccaccio seems all in favor of nakedness. Here, however, it may additionally be read as a sign of slaveability: for to be naked without shame is to be ignorant of the Fall, hence beyond the framework of Christian redemption.

In his *Esposizioni* or Dante lectures of 1373 (the year of Chaucer's visit to Florence), the now-ageing Boccaccio fulminates happily in his Paolo and Francesca section against the foppish and lust-driven youth of today, especially their fondness for growing their hair long, "*in forma barbarica,*" and for short tunics and bulging codpieces.[39] And suddenly his mind runs back more than 25 years to the Fortunate Islanders. Indians and Ethiopians, he says, take care to cover their privates, even though they live in excessive heat: but Indians and Ethiopians (and I quote) "have in them some humanity and sense of custom" ("*hanno in sé alcuna umanità e costume,*" 36). "Those people who inhabit the refound islands," however, "people one can describe as living beyond the circuit of the earth," possess "no form of speech, nor art, nor any kind of custom" conforming to the ways of "those who live civilly" ("*civilmente vivono,*" 37). Boccaccio's immediate, polemical point is that even these folks cover their loins; but of greater moment here is the revisionary classicism of his account of the Canarians, this people beyond the pale of humanity and civility. Boccaccio's classicism hardens as he ventriloquizes the youth of Florence to say: "we are following the usage of other nations: this is how the English, the Germans, the French, and the Provençals carry on" (40). Boccaccio can thus provoke himself into fierce reminiscence of the days (before current effeminization) when such peoples "were our tributaries, our vassals, our slaves"; barbarous peoples who knew or could know nothing unless first taught by Italians (*"Italiani,"* 41). It is no accident, of course, that the English are here mentioned first as a nation of, if not quite beyond, the pale. Petrarch, in the geographical survey of his *De vita solitaria*, Book II, admits that the Fortunate Islanders enjoy a solitude exceeding that of almost all mortals: but since they are but beast-like keepers of beasts, and their solitude is natural rather than wilfully chosen, this hardly counts.[40] Second in westward remoteness only to these islanders, according to Petrarch, are the Irish: a people with no interest in riches, politics, or agriculture, delighting only in *otium* and the enjoyment of *libertas*. "I'd call them a happy people," Petrarch continues, "were it not for another shameful and animalistic habit (if true)." The *"infamia"* and *"malignitas morum"* to which Petrarch alludes here derives from Strabo's account of Iernê, Ireland, which speaks of cannibalism, incest, and incestuous cannibalism.[41]

The extent to which European attitudes towards western Atlantic settlements are essayed as early as the fourteenth century, and in ways that will endure, is, I think, remarkable. As proof of this I'd like to stick with the Canary Islanders for a moment and run forward to 1494: that is, two years after Cristofero Columbo, yet another seafaring son of Genoa[42] in foreign employ, had launched himself westward. His point of departure in 1492 – indeed, for all his trans-Atlantic voyaging – was the Canaries: a fact that should further encourage us to view the discovery and colonization of the Americas as a steady, island-hopping movement across, and then just beyond, the Mediterranean.[43] And it is worth noting that it was Genoan voyaging to northern Europe that, through the compounding of Mediterranean and North Sea/ Baltic sailing technologies, prepared the way for Columbus.[44] Expressed in fanciful literary terms, we might say that Chaucer in Genoa plus Margery Kempe in Danzing (Gdansk) gets Aphra Behn to Surinam.

It was in early October 1494, then, that the Nuremberg humanist Hieronymous Münzer encountered Canarians – men, women, and children – for sale in the slave market at Valencia.[45] The peoples of the island, known as Guanche, had fought hard and very long against invasion and conquest: Gran Canaria was not officially conquered until 1493; Las Palmas and Tenerife held out for three more years.[46] The Guanche, a people that has long since disappeared from or into history, numbered only around 600 at Tenerife by 1513.[47] Münzer uses the fact of Canarian rebellion against the King of Spain, their rightful overlord, as one justification for their enslavement (p. 23); but his further reasoning adheres remarkably closely to templates laid down by slaving deeds and by Boccaccio more than a century before. The women are well-formed, he says, strong and long-limbed; but they are beasts (he says, transitioning rapidly) in morals, since they live under no law ("*sub nulla lege*," p. 24). Living under law is then directly equated with living under clothes. The victorious King of Spain gives them a bishop and has a church built; and they are ready to take on our religion.[48] Before they were naked; now they wear clothes like us: "*O quid facit doctrina et diligencia, que bestias in humano corpore facit homines et mansuetos!*"

Münzer, like Boccaccio, was a humanist of mercantile pedigree. A member of the Nuremberg humanist circle, he spent much of his share of profits in the family firm (run by his brother) on the latest humanist editions, procured by mercantile contacts, as they rolled from Italian presses. In 1483, some 11 years before the journey through Spain, he descended on Italy, toured classical and religious sites, and bought up books. One of these was the 1481 Bottonus edition of Boccaccio's *Geneologiae Deorum Gentilium*, "bought by me at Milan when returning from Rome" (the inscription proudly proclaims) "and brought back by me to Nuremberg."[49] This volume also contains Boccaccio's geographical encyclopedia, *De montibus, silvis, fontibus, lacubus, fluminibus . . . maribus* (etc.). Münzer, like Boccaccio, was dedicated to mapping the world; in 1493 he got his chance as cartographer to the *Nuremburg Chronicle*.[50] Perhaps it is not so surprising, then, that in traveling through Spain the following year his view of things shows strong Boccaccian filtration. The important point here is not literary influence, but rather how the compounding of cultural and commercial in Boccaccian humanism so suits it for catch-up migration to Nuremberg and points north.

Before finishing with Münzer I'd like to hang one footnote on him. Shortly after seeing the Canarians in Valencia (and describing local fruits and vegetation), Münzer tells of "*los marranos*," "baptized Jews," he says, "or the children of baptized Jews who publicly confess the Christian faith while secretly living according to the Jewish rite" (p. 28). It is precisely at this period that young Jews, mostly girls, begin showing up in slave markets, some sold young by panicked parents.[51] E.P. Goldschmidt, from whom almost all my knowledge of Münzer derives, writes some spirited pages about what else Münzer might have seen in Valencia in 1494: garments taken from over a thousand "*verbrannter*" Jews, for example, decorating the walls of a church.[52]

Goldschmidt, who actually discovered and catalogued Münzer's library, wrote this in German in a volume printed at Vienna in 1938. Beginning to worry for Goldschmidt, I was happy to discover (in the basement of the Warburg) that he enjoyed a long and successful career as a bookdealer in London, specializing in early printed editions.

This anecdote will have to stand in for more detailed consideration of the complex intertwining of pro-slaving and anti-semitic discourses. And one can but note, similarly, that this whole business of textual and territorial "discovery" is being observed by others beyond the frame. Ibn Khaldûn, born in Tunis on Ramadân 1,732 (May 27, 1332), begins discussion of the Canary Islands in his *Muqaddimah* with Ptolemy; "we have heard," he adds, laconically, "that European Christian ships reached them in the middle of this century, fought with [the inhabitants], plundered them, captured some of them, and sold some of the captives."[53] The best map of the Canaries from this period (1375) was made by Abraham Cresques, the Jewish cartographer from Majorca.[54]

The last Trecento passage that I'd like to consider in detail returns us to Petrarch. *Seniles* 10.2, written from Venice in 1367, is Petrarch's longest autobiographical letter and takes the form of yet another geographical survey, this time of the places where Petrarch himself has lived.[55] There are strong Golden Ageist elements here too, as Petrarch pits recollections of his halycon youth against images of embattled and degraded contemporary Europe. The heart of the letter evokes Petrarch's first visit, as a boy, to Vaucluse, accompanied by the boyhood friend to whom, more than 50 years later, he now writes: Guido Sette, Archbishop of Genoa. In writing from Venice to Genoa, Petrarch is encompassing the whole space of the Mediterranean and its slave trade: for if Genoa is the chief slaving power of this period, Venice is its only significant rival. Genoans had their chief Crimean beachhead at Caffa, the Venetians at Tana. Both were intensively involved, as Petrarch wrote, with commerce in slaves; the decade 1360–69 was actually the busiest period for the sale of young Tartars at Venice.[56] This, then, is Petrarch's view from the quayside in 1367:

*Nam Grecie calamitas vetus est, sed Scitharum recens. Ut, unde nuper ingens annua vis frumenti navibus in hanc urbem invehi solebat, inde nunc servis honuste naves veniant, quos urgente fame miseri venditant parentes. Iamque insolita et inextimabilis turba servorum utriusque sexus hanc pulcerrimam urbem scithicis vultibus et informi colluvie, velut amnem nitidissimum torrens turbidus inficit; que, si suis emptoribus non esset acceptior quam michi et non*

74

*amplius eorum oculos delectaret quam delectat meos, neque feda hec pubes hos angustos coartaret vicos, necque melioribus assuetos formis inameno advenas contristaret occursu; sed intra suam Scithiam cum fame arida ac pallenti lapidoso in agro, ubi Naso illam statuit, raras herbas dentibus velleret atque unguibus.*[57] *Et hec quidem hactenus.*

(pp. 1116–18)

The downfall of Greece is ancient, that of the Scythians recent. As a result, from where until recently huge quantities of grain would be brought every year by ship into this city, today ships come from there laden with slaves, sold by their parents under pressure of hunger. Already, a strange, enormous crowd of slaves of both sexes, like a muddy torrent tainting a limpid stream, taints this beautiful city with Scythian faces and hideous filth. If they were not more acceptable to their buyers than they are to me, and if they were not more pleasing to their eyes than to mine, these repulsive youths would not crowd our narrow streets; nor would they, by jostling people so clumsily, annoy foreign visitors, who are accustomed to better sights. Instead they would [still] be hungrily plucking the scanty grass with their teeth and nails on the stony soil of their Scythia, which Ovid once described. But enough of this.[58]

This passage, framed between reference to Greece and Rome, is humanism, hardcore. We have already seen Trecento Italian classicists imagining the extreme west as structuring the limit to all that is civilized. Here Petrarch develops a complex polarity more familiar to Greek and Roman thinking: between south and far north (but shading off into west and east). Scythia, for ancient Greeks, was antithetical to all things Hellenic, including its Asian vastness of scale; the grasslands of the Scythian steppes might go on forever. Hercules himself was more or less raped on this territory; fear of the all-consuming Scythian landscape, in Greek imagining, found expressive form in Scythian warrior women, the Amazons.[59] Ovid, evoked here by Petrarch, wrote home to Rome from his exile or "relegation" in Tomis of "a land gripped fast in frost"; "Beyond me lie the Don," he says, "and swamps of Scythia / And a few places, names scarce known at all. / Further just cold, defying habitation – / The world's end now, alas, how near to me!" Ovid's deeper fear, at this extreme physical limit, is of losing his authentically Roman voice: "Believe me," he says, "I'm afraid amid my Latin / Sintic or Pontic words you'll find I used."[60] Which is to say, a fear of cultural contamination; the same fear that grips Petrarch as he stands quayside at Venice, fantasizing repatriation.

And yet, of course, the influx of slaves reinforces and confirms *the* binome most fundamental to classical consciousness (one already

75

invoked by Petrarch earlier in this letter): liberty and servitude, Pozzo and Lucky; I know that I am free, knowing and seeing that you are not.[61] Civic debate at Genoa was clearly conditioned by awareness of 5,000 slaves in its midst: Genoa should not agree to be ruled by outsiders, according to one speaker at the 1396 assembly, "so that *we* are not shown to be slaves" (emphasis added).[62] Petrarch thus wastes his breath in measuring his superior aesthetic judgement against that of slavetraders: for these are the true purveyors of the revived classical package. Deeds of sale suggest, in fact, that the possession of a slave functioned as a marker of prestige, of classicisizing chic, for notaries (the class of intellectuals most dedicated to the development of humanist techniques); in fifteenth-century Genoa, notaries possessed four times as many slaves as all other liberal professions combined.[63]

Given the manifold contradictions of Petrarch's account, coupled with its implicit reliance upon notions of "natural" justice that have perenially subtended Western rationalizing of slavery, one grasps why techniques of deconstruction live on most powerfully in post-colonial theory: techniques of observing how a dominant discourse undoes itself through the very binaries of its self-constitution.[64] But post-colonial theory would further acknowledge that the potency of mystified self-contradictions in such a hegemonic discourse is hardly to be under-estimated, especially when it comes attached to such a personality, such an authoritative master of the expiring paradox, as Petrarch.

In returning, briefly, to Chaucer's Mediterranean – as most extensively represented by his *Man of Law's Tale* – we can only be struck by the studied archaism of its representation. His solitary, God-fearing Custance, floating her way across and out of the Mediterranean, would hardly seem to cross paths (in any sense) with the solitary slave Costanza who, in 1400, sailed into and across the Mediterranean in a ship otherwise filled with sacks of wool; yet we notice, in Chaucer's narrative, that there would be no narrative without the crucial intervention, early on, of Syrian merchants.[65] Chaucer, as London controller of customs, knew all about the bold plan of the Genoese to make Southampton (in Steven Epstein's phrase) "a Caffa or Pera of the north"; and he would have known something about the 1379 murder in London of the Genoese ambassador, Janus Imperiale, who was attempting to bring this about.[66] This murder, as Paul Strohm so memorably tells it, was achieved and covered over through an extraordinary alliance of English apprentices, merchant-capitalists and magnates: a group determined to beat the Genoese at their own game by treating the streets of London as the high seas by other means.

Slavery typically flourishes through warfare at a faith frontier of the kind mapped by the warfaring classes of the *Canterbury Tales*. Chaucer's Squire, who has fought in the Hundred Years War, tells a tale of Tartary (opening with notice of warfare and death).[67] His father, who has fought against Turks, Russians, Alexandrians, you name it,[68] tells a tale of Greece and Scythia, featuring conquered and deracinated Amazons.[69] Chaucer's Clerk tells a tale of husband and wife, deriving from Boccaccio and Petrarch, very like a tale of master and slave: Walter, you will recall, excercises absolute *dominium* over Griselde, confiscates and disposes of her children, and insists on having her stripped naked and then clothed in garments of his own devising. All three of these narratives will run and run in later English centuries.

There is also, however, a short Chaucerian text that exerted next to no influence (not appearing in print until 1866): a poem known as *The Former Age* that, in Cambridge University Library MS Hh.4.12, flowers suddenly from a crack in Chaucer's Boethius translation. "A blisful lyf, a paisible and a swete," the poem begins, "Ledden the peples in the former age."[70] The bliss of such a past, however, can only be imagined as antithetical to the ways of a ruinous present which, by the end of the poem, overshadows everything:

> For in our dayes nis but covetyse,
> Doublenesse, and tresoun, and envye,
> Poyson, manslawhtre, and mordre in sondry wise.
>
> (61–3)

The rueful self-recognition of this poem recalls that of Horace's sixteenth epode, the greatest of Fortunate Islands poems. To escape current civil strife, Horace proposes, we should cross "Oceanus" to seek "the Happy Fields and the Islands of the Blest, where every year the land, unploughed, yields corn, and ever blooms the vine unpruned"; throughout its course, however, the poem is dogged by the thought that these islands will be much less blest or fortunate once "we" show up.[71] The reflexivity of such accounts, imagined by Horace across space and by Chaucer through time, is – in the long history of Western encounters with worlds deemed simpler, more idyllic than our here and now – something to cling to.

Some of you will have thought forward to More's complex intertwinings of humanism and slavery in his island Utopia; some will have mapped Petrarch's division of Scythians from Italians onto Spenser's division of Irish from English in *A View of the State of Ireland*.[72] Such a mapping strategy usefully suggests, for Spenser, that the Irish are too western and too eastern at one and the same time; it also allows him to identify with Ovid as a poet of the imperial center translated to Scythia, the end of the world.[73] The Scythian Irish, Spenser maintains, derive their boolying (itinerant grazing) habits from the ways of "Tartarians"; Ireland and Scythia even look alike, in that they are both "waste deserts fulle of grasse."[74] Petrarch and Spenser devise pretty much the same strategy for their Scythian neighbors, namely, slow starvation.[75]

My point here is not that a live discourse of slavery migrates, like a book of ancient poetry, from one European power to the next, but rather that there has always been such a discourse throughout Europe, becoming more or less active as economic conditions dictate. The European anti-slaving Hall of Fame in the classical through early modern periods is not a very crowded place: so far I've been able to find the Sophists and Smaragde de Saint Mihiel (ninth century).[76] I thought it important to consider the relations of humanism to slavery within the context of this volume because public discourse in England is still, I think, off balance about it. As Americans flounder on how to represent the place and meaning of the Enola Gay within and as part of the Smithsonian, for example, so the English struggle over representations of slavery at Greenwich: not at the unhappy Dome, but rather at the National Maritime Museum. The permanent Wolfson trade and empire exhibition used to feature a Jane Austen-like waxwork woman taking tea in a Georgian drawing room with a bowl of Jamaican sugar on the table. Through a gap in her carpet, a manacled black hand reached up from the hatch of a slave ship. Now, following a £40,000 ($60,000) refit, this entire scene has been replaced by a gold-gilded ship's figurehead – as designed for the Prince Regent's yacht in 1817 – showing the future George IV as a benevolent emperor of Rome, surrounded by the happy faces of liberated slaves.

Personally, I prefer the first, what we might call the Ang Lee, version.

In recent years, Edward Said has made a series of important attempts to refloat "humanism" as an ideal and organizing principle of literary study. Such an effort might be aligned with the tradition of Fanon, whose *Black Skin, White Masks*[77] proposes to develop "another humanism." More pressingly, it expresses a need for regenerative civil conversation in parts of the world vitiated by sectarian and racial divides. To this enterprise, occupying this space first imagined for bell hooks, I offer this keeping of accounts.

## Notes

1   bell hooks, *Black Looks. Race and Representation* (Boston: South End Press, 1992), p. 172. In a late reshuffle of the "Republic of Letters" conference that generated this volume I found myself speaking from a slot originally conceived for bell hooks: hence my epigraph, from "Representation of Whiteness in the Black Imagination," in *Black Looks*; hence also some particular inflections of this essay.

2   Perry Anderson, *Lineages of the Absolutist State* (London: Verso, 1979), pp. 148–9. For further meditation on this passage and its ramifications, see David Wallace, *Chaucerian Polity: Absolutist Lineages and Associational Forms in England and Italy* (Stanford, CA: Stanford University Press, 1997), pp. 6–7, 55–60, 262–77.

3   See Wallace, *Chaucerian Polity*, pp. 40–54.

4   John N. King, "Henry VIII as David: The King's Image and Reformation Politics," in P.C. Herman (ed.), *Rethinking the Henrician Era: Essays on Early Tudor Texts and Contexts* (Urbana: University of Illinois Press, 1994), pp. 78–92; Richard Helgerson, *Forms of Nationhood: The Elizabethan Writing of England* (Chicago: University of Chicago Press, 1992).

5   Wallace, *Chaucerian Polity*, p. 321.

6   Anderson's dictum is "their dates are the same: their times are separate," *Lineages*, p. 10.

7   See *The Letters of Abelard and Heloise*, Betty Radice, trans. (London: Penguin, 1974); Virginia Woolf, *A Room of One's Own* (San Diego, CA: Harcourt, Brace, 1989); Barbara Newman (ed.), *Voice of the Living Light. Hildegard of Bingen and Her World* (Berkeley: University of California Press, 1998); and (fabulously illustrated), Hans-Jürgen Kotzur (ed.), *Hildegard of Bingen* (Mainz: Verlag Philipp von Zabern, 1998).

8   On Chaucer's Italian journeys, see Martin M. Crow and Clair C. Olson (eds.), *Chaucer Life-Records* (Austin: University of Texas Press, 1966), pp. 32–40, 53–61, 148–270.

9   Iris Origo, "The Domestic Enemy: The Eastern Slaves in Tuscany in the Fourteenth and Fifteenth Centuries," *Speculum*, 30 (1955): 321–66 (extract p. 329).

10   Mention of Italian cities is common in the Malebolge and there are explicit condemnations of Bologna (18.58–63), Lucca (25.10–15), Pistoia (25.10–15), Siena (29.121–32) and (lower than Malebolge) of Pisa (33.79–90) and Genoa (33.151–7). See Robert M. Durling and Ronald

L. Martinez, ed. and trans., *The Divine Comedy of Dante Alighieri*, vol. 1, *Inferno* (New York: Oxford University Press, 1996), p. 406. Citations from the *Inferno* follow this text; translations are adapted from it.

11  F.L. Mannucci (ed.), *L'anonimo genovese e la sua raccolta di rime* (Genoa: Muncipality of Genoa, 1904), as cited in Origo, "The Domestic Enemy," p. 325: *"E tanti son li Zenoexi / E per lo mondo si destexi / Che unde li van e stan / Un atra Zenoa se fan."*

12  Fernand Braudel, noting how the Genoese are effectively crowded down to the sea by sterile and mountainous terrain, makes the point succinctly: *"Elle fabrique, mais pour les autres; elle navigue, mais pour les autres; elle investit, mais pour les autres"* (Braudel, *Civilisation Matérielle et Capitalisme (XVe–XVIIIe Siècle*, 3 vols (Paris: Armand Colin, 1967–79), vol. 3, p. 134). Braudel was eloquently anticipated by a Genoese citizen, speaking in 1613: "our ancestors," this anonymous debater contends, "understood that the narrowness and sterility of our homeland" would not allow the city to thrive; they thus elected "to cultivate the ample fields of the sea" (*"in coltivare l'ampie campagne del mare"*), cited in Luciana Gatti, *Navi e cantieri della Republica di Genova (secoli XVI–XVIII)* (Genoa: Brigati, 1999), p. 13.

13  Mannucci (ed.), *L'anonimo genovese*, p. 200 (*"Tutti sono marinai . . ."*).

14  "Thus initiating," Origo remarks, "what is now called 'bacteriological warfare'" ("Domestic Enemy," p. 324).

15  Citations follow Vittore Branca (ed.), *Tutte le opere di Giovanni Boccaccio*, 12 vols (Milan: Mondadori, 1964–), vol. IV.

16  "Indeed," Burckhardt continues, "the inhabitant of the Riviera was proverbial among Italians for his contempt of all higher culture" (*The Civilization of the Renaissance in Italy*, 15th edn, S.G.C. Middlemore, trans. (London: Harrap, 1929), p. 106). Burckhardt assigns Genoa only a part-paragraph at the tail-end of his chapter on the republics of Venice and Florence; both German and English editions feature a photograph of the Palazzo di San Giorgio ("formerly the headquarters of the Bank of Genoa," figure 48 caption).

17  In 1376, the top five trading partners (as a percentage of the value of Genoese trade) were Alexandria (24.6%), Spain (18.1), Flanders (16.4), Provence (15.4), Cyprus (8.7). See Steven A. Epstein, *Genoa and the Genoese, 958–1528* (Chapel Hill: University of North Carolina Press, 1996), p. 231.

18  See Wendy Childs, "Anglo-Italian Contacts in the Fourteenth Century," in Piero Boitani (ed.), *Chaucer and the Italian Trecento* (Cambridge, UK: Cambridge University Press, 1983), pp. 65–87 (especially p. 67). The Genoese experimented with Bristol until 1383 before settling on Southampton as their main shipping center.

19  *Decameron*, 2.6.27. In 1456, more than a century later, the Doria were still a major slave-owning household (possessing 86 slaves, second only to the

Spinola): see Domenico Gioffré, *Il mercato deggli schiavi a Genova nel secolo XV* (Genoa: Fratelli Bozzi, 1971), pp. 74–5.

20  See Charles Verlinden, *L'Esclavage dans l'Europe Médiévale*, 2 vols, *I: Péninsule Ibérique – France* (Bruges: De Tempel, 1955), *II: Italie – Colonies italiennes du Levant – Levant latin – Empire byzantin* (Ghent: Rijksuniversiteit te Gent, 1977); Robert Delort, "Quelques précisions sur le commerce des esclaves à Gênes vers la fin du XIVe siècle," *Mélanges d'archéologie et d'histoire. (École Français de Rome),* 78 (1966): 215–50; Michel Balard, "Remarques sur les esclaves à Gênes dans la seconde moitié du XIIIe siècle," *Mélanges . . . de Rome,* 80 (1968): 627–80; Gioffré, *Mercato*; Jocelyn Nigel Hilgarth, *The Spanish Kingdoms, 1250–1516,* 2 vols (Oxford: Clarendon Press, 1978); John Thornton, *Africa and Africans in the Making of the Atlantic World* (Cambridge, UK: Cambridge University Press, 1992); John Brian Williams, "From the Commercial Revolution to the State Revolution: The Development of Slavery in Medieval Genoa," 2 vols (Ph.D. diss. University of Chicago, 1995); Epstein, *Genoa,* pp. 228–36, 262–70.

21  In a list of slaves sold in Florence between July 4, 1366 and March 2, 1397, 329 of the slaves are women or little girls; only four of the 28 males are over 16. This list clearly does not include all slaves sold in Florence at this period: see Origo, "Domestic Origin," p. 336. Christiane Klapisch-Zuber argues that about 98 percent of domestic slaves in Florence were female ("Women Servants in Florence during the Fourteenth and Fifteenth Centuries," in Barbara Hanawalt (ed.), *Women and Work in Preindustrial Europe* (Bloomington: Indiana University Press, 1986), pp. 56–80 (see p. 68). See further Gioffré, *Mercato,* p. 23; Epstein, *Genoa,* p. 229; Susan Mosher Stuard, "Ancillary Evidence for the Decline of Medieval Slavery," *Past and Present,* 149 (November 1995): 3–28 (especially p. 3).

22  See Delort, "Quelques précisions," p. 228. On Petrarch's understanding that desperate parents will sell their children into slavery, see *Seniles,* 10.2 (discussed below).

23  See John Boswell, *The Kindness of Strangers: The Abandonment of Children in Western Europe from Late Antiquity to the Renaissance* (New York: Vintage, 1988), pp. 415–27; Klapisch-Zuber, "Women Servants," pp. 69–70; Origo, "Domestic Enemy," pp. 347–8.

24  According to Augustine, there is a natural order (*naturalis ordo*) that compels those of lesser intellect to serve more rational beings; women should thus obey men (as children their parents and slaves their masters). "*Est enim ordo naturalis,*" he writes, "*in hominibus, ut serviant feminae viris, et filii parentibus; quia et illic haec justitia est ut infirmior ratio serviat fortiori. Haec igitur in dominationibus ut servitutibus clara justitia est ut qui excellunt ratione, excellant dominatione*" (*Quaestionum in Pentateuchum, Patrologia Latina,* J-P. Migne, ed., XXXIV, cols 547–824 (extract col. 590); Verlinden, *L'Esclavage,* II, p. 23. There is thus a clear justice in both domination and servitude. Paul's attitudes towards slavery and womanly obedience, while

broadly derived from Senecan and Stoic ideas, are complex. 1 Timothy insists that women ought not to teach or tell a man what to do (2.12); all slaves "under the yoke" must have unqualified respect for their masters (6.1). 1 Corinthians urges all converts – including slaves – to remain in their station (*"servus vocatus est? Non sit tibi curae,"* 7.20); women are to maintain silence in churches (*"taceant"*) and remain subject (*"subditas esse"*) according to the law (14.34: a verse now thought to be a post-Pauline interpellation). Paul's famous letter to Philemon, concerning the return of a fugitive slave known as "Onesimus" ("Useful"), maintains the master/slave distinction while modeling a more humane understanding – if such a paradox be considered intelligible – of ownership; in the Middle Ages, however, it was (Verlinden argues) exclusively employed to uphold the legitimacy of slaveholding (*L'Esclavage*, II, 31–2).

25   My account of discursive and material practices of slavery in this earlier period is not meant to suggest seamless continuity with later, full-blown plantation slave economies in the Americas (and I thank Crystal Bartolovich for pressing this point). In eighteenth- and nineteenth-century Surinam, for example, slave labor worked on a massive scale with little differentiation of tasks over an almost unlimited working day; in 1783, 2,133 whites commanded 51,096 blacks, a ratio of 24 : 1 that further encouraged a regime of strict brutality. In 1652, however, 200 blacks and 200 whites were reported in the same territory, suggesting working relations closer to the paternalistic, artisanal, and domestic models described elsewhere in this chapter. See Waldo Heilbron, *Colonial Transformations and the Decomposition of Dutch Plantation Slavery in Surinam* (London: Goldsmiths College, University of London Caribbean Centre, 1993), p. 13; Jacques Arends, "Demographic Factors in the Formation of Sranan," in Arends (ed.), *The Early Stages of Creolization* (Amsterdam: John Benjamins, 1995), pp. 233–85 (see pp. 259–60).

26   Non-white skin also begins to be interpreted – along with mutilation and branding – as a *sign* betokening slavery; there were elaborate arrangements for the recovery of runaways, often involving cooperation between city-states that were otherwise mutually hostile.

27   See Charles Verlinden, "Le recrutement des esclaves à Venise au XIVe et XVe siècles," *Bulletin de l'Institut Historique Belge de Rome*, 39 (1968): 83–202, esp. pp. 178–82; Gioffré, *Mercato*, pp. 33–6. For a study of ancient Greek references to *Aithiopes*, which are (it is argued) essentially free from color-based prejudice, see Frank M. Snowden, "Greeks and Ethiopians," in John E. Coleman and Clark A. Walz (eds.), *Greeks and Barbarians: Essays on the Interactions between Greeks and Non-Greeks in Antiquity and the consequences of Eurocentrism* (Bethseda, MD: CDL Press, 1997), pp. 103–26.

28   See Origo, "Domestic Enemy," pp. 331, 337, 340–1.

29   See Mario Ferrara, "Linguaggio di schiave del Quattrocento," *Studi di Filologia Italiana*, 8 (1950): 320–8. Ferrara edits and then analyzes slave

language in a sonnet (featuring two female slaves and their mistress) by the Florentine poet and notary Alessandro Braccesi (1445–1503). He then discusses a second (anonymous) fifteenth-century sonnet, which presents a dialogue between two women slaves that makes no attempt to capture linguistic peculiarities. The first of the women declares that she comes *"Da Schiavonia paisa,"* "from Slav country," thereby preserving the Slav/Slave association.

30 See S. Sobrequés, "La epoca del patriciado urbano," in J. Vicens Vives (ed.), *Historia Social y Economica de España y America*, 5 vols (Barcelona: Editorial Teide, 1957–9), II, pp. 6–406 (see p. 220); Gioffré, *Mercato*, p. 94. Gioffré states the case quite strongly; Sobrequés is a little more qualified. There is firm evidence, however, of slaves teaching other slaves the art of painting. And in his will of January 18, 1386, the Venetian painter Nicoletto Sernitecolo stipulates that his Tartar slave, Michele, should continue *"l'esercizio dell'arte sua"* (Gioffré, *Mercato*, p. 90).

31 See Origo, "Domestic Enemy," p. 330.

32 Delort, "Précisions," p. 241, n. 1.

33 See Charles Verlinden, "Lanzarotto Malocello et la découverte portugaise des Canaries," *Revue Belge de Philologie et d'Historie*, 36 (1958): 1173–1209; Felipe Férnandez-Armesto, *The Canary Islands after the Conquest: The Making of a Colonial Society in the Early Sixteenth Century* (Oxford: Clarendon Press, 1982), pp. 1–3.

34 See Valerio Manfredi, *Isole Fortunate* (Rome: Bretschneider, 1996), pp. 56–7.

35 See Mela, *De Chorographia*, Piergiorgio Parroni, ed. (Rome: Edizioni di Storia e Letteratura, 1984), III, p. 102; Frank E. Romer, *Pomponius Mela's Description of the World* (Ann Arbor: University of Michigan Press, 1998), pp. 129–30; Manfredi, *Isole Fortunate*, pp. 94–5.

36 Florence, Biblioteca Nazionale Centrale, formerly II, II 327, now Banco Rari 50; the *De Canaria* section is at ff. 123v–124r. For an edition and commentary, see M. Pastore Stocchi, "Il 'De Canaria' Boccaccesco e un *locus deperditus* nel 'De Insulis' di Domenico Silvestri," *Rinascimento*, 10 (1959): 143–56; for further commentary, see Giorgio Padoan, "Petrarca, Boccaccio e la scoperta delle Canarie," *Italia medioevale e umanistica*, 7 (1964): 263–77. For a listing of the complete contents of this *zibaldone*, see Aldo Maria Costatini, "Studi sullo Zibaldone Magliabechiano. I. Descrizioni e analisi," *Studi sul Boccaccio*, 7 (1973): 21–58 (esp. pp. 27–58).

37 That is, until Captain Cook and company caught sight of the Hawaiian islands. The peak of Tenerife's Teide rises 3,718 m above the ocean (and some 7,000 m above the ocean floor); only Hawaii's Mauna Loa and Mauna Kilauea rise higher. Almost two-thirds of Tenerife is made up by the rugged slopes of Teide (which staged the last-stand resistance of the native Guanche).

38 With this declaration, *"non dites insulas"* (104), Boccaccio may be downplaying strict identification with the *"divites . . . insulas"* dreamed of by classical tradition (see the citation of Horace's 16th epode below, n. 71).

39 *Esposizioni sopra la Comedia di Dante*, Giorgio Padoan, ed. in Branca (ed.), *Tutte le opere*, vol. VI, 5 (ii), pp. 31–4.

40 Guido Martellotti (ed.), in Francesco Petrarca, *Prose*, ed. Martellotti et al. (Milan and Naples: Ricciardi, 1955), 2.11 (pp. 522–4). Petrarch notes that these islands – celebrated by many poets, but above all by a lyric of Horace – were "penetrated" by an armed Genoan fleet "within the memory of our fathers." Petrarch's argument that Canarian remoteness does not qualify as true solitude (because it is natural, not willed) parallels that of contemporary friars against the poverty of peasants (who, similarly, do not "choose" to be poor).

41 See *De vita solitaria*, ed. Martellotti, 2.11 (p. 522 n. 5); *The Geography of Strabo*, Horace Leonard Jones, ed. and trans., Loeb Classical Library, 8 vols (London: Heinemann, 1917–32), 2.5.8 (vol. I, pp. 442–3); 4.5.4 (vol. II, pp. 258–61). Strabo deems the inhabitants of Iernê

> more savage than the Britons, since they are man-eaters as well as heavy eaters, and since, further, they count it an honourable thing, when their fathers die, to devour them, and openly to have intercourse, not only with the other women, but with their mothers and sisters; but I am saying this only with the understanding that I have no trustworthy witnesses for it. (vol. II, pp. 259–61)

42 On the Genoese lineage of Columbus, see *Columbus Documents: Summaries of Documents in Genoa*, Luciano F. Farina and Robert W. Tolf, ed. and trans. (Detroit: Omnigraphics, 1992); *Christopher Columbus and His Family: The Genoese and Ligurian Documents*, John Dotson and Aldo Agosto, ed. and trans. (Turnhout, Belgium: Brepols, 1998). The first surviving record, dated February 21, 1429, sees Giovanni Colombo, Cristofero's grandfather, take on an apprentice.

43 This was perhaps the most important aspect of the lifelong work of Charles Verlinden; see, in addition to other works cited above, *The Beginnings of Modern Colonization* (Ithaca, NY: Cornell University Press, 1970).

44 See Thornton, *Africa and Africans*, p. 22; Braudel, *Civilisation*, 3.80.

45 "Itinerarium Hispanicum Hieronymu Monetarii, 1494–5," Ludwig Pfandl, ed., *Revue Hispanique*, 48 (1920): 1–179 (see pp. 23–4); see also Jerónimo Münzer, *Viaje por España y Portugal (1494–5)*, intr. Ramón Alba (Madrid: Ediciones Polifemo, 1991). Neither Pfandl nor Alba includes the Preface in which Münzer speaks of his earlier journeying through Italy: see E.P. Goldschmidt, *Hieronymus Münzer und seine Bibliothek* (London: Warburg Institute, 1938), p. 27.

46  See Hillgarth, *Spanish Kingdoms*, pp. 576–7; Fernández-Armesto, *Canary Islands*, p. 3.

47  The Guanche – a term properly applied only to the inhabitants of Tenerife, but customarily used to include all the native islanders – may have been in place as early as 2,500 BCE; their more distant origins remain mysterious. See Fernández-Armesto, *Canary Islands*, pp. 5–12; Gilbert C. Din, *The Canary Islanders of Louisiana* (Baton Rouge: Louisiana State University Press, 1988), pp. 3–5.

48  The first Christianizing missions to the Canaries had taken place more than a century earlier; the bishropric of Teide was founded on Gran Canaria in 1351. The missionary efforts of Catalan clerics and Majorcan hermits were spoiled by the slave-raiding of other Christians. See Hillgarth, *Spanish Kingdoms*, p. 123.

49  Item 146, "Katalog von Münzers Bibliothek," in Goldschmidt, *Münzer*, pp. 115–45. On the well-established tradition of budding Nuremberg humanists traveling to Italy, see Guy Fitch Little, "The Renaissance, the Reformation, and the City of Nuremberg," in Jeffrey Chipps Smith, *Nuremberg, a Renaissance City, 1500–1618* (Austin: University of Texas Press, 1983), pp. 17–22 (see p. 19).

50  See Chipps Smith, *Nuremberg*, pp. 90, 94–5; Smith, "The Transformation of Patrician Tastes in Renaissance Nuremberg," in Smith, *New Perspectives on Renaissance Nuremberg. Five Essays* (Austin, TX: Archer M. Huntington Art Gallery, 1985), pp. 83–100 (see p. 88); Ernst Ullmann, *Geschichte der deutschen Kunst 1470–1550. Malerei, Graphik und Kunsthandwerk* (Leipzig: Seemann, 1985), pp. 206–21 (esp. p. 211).

51  See the list of "Schiavi Ebrei," sold at Genoa between 1482 and 1498, appended to Gioffré, *Mercato* (unpaginated); the first of these, seven-year-old "Tolosano," is sold "by her own father" for 12 ducats. The first ship of Sephardic refugees from Spain had arrived in 1478: see Rossana Urbani and Guido Nathan Zazzu, *The Jews in Genoa*, 2 vols (Leiden: Brill, 1999), I, p. xxxii.

52  Goldschmidt, *Münzer*, p. 85.

53  *The Muqaddimah. An Introduction to History*, trans. from the Arabic by Franz Rosenthal, 3 vols (London: RKP, 1958), I, p. 117. The Canaries, "from which Ptolemy began the determination of geographical longitude," are discussed by Ibn Khaldûn as "the Eternal Islands" (I, p. 116).

54  See M. Charles de la Roncière, *La Découverte de l'Afrique au Moyen Age. Cartographes et Explorateurs*, 3 vols (Cairo: Société Royale de Géographie d'Egypte, 1925–7), I. pp. 121–6.

55  Most conveniently available in Petrarca, *Prose*, Martellotti et al., ed., pp. 1090–1125.

56  See Verlinden, "Le recrutement," p. 126. 67.5% of Tartar slaves imported at Venice between 1360 and 1399 were women. Numbers dropped off markedly in the last two decades, probably as a result of campaigns

(1387–96) by Timur i Leng (Timur the Lame, 1336–1405, better known in the West – following Marlowe's play of 1590 – as Tamburlaine the Great).

57   Petrarch undoubtedly echoes Ovid here: Ceres sends one of her rustic minions in search of Famine to the farthest border of frozen Scythia, "a gloomy and barren soil, a land without corn, without trees" (*Metamorphoses*, 8.789); Famine is found "in a stony field, plucking with nails and teeth at the scanty herbage" (*"quaesitamque Famen lapidoso vidit in agro/ unguibus et raras vellentem dentibus herbas,"* (8.799–800). Citations follow *Metamorphoses*, Frank Justus Miller, ed. and trans. rev. G.P. Goold, Loeb Classical Library, 2 vols (Cambridge, MA: Harvard University Press, 1984).

58   The translation is my own but owes something both to the Italian of Martellotti and the English of Francis Petrarch, *Letters of Old Age. Rerum Senilium Libri. I–XVIII*, Aldo S. Bernardo, Saul Levin, and Reta S. Bernardo, trans., 2 vols. (Baltimore: Johns Hopkins University Press, 1992), II, 359–74. Bernardo et al. gloss "Scythians" as "Russians," which is quite wrong. Martellotti et al. note that "of this influx of slaves from the territories of the Black Sea there is no other report" (p. 1118 n. 1, my translation): an extraordinary statement which demonstrates, once again, the disciplinary gulf that would seem to divide expert philologists and students of humanism from the study of social and economic history.

59   See Pericles Georges, *Barbarian Asia and the Greek Experience. From the Archaic Period to the Age of Xenophon* (Baltimore: Johns Hopkins University Press, 1994), pp. xvi, 1–4, 203–4; Ludwig Edelstein, *The Idea of Progress in Classical Antiquity* (Baltimore: Johns Hopkins University Press, 1967), pp. 67–8; Frank M. Snowden, "Greeks and Ethiopians," in Coleman and Walz (eds.), *Greeks and Barbarians*, pp. 103–26 (see pp. 112–22); Renate Rolle, *The World of the Scythians*, Gayna Walls, trans. (London: Batsford, 1989), pp. 11–18.

60   Ovid, *Sorrows of an Exile, Tristia*, trans. A.D. Melville (Oxford: Clarendon Press, 1992), 3.14, lines 49–50 (*"crede mihi, timeo ne sint inmixta Latinis / inque meis scriptis Pontica verba legas,"*; Ovid, *Tristia; Ex Ponto*, trans. A.L. Wheeler, Loeb Classical Library, 151 (New York: G.P. Putnam and Sons, 1924).

61   "Hellenic liberty and slavery were indivisible," writes Perry Anderson: "each was the structural condition of the other" (*Lineages*, p. 23).

62   *"Ut non efficiamur sclavi"*: the words of Francesco de Aiguino of Voltri as cited by Epstein, *Genoa*, p. 249 and p. 357 n. 94. In 1381, the estimated number of slaves at Genoa was 5,056 (Gioffré, *Mercato*, pp. 80–81 (n. 23). Numbers fell to around 1920 by the end of the century, which is to say that at the time of Chaucer's visit in 1373 the Genoese slave trade was near its peak.

63   See Gioffré, *Mercato*, p. 83.

64   Such an impression lingers instructively from a reading of Robert Young, *White Mythologies. Writing History and the West* (London: Routledge, 1990).

65   See Origo, reporting on a document of Sept 1, 1400, "Domestic Enemy," p. 331; Wallace, *Chaucerian Polity*, pp. 183–7.

66   Epstein, *Genoa*, p. 231. On the Imperiale murder, see Paul Strohm, "Trade, Treason, and the Murder of Janus Imperial," *Journal of British Studies*, 35 (January 1996): 1–23; Benjamin Z. Kedar, *Merchants in Crisis. Genoese and Venetian Men of Affairs and the Fourteenth-Century Depression* (New Haven, CT: Yale University Press, 1976), pp. 31–7. Three months after his return from Genoa and Florence in 1373, Chaucer was dispatched by Edward III to deliver a Genoese ship, detained at Dartmouth, to her master (see Crow and Olson, *Life-Records*, pp. 40–2). The following year, Chaucer was appointed London controller of customs (a post he held until 1386: *Life-Records*, pp. 148–270). The Shipman of the *General Prologue*, who steals wine from merchants and sends captured vessels to the bottom of the ocean, is said to be "For aught I woot . . . of Dertemouthe" (1.389); Dartmouth was certainly the home of John Hawley, a rich merchant whose shipmen raided and robbed Genoese carracks and tarits (*Life-Records*, p. 42).

67   "At Sarray, in the land of Tartarye, / Ther dwelte a kynge that werryed Russye, / Thurgh which ther dyde many a doughty man" (5.9–11).

68   See Terry Jones, *Chaucer's Knight. Portrait of a Medieval Mercenary*, 3rd edn. (London: Methuen, 1994). Jones notes that in *The Book of the Duchess*, Blanche of Lancaster is commended for *not* sending knights on quests, *inter alia*, "into Tartarye" (line 1025; Jones, p. 38).

69   Explicit opposition between Scythia and Greece is underscored by the Latin epigraph to the *Knight's Tale* that appears in many manuscripts of all groups: "*Iamque domos patrias, Scithie post aspera gentis / Prelia, laurigero, etc.*" ("And now [Theseus, drawing nigh his] native land in laurelled car after fierce battling with the Scythian folk, etc."): *Riverside Chaucer*, pp. 37, 828. Scythia, early on in the *Tale*, is identified with "the regne of Femenye" and Ypolita as "The faire, hardy queene of Scithia" (1.877, 882).

70   The poem survives in two manuscripts; the other is Cambridge University Library, Ii.3.21. See *The Riverside Chaucer*, Larry D. Benson, ed. (Boston: Houghton Mifflin, 1987), pp. 650–1, 1083, 1188; Rita Copeland, "Rhetoric and Vernacular Translation in the Middle Ages," *Studies in the Age of Chaucer*, 9 (1987): 41–75 (see pp. 62–6).

71   Horace, *The Odes and Epodes*, C.E. Bennett, ed. and trans. Loeb Classical Library (London: Heinemann, 1914): "*arva, beata / petamus arva divites et insulas, reddit ubi Cererem tellus inarata quotannis / et imputata floret usque vinea*" (lines 41–4).

72   Linkage between the cannibalistic and incestuous inhabitants of Ireland

and Scythians is explicitly made by Strabo, Petrarch's source, in the passage of his *Geography* cited above (n. 41). This passage continues: "and yet, as for the matter of man-eating, that is said to be a custom of the Scythians also" (4.5.4, vol. II, pp. 260–1).

73 "Heu quam vicina," laments Ovid in *Tristia* 3.4b, "*est ultima terra mihi!*" (line 6 from the passage cited in my text above).

74 Edmund Spenser, *A View of the State of Ireland. From the First Printed Edition* (1633), Andrew Hadfield and Willy Maley, eds. (Oxford: Blackwell, 1997), p. 55. It has to be said that this volume fails to deliver the promise of its title: "we have used," the editors explain in a footnote, "the 1809 reprint of Ware's edition, which contains some minor modifications in terms of punctuation and capitalization" (p. xxvi).

75 On Spenser's elaborate plans for the slow starvation of the Irish, corralled between four English garrisons, see *A View*, pp. 95–103. The innate cannabalistic tendencies of the Irish, as noted above by Strabo and Petrarch, will speed the process of self-destruction: "for," according to Spenser's Irenius, "although there should none of them fall by the sword, nor bee slaine by the souldiour, yet thus being kept from manurance, and their cattle from running abroad, by this hard constraint they would quickly consume themselves, and devoure one another" (p. 101). Irenius goes on to equate such desperate scenes of slow starvation and cannibalism with events he had himself witnessed in the course of the Munster famine accompanying the Desmond rebellion (began 1579): "Out of every corner of the woods and glynnes they came creeping forth upon their hands, for their legges could not beare them; they looked like anatomies of death, they spake like ghosts crying out of their graves; they did eat dead carrions, happy where they could finde them, yea, and one another soone after"; this diet is varied by "water-cresses or shamrocks." (pp. 101–2).

76 See Verlinden, *L'Esclavage*, II, 15.

77 Frantz Fanon, *Black Skin, White Masks* (London: Pluto Press, 1986).

# Chapter 4

## Hamlet the Intellectual[1]

### Margreta de Grazia

According to his biographer, Rodin was thrilled with the decision in 1904 to place *The Thinker* in front of the Panthéon, the burial place of French geniuses.[2] He was devastated several weeks later, however, when a man smashed the plaster statue to bits with a hatchet crying, "I avenge myself – I come to avenge myself." When interrogated by the police, the man explained that he thought the statue was making fun of him, a poor man eating cabbages. Rodin received a letter from a sympathetic friend, "The accident with *The Thinker* is stupid. We can only feel sorry for the poor devil."

But was the incident so "stupid"? After all, how was the "poor devil" to know that a man seated with hand to mouth was supposed to be thinking instead of eating? That he was not crouching over food but absorbed in thought? That his muscles showed the strain not of hard work but of deep thought? When in 1906 a bronze statue was erected where the plaster cast had been, a plaque was placed beneath it: *LE PENSEUR*. But in the absence of such a sign (or of the ability to read it), might not the statue have been taken for *LE MANGEUR*?

If the poor devil's mistake was stupid, then so must be a good portion of Wittgenstein's *Philosophical Investigations*. For a recurring problem there is the representation of inner states: thought, pain, feeling, consciousness, even talking to oneself. The problem is concisely exemplified by the picture of a boiling kettle:

> Of course, if water boils in a pot, steam comes out of the pot and also pictured steam comes out of the pictured pot. But what if one insisted on saying that there must also be something boiling in the picture of the pot?[3]

When a kettle is steaming we know that water is boiling inside (we can lift the lid to check), but we cannot know this about a pictured steaming kettle. In this respect, the pictured kettle is no different from Rodin's statue or Shakespeare's character, Hamlet: we cannot lift their lids to see what is going on inside. So how was the poor devil to know that the *statue* was cogitating and not, say, digesting?

This essay will suggest that he could only have known if he had been familiar with *Hamlet*. Had he known about the great dramatic thinker he would not have mistaken his sculpted counterpart. He would have recognized the conventional pose for thinking: a man turned in on himself to the exclusion of the world and others. It is the claim of this essay that *Hamlet*'s first audiences did not know the convention either. Hamlet was not thinking for them any more than *The Thinker* was for the poor devil. Not until much later, closer to the time of Rodin than of Shakespeare, did Hamlet become the model of the man who thinks – the intellectual.

*    *    *

Imagine Shakespeare saying to himself: "In this tragedy I want a character who above all else *thinks*. But can thinking possibly be staged? Now if tragedy is a representation of an action, what action might a man play to indicate to an audience that he is thinking? How can that within be given show? What mirror can reflect 'the pale cast of thought'? Now I've inherited from the Middle Ages a whole roster of character types: avengers, clowns, courtiers, kings, lovers, madmen, malcontents, scholars, soldiers, villains . . . but no *thinker*. Nor are the ancients of my little-Latin-and-less-Greek of any help; they were interested only in *outer* conflict, not the *inner* affair of thought. Clearly something new is required – an action by which to dramatize thinking, when there *is* no action for thinking. But that's it! I'll stage my thinker not in action but in *in*action. I'll put him in a really tight spot, give him the cue for passion, and then have him do nothing. Instead of a tragedy of action, I'll have a tragedy of *in*action – a tragedy of thought!"

"But will they get it?" wonders this imaginary Shakespeare. "When they see my character not acting, will they say to themselves, 'Oh, he is not doing anything: therefore, he must be thinking.' Maybe I'd better give them a hint as to what's going on in his head. I'll have him on stage telling another character that he is thinking. But no, that's *dialogue*. I'll have him on stage telling the audience that he is think-

90

ing. But that's an *aside*. I'll put him on stage silent. But that's a *dumb-show*. But suppose he were on stage alone and talking – to no one but *himself*? Giving voice to his thoughts. And if I have him thinking aloud early on and then again and again and again, they'll realize that think-ing with him is an ongoing process. What he is doing when thinking aloud is what he is doing all the time, but silently. Maybe not every-one will get it at first, maybe only the wiser sort, so it will be caviar to the general, at first anyway. But in time – they *will* get it: *the per-formance of thought as inaction – as delay.*"

*   *   *

And it did take time for even "the wiser sort" to figure out that the play was about a man who thinks.[4] In fact, it took over two hundred years before Coleridge famously connected Hamlet's disposition to think with his *in*disposition to act, his "enormous, intellectual activ-ity" with his "aversion to real action."[5] And that, for him, is the point of the play, the "universal" it dramatizes: a man prone to thinking is incapable of acting, and proportionally; the more he thinks, the less he acts. Here is how Coleridge imagined Shakespeare plotting out his play:

> The poet places [Hamlet] in the most stimulating circumstances that a human being can be placed in. He is the heir-apparent of a throne: his father dies suspiciously; his mother excluded her son from his throne by marrying his uncle. This is not enough; but the Ghost of the mur-dered father is introduced to assure the son that he was put to death by his own brother. What is the effect upon the son? – instant action and pursuit of revenge? No: endless reasoning and hesitating . . .[6]

What Shakespeare did, then, was contrive the most insufferable plot imaginable just so his protagonist could then slight it. Coleridge also slights it: plot is barely mentioned in his scattered but abundant com-ments on *Hamlet*. And why should it be? What happens in the play has no bearing on Hamlet's character. His disposition to thought – his "ratiocinative meditativeness"[7] – predates the play. Indeed, it appears to be congenital, having issued from the "germ"[8] of his character. Pro-grammed by that inborn germ to do what he does (or does not), he is entirely self-determining. No need to bother with acting, reacting, or interacting. "[A] man living in meditation,"[9] possessing "a world in"[10] himself, Hamlet is all-and-all sufficient.

It is around 1800 that the saying "Like *Hamlet* without the Prince" becomes current. Take away the character and precious little remains.[11]

The inverse, however, is not true: if the play is taken away, the prince remains perfectly intact. Hamlet by this time possesses all the free-standing self-sufficiency of an icon. In any Western context, the image of a young man looking at a skull evokes Hamlet meditating: thought thinking itself. (Even with no skull, a brooding young man may invoke Hamlet. So may a skull with no brooding young man: when Hegel contemplates the relation of the skull to consciousness, Hamlet comes to mind.[12]) Without ties to plot, Hamlet is a person in his own right, ready to go anywhere, and indeed he does turn up in unlikely places – always delaying, that is – thinking.

Once plot drops away, the play becomes primarily (or even exclusively) about character, one "whose ruling passion is to think, not to act,"[13] one who expresses his character through the deferral of action. This construal shifts the domain of tragedy from the external realm of action to the inner recesses of thought. In A.W. Schlegel's much repeated phrase, Hamlet is "a tragedy of thought."[14] It is no surprise, then, that Hamlet catches the attention of the great philosopher of consciousness. Hegel, in his *Aesthetics*, views *Hamlet* as an allegory of consciousness moving haltingly – that is, dialectically – toward self-realization.[15] Hamlet is driven forward not by any external agent or principle, as was Orestes by Apollo or Oedipus by Fate. It is not the ghost's revelation, then, that stirs him to action but rather the inner prompting of his own consciousness (his "prophetic soul," 1.5.41).[16] His delays – his "stops and starts" – externalize the bumpy trajectory of that consciousness as it progresses toward its goal of absolute freedom. The plot sets him on an obstacle course of "colliding factors" (externalizations of his own irresolution) until in the final scenes, "bandied from pillar to post" he ends up "sand banked." Buffeted to his death by external circumstances, Hamlet falls short of his goal of self-determination; the mandated deed is accomplished through a convergence of accidents. While he sets the process of dialectical self-realization into motion, Hamlet himself can only go so far: delay climaxes in capitulation. For Hegel, it could not in 1600 be otherwise: history cannot move ahead of itself. Before the philosophical advances of Descartes, Spinoza, Kant, and, of course, Hegel himself, Hamlet cannot advance beyond the threshold of modern consciousness.[17]

Nietzsche loathed the Hegelian teleology that hubristically placed modern man at the pinnacle of an advancing history, as if he were the be-all and end-all of time. Yet in *The Birth of Tragedy* (1872), Hamlet is a key figure for him too, not as a stage in the development of consciousness but as a reincarnation of the Greek ideal of Dionysian man.

Hamlet's characteristic delay externalizes not dialectical consciousness but the enervating effects of "insight into the truth."[18] Having penetrated into the reality of things, Hamlet discerns its absurdity and cruelty and recoils in disgust. In Greek tragedy, such percipience was expressed ritualistically in the piercing cries and frenzied movement of the Maenads; in Hamlet, however, it is dramatized as paralysis: "Understanding kills action, action depends on a veil of illusion – this is what Hamlet teaches us." In Nietzsche's essay "On the Uses and Disadvantages of History for Life" (1874), the same ascetic resignation characterizes another Hamlet-like figure, the "suprahistorical thinker," the being who having seen the "blindness and injustice in the soul of him who acts" knows the futility of participating in history, and indeed, in life.[19]

Hamlet makes a guest appearance in another counter-Hegelian genealogy of tragedy, of baroque Germany rather than of ancient Greece. In Benjamin's *The Origins of German Tragic Drama* (1928) thought again inhibits action. Like the *Melencolia* of Dürer's engraving, Hamlet is the sorrowful Contemplator, mourning in the aftermath of the Reformation the loss of meaningful action to a world of evacuated spirituality. This is the legacy of Lutheran *solofideism* or "the philosophy of Wittenberg." With the renunciation of good works, "[h]uman actions were deprived of all value" and a numbing *acedia* or "contemplative paralysis" sets in. In the vast repertoire of German mourning drama, only one figure – a non-German – was able to overcome this world-weariness, "The figure is Hamlet." Through the unique intensity of his self-awareness, he alone is able to discern in his own reflection the providential immanence lost to the Reformation. He sees there the "distant light" or "image of redemption" that radiates on the recessed horizon of Dürer's engraving. While the contemplative *Melencolia* has his back to that gleaming horizon, Hamlet makes out its redemptive "Christian sparks," but only on the brink of his "extinction . . . The rest is silence."[20]

Perhaps it is not too much of a stretch to extend this line-up of retiring thinkers up through Derrida's *Specters of Marx*. It is, of course, true that deconstruction targets the metaphysics of thought, the great preserve of all binaries: theory and praxis, subject and object, mind and matter, inner and outer, and last but not least – thought and action. Yet it is precisely "the hero of Western consciousness"[21] whom Derrida calls upon to give direction to the future. Hamlet's proverbial delay is translated into deconstructive deferral. But what gives Hamlet pause is not a moral or psychological reluctance to take revenge. Retribution requires no delay: following the logic of tit-for-tat, it can be executed automatically. What gives Hamlet pause is rather the spectral prospect of another kind of justice, a non-retributive or incommensurate justice which requires hard deliberation. It exists as indefinite promise, deferred but with a certain performative impendency, which leaves Hamlet in a position of "indecidability" or "messianic hesitation."[23]

Hegel's dialectical set-backs, Nietzsche's nauseous recoiling, Benjamin's melancholic *acedia*, Derrida's deliberative waiting: all find their presiding genius in Hamlet, a Hamlet whose thinking curbs action. These great analyses of consciousness, insight, reflection, and deliberation all assume the aversion to action postulated by Coleridge's hermeneutic almost two centuries ago. If there is a *locus classicus* for the traditional model of the intellectual which Gramsci would overturn – aloof, passive, with no interest in action, construction, production – it is Hamlet.

*    *    *

In Shakespeare's time, Hamlet was applauded for his antics, not his thoughts. Rather than his inaccessible interiority, it was his knockabout clowning that audiences appear to have loved. The earliest playgoers leave record of his lunatic rant, not his intellectual musings; his madman's deshabille, not his melancholy "inky cloak." One author in 1604 envies Hamlet's capacity to "please all," but since it is the result of his having "runne mad," the author would rather "*dis*please all" and stay sane.[23] When a character named Hamlet appears in *Eastward Ho* (1605), he enters quite literally in that state: "Enter Hamlet a footeman in haste," reads the stage direction, and so he does, "Sfoote Hamlet: are you madde? Whither run you now . . . ?"[24] That so many of the few early comments we have on Hamlet refer to him in frantic motion suggests that this may have been something of a signature stage stunt. Dekker twice alludes to Hamlet in such commotion: "break[ing] loose like a Beare from the stake" and rushing in furiously ("by violence") to disperse a crowd.[25] Richard Burbage, the first to act the part of Shakespeare's Hamlet, was remembered in his eulogy for his gymnastic leap into Ophelia's grave ("Oft have I seen him leap into the grave"),[26] though later critics, reluctant to allow their brainy protagonist such a display of brawny bravura, deny that the text calls for such a leap.[27]

After 1660 the newly opened private theaters might have catered to recently classicized taste by offering a more decorously sedate Hamlet. But reviewers throughout the eighteenth century repeatedly comment on the energetic physicality of the famous Hamlets. Betterton was said to have played the part with great "Vivacity" up to age 74.[28] His successor Wilks had "a Spirit that ran away with his Body," "He seem'd animated, without Purpose," racing through his part "without Rub, Rest, or Marking."[29] Garrick distinguished himself from his predecessors by framing his energies into discrete poses; he held gesture and expression in "picturesque attitude," as in his "terror-struck" response to the ghost, captured in both contemporary painting and engraving.[30] Yet Garrick's decision to omit Hamlet's great meditative occasion – the graveyard scene – suggests no great regard for Hamlet's thought. By the nineteenth century, Hamlets begin to show traces of introspection. Indeed Charles Kean's introverted Hamlet – "So immersed in the soundless depths of a divine philosophy as to become indifferent to the agitations of the surface"[31] – seems to have been lifted straight out of Coleridge's lectures quoted above. At the same time, Kean hardly sacrificed the vulgar buffoonery of earlier productions. Outraged reviewers remarked on how "he not only exposed his derriere to [Ophelia], but positively crawled upon his belly toward the King like a wounded snake in a meadow."[32]

Such antics no doubt contributed to the nineteenth-century prejudice against performing *Hamlet*. Lamb found it regrettable that Hamlet had to appear on stage at all when "nine parts in ten" of his part are the "effusions of his solitary musings, which he retires to holes and corners and the most sequestered parts of the palace to pour forth."[33] What sense does it then make, asks Lamb, for "these light-and-noise-abhorring ruminations" to be uttered by an actor "who comes and mouths them before an audience, making four hundred people his confidants at once?" Hazlitt maintained that there was "no play that suffered so much from being transferred to the stage." And for him, too, the problem was how to enact thought on stage, "Hamlet seems hardly capable of being acted . . . He is, as it were, wrapped up in his reflections, and only *thinks aloud*."[34] The volume on his thought must be turned up, but only slightly: "There should therefore be no attempt to impress what he says upon others by a studied exaggeration of emphasis or manner; no *talking at* his hearers." By the middle of the nineteenth century – the century Emerson identified with Hamlet's "speculative genius"[35] – performances of Hamlet are still largely seen as rowdy travesties of the character Shakespeare intended, *"overflowing* with *bustle, starts,* and *rant,* and *entirely destitute* of that *meditative* and *philosophic repose,* which Shakespeare has made the *leading feature* of the *character*."[36]

In the prompt-books, too, there is evidence that the post-Restoration theater had scant interest in Hamlet's mind. The stage version of the play published in 1676, known as the Players' Quarto and attributed to Sir William Davenant, cuts some 800 lines from the text of the 1604 Quarto. A good percentage of those lines are taken from Hamlet's main soliloquies: all five of which were either halved, gutted, or omitted in performance, except "To be or not to be," which appears from its numerous imitations and parodies to have been popular from the start.[37] The prefatory note explains the principle behind the cuts: whatever was not "prejudicial to the plot" was deleted. Hamlet's antic lines, however, though entirely superfluous to the plot, are retained, except for the most obscene. The cuts were largely preserved in the next prompt-book, the Hughs-Wilks version published in 1718, which continued to be staged well into the next century. These prompt-book cuts may reflect stage practice before as well as after the Restoration. According to the prompter of Davenant's company, Davenant's *Hamlet* had a direct link to Shakespeare: Davenant had seen the part performed at Blackfriars by Joseph Taylor who had been instructed in the role by Shakespeare himself.[38] While the particulars are dubious (Shakespeare had been dead for three years when Taylor first played Hamlet in 1619), the alleged link between Shakespeare's stage and Davenant's is born out by other evidence. In the 1676 Players' Quarto, Davenant's cuts from the 1604 Quarto closely correspond to the lines missing from the 1623 Folio, suggesting some kind of continuity, textual or theatrical, between the two texts. Both texts, for example, omit the soliloquy Hamlet delivers upon encountering Fortinbras's army (4.4), the one soliloquy directly connecting Hamlet's thought ("some craven scruple / Of thinking too precisely on th'event," 39–40) to his failure to act ("I do not know / Why yet I live to say this thing's to do," 43–4).[39]

While the text performed on the eighteenth-century stage was abbreviated, the one reproduced in editions was enlarged. The first editors, Rowe and Pope, start to add passages to the Folio text from the 1604 quarto; in 1733 Theobald completes the job by conflating the two to produce the composite that became standard until the late twentieth century. Yet even the expanded version replete with soliloquies fails to suggest to editors the crippling effects of thought in *Hamlet* until the Boswell–Malone edition of 1821.[40] For the play's first two hundred years – about half of its entire history – Hamlet's delay, for actors and editors, was not an issue.

*    *    *

This is not to say that no one noticed that there was delay. Clearly there was a long lag between Hamlet's breathless resolution to swoop to his revenge at the play's start and his eventual killing of Claudius at its end. (Hamlet himself draws attention to this delay; so does the ghost.) It is no surprise, then, to find it noted in the first extensive critical work on *Hamlet*. In *Some Remarks on Hamlet* (1736), George Stubbes writes: "To speak the truth, our poet, has fallen into an absurdity: there appears no reason at all in nature why this young Prince did not put the usurper to death as soon as possible."[41] But the problem here, as through most of this century, was not with the *character* but rather with the *plot*. Shakespeare turned to the "old wretched Chronicler" (Saxo Grammaticus) rather than to one of "the noble Originals of Antiquity" (Sophocles or Aeschylus) and followed it so closely as to produce "an Absurdity in the Plot." In Saxo, Hamlet's counterpart must wait for years – until he has grown up – before he can exact revenge, and he bides his time for this long span by feigning idiocy. Having determined to follow his source, Shakespeare was left with a problem, "Had [Hamlet] gone naturally to work . . . there would have been an End of our Play." He, therefore, "was obliged to delay his Hero's Revenge." But it is not Hamlet's contemplative nature that holds up the action; for Stubbes, it is his "antic disposition." The editor George Steevens concurred, noting the lack of "Progress in the Fable": no sooner does Hamlet vow to exact revenge than "he goes from Act to Act playing the fool."[42] Thus on the rare occasion before the end of the eighteenth century, when delay is noted, the problem belongs to plot not character, and Shakespeare is thought to have addressed it, as had his source, through the expedient of the "antic disposition."

So the criticism shared by Stubbes and Steevens suggests an approach to delay that is dramaturgical rather than psychological, inherent in plot rather than symptomatic of character. A plot that begins with the command to revenge ("Revenge his foul and most unnatural murder," 1.5.25) and ends with the satisfaction of the command ("Here . . . thou damned Dane, / Drink of this potion," 5.2.330–1), is left with a gap in between that needs to be filled up. And this was done not by extending, thickening, or multiplying the plot line, as a novel might do, but by filling up the interval between endpoints with Hamlet's clowning. This was, after all, the purpose of farce, as its etymology reveals: *enfarcir*, to stuff. Like the interludes designed to pass the time between the acts of medieval mystery and morality plays, Hamlet's "pranks" fill up the "meantime" between two termini: the command to revenge and its execution.[43]

As Robert Weimann has shown, the clown's routine was from the start interpolative; the lines he spoke from the downstage *platea* were directed more to the audience (particularly the groundlings closest to the rim of the stage) than to the characters enacting the fiction at the center of the stage or *locus*.[44] Impertinent extemporizing from the side-lines, superfluous to the matter at hand, traditionally served to eke out and hold up the action of the play. It is this improvisational license that Hamlet attempts to discipline in his instruction to the actors: "And let those that play your clowns speak no more than is set down for them" (3.2.38–9) he warns, and berates those clowns who hold forth "when in the meantime some necessary question of the play be then to be considered" (42–3). "That's villainous," he concludes, reminding us that such impertinence was also characteristic of the Vice of the moralities.[45]

And indeed in this itinerant acting company the closest kin to the clown might well be the actor cast as Lucianus in the "Murder of Gonzago." Though he doesn't speak more than is set down for him, he certainly holds up the action, and an especially climactic action: the pouring of the poison in the king's ear that is intended to "unkennel" Claudius's "occulted guilt" (3.2.80–1). Before he pours the poison, Lucianus pauses – perhaps holding the vial up in the air, just as Pyrrhus held his fatal sword suspended over his victim's head in "Priam's slaughter" (2.2.473–88). Hamlet's expression of impatience indicates that Lucianus (or rather the actor playing Lucianus), has been draw-ing out the act: "Begin, murderer. Leave thy damnable faces and begin/Come. The croaking raven doth bellow for revenge" (3.2.246–7). Between his entrance and his first speech, Lucianus is on stage for 10 lines while Hamlet banters bawdily with Ophelia. For this duration, Lucianus has the stage to himself (or rather the stage-within-the-stage), all eyes (of the court audience) upon him, and he takes the opportunity to ham it up, apparently by making grotesquely diabolic faces. This kind of mugging must have been routine for clowns; Kempe, we know, would famously poke his head out of the tiring house and make "scurvey faces" at the audience, stretching out the time before his entrance for as long as laughter lasted.[46] Lucianus's antics obviously displease Hamlet, and the feeling might well be mutual, for Hamlet has been holding up the show with his off-color repartee with Ophelia. They must have delighted the "barren spectators", however, who, as Hamlet attests, "for the most part" love dumbshows (3.2.11).

As Lucianus is to "The Murder of Gonzago," so is Hamlet to "The Murder of Claudius." Both characters are "nephew[s] to the king" (3.2.239) they would murder; and both actors share the same ancestry in the Antic-Vice figure of the Tudor moralities. It is quite possible that Hamlet, too, makes "damned faces" when, for example, he fiendishly boasts, "Now could I drink hot blood" (3.2.381). Grimacing might well have accompanied the other forms of physical disfiguration Hamlet "puts on" in order to play the antic, "with arms encumber'd thus" and with "this head-shake" (1.5.182); perhaps it is his "damned faces" which make him appear to Ophelia "[a]s if he had been loosed out of hell" (2.1.83). And perhaps he, like Lucianus, sometimes hams it up by "making mouths" or "mopes and moes" (Q1, E3r). In the *Hamlet* text believed to bear the closest relation to performance, there is evidence that Hamlet (or the actor playing Hamlet) did delay the play's progress by speaking more than was set down. At one point only is the notoriously truncated Q1 *Hamlet* longer – by 10 lines – than either Q2 or F. Weimann has recently argued that these lines record an actor's interpolations.[47] Having just warned the clown against ad libbing, Hamlet (or the actor playing Hamlet) himself ad libs, rattling off the punch lines to four stock jests, and topping them off with a fifth of his own to complete a "cinkapase of ieasts":

> Cannot you stay till I eate my porrige? *And*, you owe me
> A quarters wages: *and*, my coate wants a cullison:
> *And*, your beere is sowre: *and*, blabbering with his lips,
> *And* thus keeping in his cinkapase of ieasts,
> When, God knows, the warme Clowne cannot make a iest
> Unlesse by chance, as the blinde man catcheth a hare.
>     (Q1 F2r) [italics added]

These lines record the theatrical moment when the actor holds on to the spotlight, as it were, by saying "more than is set down." He drags out the time between the scripted lines assigned to him and those of the next speaker (in this instance, the Player) by stringing together jests familiar from jestbooks as well as from recitation. That the jests are linked together with *ands* suggests that in performance additional ones could be strung on indefinitely, as long as the audience kept laughing. By drawing out this series in Q1, Hamlet quite literally delays the scheduled performance so that he then, as if to make up for lost time, whisks off the actors, "Well, goe make you ready"; in Q2 and F he also instructs Polonius to do so, "Bid the players make haste," as well as Rosencrantz and Guildenstern, "Will you two help to hasten them?" (3.2.49–50).

While the interpolated lines are present only in Q1, they are quite typical of Hamlet's performance of madness. He repeatedly draws on the clown's privilege of directly addressing the audience, establishing a verbal rapport with the low members of the audience through direct address, puns, proverbs, obscenities, and scurrilities. His own "blabbering" is made up of similarly eruptive gags; because they routinely take the form of non sequiturs, often triggered by a pun, they appear improvisational even when scripted. And they invariably forestall the action at hand, "some necessary question," whether it be the swearing ceremony, the various attempts to fathom the cause of his "transformation," his conference with his mother, the search for Polonius's body, the burial of Ophelia. While exasperating the characters within the play, his "wild and whirling words" (1.5.139) undoubtedly amused the audience.

\*      \*      \*

As we have seen, the dilational plot that follows the structure of command (or vow) and fulfillment with a gap in between, may have been less a problem (how to fill the gap?) than an opportunity to exploit a popular tradition of ludic pastimes. But what about that popularity? Was the "mirth" which Hamlet's antics caused universal? Hamlet maintains otherwise. In his instructions to the actors, he postulates an audience that is divided both socially and spatially, with the "judicious" in the galleries and the "unskillful" in the yard. Each division has its own taste in theater, so what pleases the one, displeases the other: what "makes the unskillful laugh, cannot but make the judicious grieve." For Hamlet, at least, there is no question about whose taste should be considered: "one" of the seated "judicious" should "oe'rweigh a whole theatre" of the standing "unskillful" (3.2.26–7). Hamlet's antics would surely satisfy the vulgar appetite for "dumbshows and noise" (3.2.12); but what catered to the elite? What did Gabriel Harvey mean when he jotted in his margin that *Hamlet* could "please the wiser sort"?[48] Was it the prince's humanist learning that they found so delectable? His education at Wittenberg? His "hand of little employment" (5.1.68)? His sententious speeches and dilated rhetoric? The fact that he customarily walks in the lobby four hours together reading a book? That his best friend is a scholar with a Roman name who counts himself more an "antique Roman than a Dane" (5.2.346)? Is it connections to the ancient world of the classics that appealed to their cultivated palates? Is this – like Hamlet's favorite speech adapted from Virgil – what "pleased not the million, 'twas caviare to the general" (2.2.432–3) but pleased instead "the wiser sort"?

Hamlet's dilatory antics have a precedent in ancient history as well as in native performative practice. The very description of his part as "antic" may have implied this ancient source at a time when "antic" and "antique" shared the same spelling and pronunciation.[49] Whether Shakespeare came to know the story of Hamlet from Belleforest's *Histoires Tragiques* (1570) or from its English translation, *The Hystorie of Hamblet* (not published until 1608 but possibly circulating in manuscript before that), he would have learned from either version that the model for Hamlet's feigned idiocy was Lucius Junius Brutus. In the English translation, Hamlet is said to have known how to counterfeit madness because he "had been at the schoole" of this Brutus. It was from him that he learned how to bide his time by playing the fool: "running through the streets like a man distraught," begriming himself, speaking nonsense, "all his actions and jestures" proper only to a man deprived of his wits, "fitte for nothing but to make sport." In the margin flanking this account, the reader is told where to look for a fuller account of Brutus' "counterfeiting the foole": "Read Titus Livius."[50] In his recently translated *The Romane Historie* (1600), Livy explains that this Brutus counterfeited "a noddie and a verie innocent" in order to conceal his conspiracy against the tyrannous king Tarquin, suffering to have himself called *Brutus*, "a name appropriate to unreasonable creatures." His disguise enabled him to "abide the full time and appear in due season."[51] As Shakespeare recounts at the end of *The Rape of Lucrece*, when the moment came, he dropped his "folly's show" (1810) or "shallow habit" (1814), and led an insurrection against Tarquin that ended in his "everlasting banishment" (1815). In Livy, this event put an end not only to the Tarquinian line of kings, but to kingship itself, and ushered in the Roman Republic.[52] In his republican commentary on Livy, Machiavelli also describes Lucius Junius Brutus' dilatory folly and hails him as founder of the Roman republic and father of Roman liberty.[53]

Hamlet also takes after Junius Brutus' more famous descendant, Marcus Brutus, the man who tried to save the Republic by opposing Caesar's ambition for the crown. When he slays the man who once played Caesar, Hamlet takes on the "brute part" of the younger Brutus. Hamlet and Brutus would have been further connected if, as has been argued, Richard Burbage played both parts to John Heminges' Polonius and Caesar. The two Brutuses were often paired, one at either end of the 500-year duration of the Republic. Plutarch connects them in the opening sentence of his Life of the younger Brutus, "Marcus Brutus came of that Junius Brutus." Both were identified as haters of monarchy and champions of republicanism. Lucan in his *Pharsalia* has Junius Brutus applauding the Caesarian line, knowing that his descendant and namesake in time will succeed in killing Caesar.[54] As the elder Brutus ushered in the Republic so the younger Brutus attempted to preserve it by eliminating the man who aspired to the sovereignty that became synonymous with his name. Shakespeare stresses their kinship in *Julius Caesar*, both when Cassius reminds Brutus of his ancestor's hatred of kingship ("There was a Brutus once," 1.2.160) and when Brutus himself remembers him, "My ancestor did from the streets of Rome / The Tarquin drive when he was called a king" (2.1.53–4).

Is it possible that Gabriel Harvey's "wiser sort" consisted of a faction of men who took interest in the Roman Republic? We know for a fact that he pored over his Livy;[55] so, too, did the Earl of Essex whose authority he cites in the same marginalia and whose rebellion may be encoded in *Hamlet* itself.[56] Why does Harvey couple *The Rape of Lucrece* with *Hamlet* as the two Shakespearean works which "haue it in them, to please the wiser sort"? Is it because both invoke the founding moment of the Republic during a time when Roman history was intensively studied for the instability of its constitutional forms?[57] If Hamlet is affiliated with both prominent Brutuses, might he have been thought to share in their politics?

Although out to kill one in particular, Hamlet seems to relish the felling of kings of all stripes. His favorite speech describes the slaughter of Priam, King of Troy; the performance he sponsors requires that a king be poisoned (and twice over); he stabs the man he thinks is king ("Is it the King?" [3.4.26]; "I took thee for thy better" [32]); considers, "too curiously," the reduction of two men associated with kingship – Caesar and Alexander – to dust, as well as the passage of a king through the guts of a beggar. All these regicides – represented, mistaken, imagined – are rehearsals for the final debacle when he both stabs and poisons the King of Denmark, to the cry of "Treason! treason!" (5.2.328). In light of such a past, one wonders if a certain irony is not intended in Fortinbras's tribute, "he was likely, had he been put on, / To have prov'd most royal" (5.2.402–3). For the course of the play, Hamlet has "put on" an antic disposition rather than royalty, a "transformation" which debases his princely status. This would not have gone unnoticed by those who recognized that the decorums separating tragedy from comedy were political as well as generic. As Stubbes pointed out, a prince playing the fool makes a mockery of kingship: it is "as if we were to dress a Monarch in all his Royal Robes, and then put a Fool's Cap upon him."[58]

Like Hamlet, *Hamlet* also seems to take pleasure in the death of kings. It features a long narrative of a king's poisoning and an extended discursus on the consequence of a king's death or the "cess of majesty" (3.3.15). Sentries identify the ghost with the king ("Looks a not like the King?" [1.1.46] and "Is it not like the King?" [61]) and then strike at the "majestical" figure with their partisans, and thereby "do it wrong." The same majestic figure suffers literal degradation when dropped beneath the level of the stage, on a par with the groundlings, where he is addressed as "old mole," the lowliest of creatures. Regicide is threatened in deed when Laertes and his "riotous head" ("halfe the heart of all our Land," Q1, Hr) raise arms against the king and are heard clamoring outside the palace gates before ramming their way into the palace ("The doors are broke," 4.5.111]). The messenger, panic-stricken, describes the rebellion as a reversion to primordial chaos – "Antiquity forgot, custom not known" – and indeed what it demands is a monstrous constitutional hybrid in which the rabble elect the king: "The rabble call him lord"; "They cry, 'Choose we! Laertes shall be king'" (4.5.102, 106). A recent historical rebellion, Essex's plot to overthrow Elizabeth, is alluded to as "the late innovation" which drove the players out of the city.[59] It is astonishing that so many threats to monarchy are represented in this play in an age that equated even the imagining of the king's death with treason.[60]

After so many assaults on the king's person and office, the play leaves Denmark with no king on the throne, at least no Danish king. The present king has been killed to the cry (by *All*) of "Treason! treason!" (5.2.328). A quarry of royal bodies ("so many princes at a shot," 371) strews the stage. "[M]en's minds are wild" (399), warns Horatio; "unhappy country,' laments the English ambassador (Q1, I4r). What is to become of the state of Denmark?

The final lines of the play take every measure to prepare for an election. Hamlet's last thoughts turn to the process: with the clairvoyance of the dying, he foretells its outcome: "I do prophecy th'election lights / On Fortinbras" (5.2.360). With his final breath – his "dying voice" (361) – he gives his vote to Fortinbras, bids Horatio to deliver it, and Horatio is confident that other votes will follow upon it (5.2.397). Fortinbras commands that the electoral body be convened, "call the Noblest to the audience," and Horatio urges that "this same presently be performed" in order to avoid further turmoil. On the other hand, why should Fortinbras bother with the Danish electoral system? A sovereign prince with imperial designs, whose name connects him with the force of arms, backed by a triumphant army of as many as 20,000 men (4.4.60) "with conquest come from Poland" (5.2.355) and heralded by cannon fire, Fortinbras hardly needs this parliamentary ritual, especially when his own country's history provides him with a claim, "I have some rights [rites] of memory in this kingdom, / Which now to claim my vantage doth invite me" (5.2.394–5). In the Folio's concluding stage direction, the play ends with a resonating assertion of his military triumph: "Exeunt Marching: after the which, a peale of Ordenance are shot off."

Why this last-minute fussing over constitutional politics? Or is it last-minute? What if the effect of Hamlet's prolonged antics was a social leveling? What if Hamlet's delay was seen on the model of the Brutuses awaiting the opportunity to overthrow monarchy? What if his anti-hierarchic jabs and jibes were seen to be operating on both registers? It has been the purpose of this essay to indicate how *Hamlet* might have been regarded before the play was swept into the vortex of Hamlet's tortuous mind. Once delay was construed as psychological symptom, the play's focus shifted from the constitution of the body politic to what Coleridge termed the "constitution of mind." As a result, the play's intellectual energies have been largely restricted to what could be imagined to be occurring "within" Hamlet. Yet the play that has generated more commentary than any work in the language has been, it must be said, strangely under-determined. This is not to say that Hamlet is not a Thinker – but that thinking is "an action that a man might play." Hamlet plays that part by putting on an antic disposition and by recalling, for those who know, the great historical alternative to monarchy. That the modern tradition has cast him otherwise – as a deep thinker turned in on himself with his back to the world – is a sign of how badly it has needed a very different model.

## Notes

1  I wish to thank Peter Stallybrass for the exchanges with which this essay begins and ends, and Colin Thubron who helped it through its final stages.

2  Ruth Butler, *The Shape of Genius* (New Haven, CT, London: Yale University Press, 1993), pp. 426–7.

3  Ludwig Wittgenstein, *Philosophical Investigations*, G.E.M. Anscombe, trans. (New York: Macmillan, 1958), Part I, p. 297.

4  In his copy of Chaucer's *Works* (1598), Gabriel Harvey notes that both *Lucrece* and *Hamlet* "have it in them to please the wiser sort". For a transcription of this manuscript note, see the Appendix in Harold Jenkins (ed.), Arden *Hamlet* (London, New York: Methuen, 1982), pp. 573–4.

5  *Critical Responses to Hamlet 1600–1900*, David Farley-Hills, ed., 3 vols. (New York: AMS Press, 1996–99), from Letter of H.C. Robinson to Mrs Thomas Clarkson (January 3, 1812), 2, p. 62. Unless otherwise indicated, citations to seventeenth-, eighteenth, and nineteenth-century comments on the play will follow Farley-Hills's three-volume compendium.

6  From J.P. Collier's report of Lecture 12 (1811–12), Farley-Hills, 2, p. 54.

7  From "Notes on Hamlet," collected and edited by Henry Nelson Coleridge (1836), Farley-Hills, 2, p. 72.

8  Ibid., 2, p. 80.

9  Ibid., 2, p. 59.

10  From J.P. Collier's report, 2, p. 55.

11  The OED gives 1818 for the first figurative use of the expression to mean a production without the key figure. See also A.C. Bradley's reference to the expression in the context of the late eighteenth-century "discovery" of the centrality of Hamlet's character to the play, *Shakespearean Tragedy: Lectures on "Hamlet", "Othello", "King Lear" and "Macbeth"* (London: Penguin, 1991), p. 94.

12  *Hegel's Phenomenology of Spirit*, J.N. Findlay, trans. (Oxford, New York: Oxford University Press, 1977), p. 201.

13  From William Hazlitt, *Characters of Shakespear's Plays* (1817), in Farley-Hills, 2, p. 117.

14  From August Wilhelm Schlegel, *Lectures on Dramatic Art and Literature* (John Black, trans., 1815), in Farley-Hills, 2, p. 49.

15  See *The Philosophy of Fine Art*, F.P.B. Osmaston, trans. (New York: Hacker Art Books, 1975), IV, pp. 334–6, 342.

16  Hegel, *Phenomenology*, p. 447.

17  At the conclusion of his *History of Philosophy*, Hegel turns to *Hamlet* for a metaphor by which to describe its long, hard, 2,500-year trajectory, and finds an unlikely one: "Well said, old mole. Cans't work in the earth so fast?" The old mole, like the spirit of consciousness, like Hamlet himself until the play's end, tunnels arduously through earth toward the light that is the freedom of absolute self-determination. For further discussion

of the mole's importance to Marx's materialism as well as Hegel's idealism, see Peter Stallybrass, "'Well Grubbed, Old Mole': Marx, Hamlet, and the (Un)Fixing of Representation," *Cultural Studies*, 12, 1 (1998): 3–14; and Margreta de Grazia, "Teleology, Delay, and the 'Old Mole'," *Shakespeare Quarterly*, 50 (Fall, 1999): 3, 251–67.

18  Friedrich Nietzsche, *The Birth of Tragedy*, Shaun Whiteside, trans. (London, New York: Penguin, 1993), p. 39.

19  Nietzsche, *Untimely Meditations*, R.J. Hollingdale, trans. (Cambridge, UK: Cambridge University Press, 1983), p. 65. For another account of Hamlet's relevance to this essay, see Marjorie Garber, *Shakespeare's Ghost Writers: Literature as Uncanny Causality* (New York, London: Methuen, 1987), esp. pp. 154–7.

20  Walter Benjamin, *The Origin of German Tragic Drama*, John Osborne, trans. (London: Verso, 1977), pp. 138, 139, 140, 157.

21  This is Harold Bloom's phrase, in *Shakespeare: The Invention of the Human* (New York: Riverhead Books, 1998), p. 109.

22  Jacques Derrida, *Specters of Marx: The State of the Debt, the Work of Mourning, and the New International*, Peggy Kamuf, trans. (New York, London: Routledge), p. 169.

23  From "The Epistle to the Reader," *Daiphanthus, or The Passion of Love* (1604), in Farley-Hills, 1, p. 2.

24  From George Chapman, Ben Jonson, and John Marston, *Eastward Ho* (1605), in Farley-Hills, 1, pp. 3–6.

25  See Paul S. Conklin, *A History of Hamlet Criticism 1601–1821* (London: Frank Cass & Co., 1968), pp. 18–19.

26  From "A Funeral Elegy on the Death of Richard Burbage" (1618), in Farley-Hills, 1, p. 9.

27  Because the stage direction *"Hamlet leapes in after Leartes"* appears only in Q1, editors and directors have often chosen to spare Hamlet the undignified leap (see, for example, Harley Granville-Barker, *Prefaces to Shakespeare* [Princeton, NJ: Princeton University Press, 1946], p. 139, n. 19). In both Q2 and F, however, Hamlet's words (5.1.272–4) make clear that he is following Laertes whose jump is called for by the stage directions in both Q1 and F. That Nicholas Rowe introduced the stage direction into his 1709 edition (before the discovery of Q1 in 1825) suggests that the leap was also staged after the Restoration.

28  From Sir Richard Steele, *The Tatler* (September 20, 1709), in Farley-Hills, 1, p. 33.

29  From Aaron Hill, *The Prompter* (October 24, 1735), in Farley-Hills, 1, pp. 94, 96.

30  From Francis Gentleman, *The Dramatic Censor* (1770), in Farley-Hills, 1, p. 213.

31  From F.W. Hawkins, *The Life of Edmund Kean* (1869), in Farley-Hills, 2, p. xlvii.

32  See John A. Mills, *Hamlet on Stage, the Great Tradition* (Westport, CT: Greenwood Press, 1985), p. 83. Mills gives additional evidence of hyperactive Hamlets in the seventeenth and eighteenth centuries, pp. 4–5.

33  Charles Lamb, *The Tragedies of Shakespeare* (1811), in Farley-Hills, 2, pp. 102–3.

34  Hazlitt, *Characters*, in Farley-Hills, 2, p. 119. For a critique of soliloquies as *"thinking aloud,"* see de Grazia, "Soliloquies and Wages in the Age of Emergent Consciousness," *Textual Practice*, 9, 1 (1995): 67–92.

35  Ralph Waldo Emerson, *Representative Men: Seven Lectures* (Boston: Houghton, Mifflin, 1921), pp. 201–2.

36  Jas. H. Hackett, Correspondence (July 24, 1839), in Farley-Hills, 3, p. 14.

37  For the immediate popularity of the "To be or not to be" soliloquy, see Conklin, *A History of Hamlet Criticism*, pp. 20–1.

38  From John Downes, *Roscius Anglicanus* (1708), in Farley-Hills, 1, p. 29.

39  In the "To be or not to be" soliloquy, Hamlet also makes the connection between "the pale cast of thought" and the stemming of "enterprises of great pitch and moment," but without applying it to his own situation. Unless otherwise noted, all citations from *Hamlet* will follow Jenkins' Arden *Hamlet* and appear parenthetically in text. Citations to other works by Shakespeare are from *The Norton Shakespeare* (New York, London: W.W. Norton, 1997).

40  In the Malone/Boswell *The Plays and Poems of William Shakspeare* (1821), James Boswell the younger refers to Hamlet's "incurable habits of procrastination" and "that irresolution which forms so marked a part of his character" (pp. vii, 535, 539). Boswell cites both Schlegel and Goethe, though not Coleridge.

41  Published anonymously in 1736, *Some Remarks on the Tragedy of Hamlet* has recently been attributed to George Stubbes. References are from the reprint by AMS Press (New York, 1975) and page numbers will henceforth appear in text. Malone in 1790 and Boswell/Malone in 1821 reproduce much of the essay at the end of their edition of *Hamlet*. If Stubbes is the first critic to comment on delay in *Hamlet*, it may be because he was the first to use Theobald's edition, the first to conflate the Folio and Quarto *Hamlet*s. As many have noted, the problem of delay is less likely to have been noted in the highly truncated Q1 version.

42  George Steevens, *St James's Chronicle* (February 18–20, 1772), in Farley-Hills, 1, pp. 220–1.

43  Patricia Parker at several points relates "farce" to material to be "stuffed," "crammed," or "forced" between two endpoints. See *Shakespeare from the Margins: Language, Culture, Context* (Chicago, London: University of Chicago Press, 1996), pp. 76, 216, 223.

44  See Robert Weimann in Robert Schwartz (ed.), *Shakespeare and the Popular Tradition in the Theater: Studies in the Social Dimension of Dramatic Form and*

*Function* (Baltimore, London: The Johns Hopkins University Press, 1978), esp. pp. 230–5.

45  On the clown's origins in the Tudor "Vice," see David Wiles, *Shakespeare's Clown* (Cambridge, UK: Cambridge University Press, 1987), pp. 1–10.

46  See J.B. Leishmann (ed.), *Pilgrimmage to Parnassus* in *The Three Parnassus Plays, 1598–1601* (London: Nicholson & Watson, 1949), pp. 129, 223.

47  See Robert Weimann in Helen Higbee and William West (eds.), *Author's Pen and Actor's Voice: Playing and Writing in Shakespeare's Theatre* (Cambridge, UK: Cambridge University Press, 2000), pp. 23–5.

48  See n. 4 above.

49  Hamlet assumes an "Anticke" (Q1, Q2, F) disposition; Priam wields his "antike" (Q1) or "anticke" (Q2, F) sword; and Horatio is more an "antike" (Q1, F1) or "anticke" (Q2) Roman than a Dane.

50  *The Hystorie of Hamblet* (1608), in Geoffrey Bullough (ed.), *Narrative and Dramatic Sources of Shakespeare*, 8 vols (London: Routledge and Kegan Paul, 1973), Vol. 7, pp. 7, 90 and n. 4.

51  From *The Romane Historie* by Titus Livius translated by Philemon Holland (1600), in Bullough, *Sources*, Vol. 7, p. 80.

52  See also the comparison of Prince Hal's vanities to "the outside of the Roman Brutus, / Covering discretion with a coat of folly," in *Henry V* (2.4.37–8).

53  Machiavelli, *Discourses upon Livy*, Book III, ch. V, 448–50. Though not printed in England until 1636, three manuscript translations of the Italian edition circulated in the early seventeenth century.

54  See David Norbrook, *Writing the English Republic: Poetry, Rhetoric and Politics, 1627–1660* (Cambridge, UK: Cambridge University Press, 1999), p. 451.

55  See Lisa Jardine and Anthony Grafton, "How Gabriel Harvey Read his Livy," *Past and Present*, 129 (November, 1990): 55.

56  See Jenkins's gloss on "the late innovation" (2.2.331), pp. 470–2, and Annabel Patterson, *Shakespeare and the Popular Voice* (Cambridge, MA: Basil Blackwell, 1989), p. 31. For fascinating speculations on Harvey's marginalia, Essex's faction, and *Hamlet's* "performance of philosophy," see John Guillory, "To Please the Wiser Sort," in Carla Mazzio and Douglas Trevor (eds.), *Historicism, Psychoanalysis, and Early Modern Culture* (New York, London: Routledge, 2000), pp. 82–109.

57  See R. Malcolm Smuts, *Culture and Politics in Early Stuart England, 1585–1685* (New York: St. Martin's Press, 1999).

58  Stubbes, *Remarks*, p. 19.

59  See n. 56 above.

60  See John Bellamy, *The Tudor Law of Treason* (Buffalo: University of Toronto Press, 1979). On the statute passed in the reign of Edward III defining

treason as "when a man doth compass or imagine the death of our lord the king," and the complications around its application at the end of the eighteenth century, see John Barrell, "Imaginary Treason, Imaginary Law," in *The Birth of Pandora and the Division of Knowledge* (Philadelphia: University of Pennsylvania Press, 1992), pp. 119–43.

# Chapter 5

## Deaths of the Intellectual: A Comparative Autopsy

### Jeremy Jennings

As the American electorate reflected upon the flawed outcome of its Presidential contest, Todd Gitlin, chronicler of the twilight of America's common dreams,[1] voiced further cause for unease and disquiet: the arrival of Gov. Malaprop at the White House, he suggested, spoke "clearly about the value accorded intellectuals and intellectuality in American culture," and what it said was "inauspicious." In choosing "the amiable common man," rather than someone who, by general acknowledgement, was too smart for his own good, America had fallen back upon her long and robust tradition of anti-intellectualism. That tradition, brilliantly analyzed by Richard Hofstadter, valued brains to the extent that they provided technical, practical knowledge and, no less importantly, to the extent that the "nerd" and the "geek" remained firmly in their place.

Yet, if Gitlin was eager to highlight the renaissance of an anti-intellectualism that had roots deeply embedded in a popular resentment of cultural elitism, so too he sought to draw attention to a variety of anti-intellectualism that post-dated Hofstadter's earlier account. This he diagnosed as "the rise of a new form of faux cerebration: punditry." "Punditry," Gitlin commented, "is to intellectual life as fast food is to fine cuisine": it provides "pre-cooked opinion," endless talk that amounts to no more than "signals, gestures and stances," it reviews and rates performances, rather than assessing arguments, "cornering intellect in the name of chat."

The pundits, Gitlin argues, are hired "for the facility and pungency of their presentations and the ferocity and acceptability of their opinions." As such, they represent "the rise of the pseudo-intellectual," where the "premium" is placed on "smirking and glibness." "The pundit," Gitlin concludes, "is a smart person in both senses – intelligent and a smarty pants – and his knowingness about how the game is played is a substitute for knowledge about what would improve society." Punditry and pundits, in short, debase both intellectual life and the demanding function of the intellectual.[2]

There is much that is worthy of comment in Gitlin's argument – especially when it is placed in the broader context of American debates about the future of the public intellectual – but for the moment I wish simply to make the point that Gitlin's dismissal of an American anti-intellectualism that places style before content and which reduces intellectual life to chat-show celebrity is one that finds echoes only too easily elsewhere, most notably in Great Britain and France. The conclusion would seem to be that intellectuals have died similar deaths in dissimilar countries and dissimilar circumstances.

Let me take the diagnosis of the decline of the intellectual in Britain recently advanced by writer and broadcaster Michael Ignatieff.[3] Posing the question: "where are the independent intellectuals now?," his answer is brutally to the point. "In place of thought," he contends, "we have opinion; in place of argument we have journalism, in place of polemic we have personality profiles." The refrain is completed with the rousing claim that "in place of . . . public dialogue, we have celebrity chat shows. In place of a public forum for debate, we have academic conferences." How, according to Ignatieff, should these deleterious trends be interpreted? Intellectuals, he concludes, have lost their independence and moral authority. Ashamed of their elitism, they have abandoned public debate and plain speech, the victims of a democratization of culture that "has bred a populist loathing of high culture itself." Only the scientists have escaped the crisis (they alone "appear to know something"): for the rest, we have "worthy professors, cultural bureaucrats, carnival barkers and entertainers."

Like Gitlin, Ignatieff regrets these developments, identifying a "void in public life" that cannot be filled by "bankers, economists and politicians." However, it is far from clear how he thinks that they might be reversed, especially when, on this account, intellectuals themselves are sacrificing the "historical function of defending the universal against the violence and the closure associated with the tribal, national and ethnic." Little, it seems, can raise the British intellectual from the deathbed or avert the respectful, if rather thin, obituary notices that follow inevitably upon such a painful demise.

As one might expect, French accounts of this process of decline, amounting as they do to a description of the disappearance of an iconic figure in French national culture, come replete with an intensity of emotion and political passion that is lacking in their American and British counterparts. The death of the French intellectual is a death that has been foretold for much longer, the dying patient clinging to life despite mounting terminal illness for 20 years or more. Indeed, such is the physical tenacity of this particular specimen that death has seemed frequently cheated of this, its most cherished prize, the intellectual who, from Voltaire to Sartre, made governments sit up and listen. Yet, for all that, the diagnosis offered bears a striking resemblance to those provided in America and Great Britain.

Topicality alone might be sufficient to justify examination of the arguments recently advanced by Régis Debray, were it not for the fact that Debray's initial forays into this territory were of such originality that they have since served to define the parameters of a debate that has resurfaced in France with astounding regularity and considerable public attention. His latest offering, *i. f. suite et fin*, as its title might suggest, only serves to personalize (and also possibly trivialize) a polemic whose outlines were originally sketched out in *Le Pouvoir intellectuel en France*, published first in 1979.

In contrast to Todd Gitlin, Debray could at least in his earlier text evoke a lost golden age characterized by the founding myth of the Dreyfusard intellectual – now described as *"l'intellectuel original, version 1900"* – and such literary reviews as André Gide's *Nouvelle Revue Française*. With the advent of what Debray describes as "the media cycle," dated from 1968 onwards, such cultural glories came to an end, the "information apparatus" reducing thought to the equivalent of fast food. "The mass media," Debray wrote, at a time when the seductive powers of French television were severely under-developed, "run on personality, not the collective, the sensational, not the intelligible, and the singular, not the universal."[4] They produce simplicity by eliminating complexity. Valued above all was "the ability to speak on a subject about which one knows virtually nothing." Ambition, corruption, and conformism, rather than principle, were the order of the day in a world dominated by image ("good teeth, nice hair") rather than content. The "great mediacrats" had replaced the "golden age of French thought" of yesteryear.

Twenty years later Debray saw only the decomposing remains of *"l'intellectuel terminal, version 2000,"* the sad victim of an "almost biological process" of decline brought about by the growing presence of the mass media. The pathological symptoms of this terminal condition are analyzed in detail and are sufficiently obvious not to need translation: *"autisme collectif," "déréalisation grandiloquente," "imprévision chronique," "narcissisme moral,"* and *"instantanéisme."*[5] It is clear, however, that beneath the pseudoterminology of the medical diagnostician lies a deep irritation with what Debray sees as the decline of reasoned debate and argument and its replacement by invective, sloganizing, and intellectual conformism. That Debray recognizes that he himself has not been free of these tendencies only serves to give greater force to a polemic that has many of France's public intellectuals firmly within its sights.

Yet, as Debray is the first to acknowledge, at the heart of his analysis lies a fundamental paradox. If the intellectual has never been subject to so much sarcasm and ridicule, so too the intellectuals have never been *"aussi envahissants"* (as ever-present). For all Debray's talk of *"l'intellectuel terminal,"* in other words, none of this would seem to suggest that the French intellectual is ready to be quietly carried away from the scene.

Indeed, this is an impression that is quickly confirmed by the perusal of France's still-thriving periodical press. Here France's post-World War II history provides us with some of the context. When Jean-Paul Sartre established *Les Temps Modernes* in 1945 he did so with the explicit intention of dethroning Gide's *Nouvelle Revue Française* and its philosophy of art for art's sake. Thirty-five years later Pierre Nora, launching *Le Débat*, repeated the strategy, seeking to kill off the Sartrian doctrine of intellectual commitment amid calls for the recognition of a new "intellectual democracy." Whether that transformation brought a golden age of partisan engagement to an end, or simply put paid to a parenthetic aberration, has since been the subject of much heated dispute, but the fact remains that Nora began a debate about the appropriate role of the intellectual that has continued to this day and which, given recent attempts to reassert the canonical status of Jean-Paul Sartre,[6] has lost none of its pertinence. Restated in a 20th anniversary celebratory issue, the case was succinctly made: if the goal was to secure "the independence and autonomy of intellectual activity" this could only be achieved through "a veritable metamorphosis of the model of the intellectual itself." This, according to Nora, had been one of the principal tasks that *Le Débat* had set itself throughout its existence.[7]

Accordingly, the frequently announced death of the French intellectual has been accompanied by a proliferation of competing models and descriptions which challenge the Sartrian account and which, in some cases, are intended to offer possibilities for the future. Intellectuals now appear to come in all shapes and sizes. Historian Michel Winock, for example, recently provided a threefold classification, dividing intellectuals into the categories of *"professionel," "spécifique,"* and *"anonyme."* If the first group appears with annoying regularity on our television screens, consumed by a narcissistic belief in the importance of their message, the second seeks, in the manner of Michel Foucault, to deploy their technical competence to aid the oppressed, only themselves occasionally falling victim to their own prestige by reverting back to the now-discredited Sartrian "universal" model.[8] As for the "anonymous" intellectual, he or she denoted not the "end of the intellectual" but rather their "proliferation" and with that the eradication of earlier "aristocratic" patterns of behavior and claims to superiority. On this view, intellectuals are individuals who "make sense of our collective life"; they are, in Winock's phrase, *"les penseurs du contemporain."*

It would easily be possible to cite further evidence of such interpretative accounts of the function of intellectuals in contemporary France. In the spring of 2000, the influential review *Esprit* provided two substantial issues devoted entirely to the examination of what it termed the *"splendeurs et misères de la vie intellectuelle,"* and with that came further typological definitions and classifications. The aim was to clarify the past, present, and future of this enigmatic and elusive figure.[9] More substantially, however, the point needs to be made that patterns of activity and protest by intellectuals in France have remained substantially unchanged over a considerable period of time and the French public still seems to accord a special status to pronouncements made by intellectuals on a wide range of political and social issues. I have explored these patterns of continuity in detail elsewhere,[10] focusing upon the manner in which intellectuals in France still resort with remarkable frequency to the tried and tested strategy of the public petition, first established as their favorite weapon over a hundred years ago during the Dreyfus Affair. By the same token, the quality press continues to show itself ready to give space to such statements. In January 2000, for example, *Le Monde* published an editorial entitled "Les intellectuels et nous" in which, with admirable dexterity, it announced its continued acceptance of its long-established responsibility "to open up its columns, without favor, to all those who lead intellectual debate."[11]

That editorial, written in the context of the publication of Bernard-Henri Lévy's much discussed *Le Siècle de Sartre*, could not but mention Pierre Bourdieu, described as "without doubt the intellectual figure who today most resembles Sartre through the strength of his commitments and the international reputation of his work." Few would disagree with this characterization. Moreover, Bourdieu until his death in January 2000, came increasingly to occupy the political stage, himself acknowledging this process of evolution. In his last collection of essays, for example, he wrote that "I have come to think that those who have the opportunity to devote their life to the study of the social world cannot remain neutral or indifferent, distanced from those struggles where the future of the world is at stake."[12] The same collection provides a powerful defense of what he terms *"un savoir engagé"* or, to use Bourdieu's own English expression, "scholarship with commitment," thereby inviting scholars and researchers to transcend "the sacred frontier" transcribed by the "academic microcosm."[13]

Bourdieu himself was as critical as anyone of what he saw as the loss of "autonomy" that has followed the emergence of the much-despised *"intellectuel médiatique"* and their longing for "temporal success." Like Régis Debray, he focused much of the blame upon television, a medium which privileges the banal and insignificant over information and culture, inviting those academics turned journalists who participate in its mind-numbing debates to subject themselves to a self-imposed censorship in line with what is repeatedly described as the ideological dominance of economic liberalism.[14] Few have been spared the opprobrium contained in their description as the *"nouveaux maîtres à penser sans pensée,"* not even the editors of *Esprit*, a review which has continually sought to challenge the stultifying orthodoxy that so often characterizes what passes for intellectual debate in France.[15]

Nevertheless, Bourdieu repeatedly refused to accept the "death" of what he described as "one of the last critical countervailing powers capable of opposing the forces of the economic and political order."[16] Defending what he has termed a *"Realpolitik de la raison"* Bourdieu outlined a *"corporatisme de l'universel"* which, in his opinion, could still be represented by an *"Internationale des intellectuels."* Such an "International" would bring together "specific intellectuals" (in the Foucauldian sense of the term) to form a "collective intellectual" capable of defining its own goals and objectives in a situation of "autonomy." It would, moreover, ally itself with an emerging European social movement, still in its infancy, providing the latter not just with critical analysis and documentation but also with a set of "realistic utopias."[17]

What conclusions, if any, can be drawn from these developments? It would be foolish to deny that the passage from Sartre to Foucault to Bourdieu has involved a significant metamorphosis, reshaping both the status and function of the intellectual in France. Yet, for all the talk of the death of the intellectual, the public clamor and attention that attended virtually every statement made by Bourdieu is sufficient on its own to indicate that the figure of the public intellectual has far from vanished. Moreover, Bourdieu, unlike many of his contemporaries and despite his own philosophical reservations, conformed very closely to the traditional model of the Dreyfusard intellectual, deploying the authority that derived from his "scientific" status and his academic eminence at the *Collège de France* not only to articulate a set of political positions but also to co-ordinate what amounted to a sophisticated network of like-minded supporters (most notably through the columns of *Le Monde diplomatique* and such highly successful publishing ventures as *Editions Raisons d'Agir*).

The question then becomes not only one of why this should be the case but also whether this refusal on the part of the French intellectual to depart from the scene represents perhaps only a temporary reprieve. The latter is the view of Jean-François Sirinelli, one of the most distinguished historians of the French intellectual. Here is not the place to analyze in detail the arguments put forward by Sirinelli: in essence his claim is that the socio-cultural context in which the Dreyfusard and (later) committed or "revolutionary" intellectual operated has so changed beyond recognition that there is no possibility of permanent rehabilitation. Specifically, he argues that "the rise to preeminence of the *clerc* in French society occurred at a time when the printed word was King. Since that time a change of dynasty has occurred, the printed word has been dethroned as the principal form of communication, replaced by the audio-visual." Thus, according to Sirinelli, Bernard-Henri Lévy's attempt to re-instate Sartre amounts to no more than the return of Napoleon's remains from Saint Helena; the *cinéastes* who led the campaign of civil disobedience in 1997 are "*les enfants de l'éclipse*"; whilst the signs of renewed activity that we have witnessed since 1995 are nothing but "a lunch in the sun during an Indian summer that moves slowly and inevitably towards winter."[18]

For the remainder of this article I want to explore an argument which suggests that Sirinelli's seasonal metaphors might be misleading, and which might give grounds for believing that the French intellectual is not dead after all. In part I want to pursue this argument by paying closer attention to the diagnoses that have sought to explain the passing of the intellectual in Britain and America, for it seems likely that the conditions which prevail there might, in very significant respects, be different from those that pertain in France. At best my conclusions will be both tentative and provisional. I acknowledge in particular that there are those on either side of the Atlantic who do not share these pessimistic analyses, believing that the public intellectual might yet have a role to play in shaking the prevailing political consensus and that they might yet draw sustenance from the possibilities offered by new technologies. In America, in particular, there is clearly no agreement about the consequences of what Bruce Robbins has described as "the grounding" or professionalization of the intellectual and the passing of the "free-floating" autonomous intellectual as outsider described by Karl Mannheim.[19] Nor is there likely to be in the near future, given the legitimacy and resonance of disagreements between foundationalists and anti-foundationalists. However, both the American and British situations might cast light upon the likelihood of the continued existence of the French intellectual. This, at least, is worth exploring.

No one has done more than Russell Jacoby to provide an account of what is characterized as the disappearance of the intellectual in America. He has drawn our attention especially to two important, interrelated developments. The first, examined in *The Last Intellectuals: American Culture in the Age of Academe*[20] focused upon a generational transition that saw independent intellectuals – "the last bohemians" – abandon their urban habitats for the university campus. The consequence was professionalization and specialization, the turning away from a public sphere that had been the focus of the republic of letters from the eighteenth century onwards. With specialization came not just fragmentation (the targeting of ever smaller audiences and the abandonment of the vernacular), but also depolitization and (if truth be told) careerism, academic life increasingly coming to imitate corporate practices (most notably through inflated salaries for the celebrity superstars who supposedly bring prestige and glamor to their employers). Physical comfort also bred conformism and the absence of serious intellectual endeavor.

Worse, however, was yet to come: the culture wars. Here we need briefly to acknowledge the intimate ties that bind the emergence of the intellectual with modernity and the tradition of enlightenment. The post-modern, to critics and friends alike, amounts to a theoretical attack upon the beliefs of the *philosophes* in the claims of normative rationality, and thus, on this account, undermines the epistemological authority of the intellectual. Richard Rorty, for example, provides a compelling portrait of the post-modern intellectual as ironist.[21] For Jacoby, on the other hand, the demise of this progressive tradition "makes way for the party of multiculturalists."

The arguments of Jacoby's *The End of Utopia: Politics and Culture in an Age of Apathy* are far-reaching and would presumably evoke strong reaction from the campus radicals he so readily dismisses as irrelevant. The charge, however, is a simple one. Multiculturalism "has become the opium of disillusioned intellectuals, the ideology of an era without ideology." It relies, he goes on, "on an intellectual rout, the refusal or inability to address what makes up a culture." Despite a rhetoric of subversion, therefore, "it leads intellectuals down the path of acquiescence." And here is the punch line: "to put this sharply, once intellectuals were outsiders who wanted to be insiders. Now they are insiders who pretend to be outsiders – a claim that can be sustained only by turning marginality into a pose."[22] For the self-defined outsider intellectual marginality is no more than a shrewd career move.

Jacoby is by no means alone in telling this story. Todd Gitlin makes similar claims,[23] accusing the multiculturalists of turning their backs upon the real issues of economic poverty that daily disfigure American public life (the Bangladeshi male, he points out, has a longer life expectancy than the black male from Harlem); so too does Jeffrey Goldfarb in his thought-provoking *Civility and Subversion: The Intellectual in Democratic Society*, where multiculturalism is redescribed as "multitribalism" and where even Edward Said's model intellectual is castigated for being "not an agent for public deliberation but for political assertion." Taken together, the charges amount to saying that multiculturalism condemns the intellectual left in America to a position of permanent marginality and condemns the intellectual, now safely cocooned in the warm embrace of the university, to endless debates about the political correctness or otherwise of the faculty curriculum. As Goldfarb comments: "Academic politics have become more real to some post-modern critics than the consequential democratic politics of the general society."[24]

Given the sheer power and size of the American economy and the extent to which corporate interests determine the political agenda in America, it is difficult to know what, if anything, might dent the triumphalist expectations associated with the ideology of global capitalism. The fact remains, however, that on this view Bill Gates has more to fear from street demonstrators of the kind we have recently witnessed in Seattle and elsewhere than he ever does from America's domesticated and institutionalized intellectuals.

It is only with great hesitation and trepidation that an English academic would venture upon a comparative examination of the role of the British and French intellectual, such has been the assumed lowly status of the former. Even Régis Debray speaks of the "benign neglect" that exists this side of the Channel. It is as well, therefore, to begin by briefly addressing the cliché that Britain has not had any intellectuals. Thomas William Heyck attributes this misconception to three factors: "first, a tradition in modern British history carrying an image of British society as non-intellectual: second, paradoxically, the high degree of integration of the intellectuals with the ruling elite, and third, a problem of multiple meanings of the term "intellectual."[25] How might each of these elements be characterized? The first ironically owes much to a deep antipathy to all things French and predates even the French revolution of 1789. The sturdy, commonsensical British (Protestant) yeoman was contrasted first with the artificial and effete *habitué* of the Parisian *salon* and then with the diabolical, atheistic *philosophe* that Jeremy Bentham, like Edmund Burke, found guilty of producing "nonsense upon stilts," with such terrible consequences. If that antipathy toward French intellectualism was shared by such a nineteenth-century Conservative statesman as the British Prime Minister, the Marquess of Salisbury (who openly delighted in the bloody repression of the Paris Commune) it was equally evident in the opinions of such quintessential members of the British Left as George Orwell and E.P. Thompson, for whom respect for "the peculiarities of the English" went hand-in-hand with a profound contempt for Althusser.[26] One contemporary example serves to highlight this continued self-perception that British society is non-intellectual. The novel *White Teeth* by Zadie Smith has generally been perceived as having its finger firmly upon the pulse of a modern, multicultural Britain. It is therefore interesting to note that when one character describes the unusual members of the Chalfen family as intellectuals, it is whispered "as if it were some exotic disease of the tropics."[27]

The integration of British intellectuals into the ruling elite has been well chronicled, even if the picture presented has to an extent been misunderstood. In Britain, as Stefan Collini has shown,[28] political and intellectual élites became highly integrated during the latter half of the nineteenth century and remained so for much of the twentieth century, producing the phenomenon of the "public moralist." "All," to quote Julia Stapleton, "sought a prominent role for intellectuals in defining the central "public" values and identities of their society through their scholarship and personal conduct alike."[29] Their natural habitat could not have been further removed from the Parisian café of their French counterpart, being rather the Senior Common Room of the Oxbridge college and the gentlemen's club in London. To this might be added the exclusive apartments of Albany. Political integration, it is argued, was also matched by ties of family kinship. Noel (later Lord) Annan not only gave this trend personal embodiment but also coined the phrase "intellectual aristocracy" to characterize the remarkable proportion of the nation's academic elite that was drawn from a relatively small number of interconnected families. To this picture of untroubled tranquillity was added the fortunate occurrence that Britain, to the dismay of the Marxist New Left, received the wrong sort of intellectual immigrant: it was settled by "a 'White', counter-revolutionary emigration" from Central and Eastern Europe.[30] Rather than receiving such revolutionary firebrands as Herbert Marcuse, Britain had welcomed the likes of Isaiah Berlin, for whom it epito-mized "tradition, continuity and orderly empire."

Confusions about the meaning of the term intellectual need not detain us, especially as they have been adequately explored elsewhere. However, one source of the confusion might be worthy of note. As T.W. Heyck has commented: "no single event like the Dreyfus case in France riveted British attention on one aspect or function of intellec-tuals." The truth of this assertion can be shown by reference to another literary work. In 1999 Bernice Rubens published a novel entitled *I, Dreyfus*.[31] It is a reworking of the Dreyfus case in a British setting, the French army officer reappearing rather predictably as a public school master. Apart from its literary qualities, what adds to the fascination of the account is that the fate of Dreyfus is seen entirely in terms of his personal tragedy as a victim of anti-Semitism. At no point does the wider political controversy of the original Dreyfus case intrude into the story and at no point do intellectuals, as either individuals or a group, make their entry.

Yet Britain arguably has had intellectuals who have enjoyed both autonomy and influence, matching that accorded them in France from the Dreyfus affair onwards. Again, it is as well to refer to the conclu-sions reached by Julia Stapleton. Recent studies of British intellectual culture in the late nineteenth and early twentieth centuries, she points out, have identified five distinguishing aspects of "public intellec-tuals": "their exclusivity; pursuit of intellectual inquiry within distinc-tive English 'national' traditions; adherence to an ideology of 'liberal pluralism'; commitment to social improvement through individual exertion, and accordance of a purely formal role to the State." Part of the argument is that those distinguishing features have been progressively undermined in the years that followed World War II, producing an increasingly antithetical relationship between intellectuals and the broader public culture in Britain. Moreover, as Stapleton has pointed out elsewhere, these British intellectuals shared certain common features with their counterparts in France, most notably their perception of themselves as an oppositional voice, as public rather than civil servants. They were, as she writes, "politically engaged, kept up a high public profile and set great store by their own independence and by free debate more generally."[32] This is a conclusion endorsed by Noel Annan. The intellectual aristocracy, he comments, "did not think of themselves, whatever their connections, as being part of the ruling class and the established circles of power."[33] So too, British intellectuals, like those in France, were conscious that their authority and effectiveness were dependent upon a strong sense of national identity, however contested that identity might be. But here there is a point of obvious contrast. From Zola onwards, if not from before, the French intellectual has defined the identity of France in terms of universal ideals of truth, justice, and the rights of man and has chosen to locate their physical embodiment in the institutions of the Republic, one and indivisible. In England, a distrust of abstract ideas combined with a delight in particularity focused patriotic nostalgia upon the peoples, places, and architecture of a much-revered English landscape. If in France intellectuals presumed to speak in the name of humanity, in England the inspiration was as likely to have been the parish church.

What, if anything, remains of the distinctive features of this earlier period? If we are to believe Richard English and Michael Kenny, we are now left with little more than "the tradition of the intellectual as public doom-monger,"[34] a tradition far removed from the triumphalist narratives of British exceptionalism. Within this declinist literature, of which there is undoubtedly an abundance, the traditions and identity of the English *patria* which provided such inspiration for earlier public moralists are on the point of extinction, with the potential break-up of the constituent parts of the United Kingdom matched only by the fragmentation associated with the emergence of a multicultural Britain. Roger Scruton's recent, otherwise disappointing, foray into this terrain[35] is at least accurate in one respect: to write about "England" today is to compose an elegy.

If this account of Britain's decline rests heavily upon a characterization of poor post-war leadership by both its political and economic elites, it also arguably has contemporary expression in what appears to be the near unanimous acceptance of what are taken to be the political consequences of globalization.[36] As English and Kenny state: "a wave of recent commentary has rightly observed the way in which contemporary politicians and intellectuals have redefined (and often reduced) the parameters of 'the possible' by presenting the global economy (through the ambiguous notion of 'globalization') as a set of ineluctable forces which produce immovable structural constraints for public policy-makers."[37] Here is not the place to begin a debate on the correctness or otherwise of the globalization thesis, but we can at least confirm that, in the form of "the third way," it has now attained something near to both political and intellectual orthodoxy in Britain, its dominance succinctly embodied in the figures of Tony Blair and Anthony Giddens.

The doom-mongery of British intellectuals has also been accompanied by a perceived loss of status. The exclusivity born of the "clerisy" tradition looks, for good or ill, to be a thing of the past. The election of 1979 brought with it not just what Stefan Collini has described as "the anti-intellectualism of the intellectual"[38] but also a concerted challenge to the culture of British universities, bringing to an end the cosy relationship of mutual admiration that had characterized the relationship between government and academics. More than this, however, the vast expansion of higher education that accompanied this decline in privileged status for both academic institutions and their members alike came replete with demands not only that British universities should increase their contribution to the competitiveness of the economy but also that their staff – the descendants of the Trevelyans, Stephens, and Stracheys – should increase their own productivity. If the research priorities of the British funding councils took care of the former, the vast array of increasingly sophisticated mechanisms of external audit was sufficient to ensure that the public moralist of old gave way to the disciplinary specialist, the height of whose ambition is to pen a learned article in a scholarly journal with a circulation that rarely exceeds 300 copies. By any standards, this transformation has been a success story. Britain's higher education system now educates far more undergraduates than ever before, at a much reduced cost, with a disciplined workforce which not only scarcely ever raises a murmur of complaint but which also seems content to accept its domesticated role in what is seen as an emerging academic public sphere.

If, in these ways, we might account for the disappearance of the public intellectual in both the United States and Great Britain, how might the situation in France be different and to what extent might this lead us to conclude that there, at least, the public intellectual might have a future? A response can draw upon four possible contrasts. The first, paradoxically, derives from the very weaknesses and deficiencies of the French university system; the second focuses upon the continued existence of what is invariably described as "the radical left" in France; the third highlights a related widely held public antipathy toward liberalism and globalization; while the fourth stresses what remains a relatively strong sense of national identity combined with a relatively homogenous republican political culture that eschews multiculturalism.

The problems that afflict the French university system are both profound and long-standing. They have repeatedly defeated the reforming intentions of successive governments. Occasionally, however, they receive a very public airing, as when the philosopher Jean-Fabien Spitz published an article in *Le Débat* detailing the three misfortunes – "material, intellectual, and moral" – that afflict the average university teacher. The material conditions of the French university are too well known to require enumeration: too many students taught by staff with inadequate resources, inadequate administrative support, and inadequate salaries. In summary, as Spitz writes, "the French university resembles those of the third world rather than those of the developed countries with which we claim to compare ourselves." The intellectual conditions are arguably even more debilitating; the inability to carry out research (Spitz draws particular attention to the state of France's libraries) is matched by an institutionalized anti-intellectualism and a clientelism that thrives on servility. Faced by such appalling conditions the moral outcome is one of generalized cynicism, in which teachers pretend to teach, students pretend to study, and examiners pretend to examine. "The function of the university," Spitz writes, "is reduced to that of ensuring the social safekeeping of the young, perceived as the dangerous class of the end of the twentieth century."[39]

The solutions proffered to rectify this situation of near collapse do not concern us, but it is as well to recognize, as Antoine Compagnon has done,[40] that if the system continues to work at all, it is due in great part to the continued dedication of its participants. The fact of the matter is, however, that in France, unlike the United States and Great Britain, the natural starting point in any search for intellectuals, is not likely to be in the universities, and therefore the question of whether the notion of the academic intellectual is an oxymoron is one that is far less likely to be heard. For example, certain consequences follow from the absence in France of university presses of the kind so readily found in Britain and the United States. Jean-Luc Giribone, from the publishing house *Seuil*, recently commented that:

> whether one considers it to be a good or bad thing, the absence of a large university publisher contributes to preserving the figure of *homo intelluallis gallicus* who, in one way or another, is more than a simple specialist, because the publisher obliges the researcher who knocks on his door to reformat his work to suit the publishing profile of a more general publishing house. We therefore create a type of author who does not have an exact equivalent in the United States, for example.[41]

Joël Roman, one of the editors of *Esprit*, simply makes the point that "in France, intellectual life has never been limited to the University."[42] The French University system, in short, might crush its participants but it does not always, as elsewhere, domesticate and compromise them. Nor is it all-consuming. Moreover, when they do occasionally protest, they do so not in the Anglo-American guise of academic professionals but as "autonomous intellectuals."[43]

It is only seven years ago, in 1994, that Mark Lilla, introducing a volume on *New French Thought*, could speak of "the legitimacy of the Liberal Age."[44] The prominence of three reviews in particular, *Esprit*, *Le Débat*, and *Commentaire* (the latter founded under the auspices of the once much-maligned liberal philosopher Raymond Aron), seemed proof alone that something had changed dramatically on the French intellectual landscape. Moreover, this was a view shared by those on the Left who came increasingly to condemn what they saw as the dominant *"pensée unique"* associated with "neo-liberalism." Since the mid-1990s, however, liberalism has again found itself on the defensive while the Left, despite earlier predictions of its imminent disappearance, finds itself still being heard and read (to take one example, the left-leaning *Le Monde diplomatique* has a regular circulation within France of around 200,000). Ironically, as critics on both the Right and the Left have acknowledged, this renaissance has in part been aided by the demise of the Soviet bloc. If, for example, Jean-François Revel thinks that this is because the Left has never faced up to the reality of the Communist system, Pierre Bourdieu took the view that the collapse of these regimes and the decline of communist parties in the West "has liberated critical thought."[45]

The precise nature of this "radical Left" has been the subject of much discussion.[46] It is heterogeneous. It is built less around political parties than around a range of single-issue organizations (for example, *Les Comités des sans-papiers* and *Les Restos de Coeur*) as well as clubs and associations (for example, *Pétitions* and *Copernic*, the latter of which explicitly set itself up to oppose the reformist *Fondation Saint-Simon*). For opponents such as Pierre Rosanvallon, it represents a "distrust" of modernity, a "vague" anti-establishment "radicalism," a "moral posture" of "resistance" and "a culture of criticism rather than a culture of action."[47] For its members this new radicalism draws its strength from the real problems experienced by modern society and from the need to defend the "French model" from the destructive intrusions of the emerging technocratic world economic order. To cite Pierre Bourdieu once more, what is at stake is "the defence of a *civilization*, associated with the existence of public services, the republican equality of rights, the rights to education, to health care, to culture, to knowledge, to art, and above the rest, to work."[48]

How does this impact upon the claim that intellectuals still exist in France? The recent interventions of Pierre Bourdieu and of those allied to him have relied explicitly upon the claim that the "neo-liberal vulgate" needs to be subjected to a radical critique. Given that this cannot be performed by those dismissed as "doxosophes" it might, however, be achieved by those that retain "an interest in the universal." The grounds of this argument are sketched out in Bourdieu's *Méditations pascaliennes*. Thus, despite all the distortions and ambiguities associated with claims to represent an abstract universalism – Bourdieu specifically recognized that France, more than any other country, has embodied the "imperialism" of a "false Western universalism" – the process of autonomization that followed the Enlightenment allowed the development within society of sectors which had an "interest in the universal" as well as "an interest in being disinterested." This argument produces two overt strategic outcomes. The first focuses upon the mobilization of all those whose interests are perceived or presented as being in line with the "universal" or the "general interest." In practice this meant, for example, support for the railway workers during the 1995 strikes which brought France to a virtual standstill. Crucially, this stance depends upon a distinction within the *noblesse d'Etat* between those who defend the interests of the dominant class, in other words those who have turned a "public" into a "private good," and those referred to as the *petite noblisse d'Etat* who defend *"les acquis universels"* associated with the State and the general good. Secondly, as such documents as *Le "décembre" des intellectuels français* reveal, this strategy rests upon an opposition between those specialists drawn from the social sciences who, modeling themselves upon the Dreyfusard intellectuals, deploy their "intellectual and scientific capital" in the defense of "the victims," and the vast cohort of "mediatic" intellectuals and so-called experts who, through either cynicism or self-interest – not to mention "narcissism" – collude or "collaborate" with "the dominant discourse." Here, then, is a clear role for "the collective intellectual" as described by Bourdieu.[49]

The last two elements of this account serve further to confirm that the context in which French intellectuals operate is quite different from that experienced by their disappearing British and American counterparts. If a survey of the ideology of the radical Left in France reveals that it turns its attention to a wide variety of issues – immigration, the rights of women, campaigns for the homeless, and so on – its overriding themes are undoubtedly an opposition to "the neo-liberal invasion" and the related phenomenon of "globalization" (or *mondialisation*). There is much that might be said here about the failure of liberalism ever to develop deep roots in French political culture and it is as well to remember that French and American "exceptionalisms" share little in common. The fact of the matter is, however, that both free-market liberal capitalism and globalization have been subject to strident and sustained criticism in France over recent years. Again, it has been a message that has had a sizeable readership. *L'Horreur économique*, published by literary critic Viviane Forrester of *Le Monde*, not only won the *Prix Medicis* in 1996 but also sold well over 350,000 copies in France alone. *Une Etrange dictature*, which continued Forrester's polemic against "the fiasco of ultraliberalism," had only slightly less success.[50] Other works attacking the *"chienlit mondialiste laisser-fairiste"* could easily be cited.

Viewed from the radical Left – although this is quite decidedly not an interpretation shared by writers in such reviews as *Commentaire*, for whom France remains wedded to its inflexible and outmoded statist model – not only is "neo-liberalism" the new "economic orthodoxy" (threatening a form of "exploitation without limits") but "globalization" is itself "a political creation," the result of a self-conscious policy of trade liberalization. As our inevitable destiny it has therefore only the status of myth.

If, however, it has been accepted as a reality, this is because, in France as elsewhere, what is now seen as self-evident is the result of a determined, well-thought-out attempt to influence and change opinion by government and by a whole variety of think-tanks, associations, and so on. How might France respond to the imposition of this foreign model? Bourdieu writes:

> The most urgent task appears to me to be that of finding the appropriate material, economic, and, above all, organizational means in order to encourage all those competent experts [*chercheurs*] to unite their efforts with activist leaders to discuss and elaborate collectively a set of analyses and propositions for the future which today only have a virtual existence in private thoughts or in marginal publications.[51]

In brief, Bourdieu believed that "globalization" should be matched by a "new internationalism" and that, within this, "critical" and "autonomous" intellectuals should play a key role.

The final point of contrast highlights issues of national identity. The claim, it should be remembered, is that in America multiculturalism has reduced intellectuals to marginality, while in Britain (and especially in England) the loss of a settled sense of national identity has deprived intellectuals of the object in whose name they have been likely to speak. In France, the authority first accorded to intellectuals owed much to the need of the Republic to challenge clericalism and the Republic was therefore prepared to reward its scientists and philosophers with status and prestige. If today, in the eyes of many of France's intellectuals, the Republic itself is rather tarnished, the same cannot be said for the ideology of republicanism, which secures almost universal assent. That ideology is itself remarkably complex: it is also subject to evolution. Historically, however, it has placed great emphasis upon the character and integrity of nation and this is a feature still visible amongst its adherents (including, for example, Régis Debray). There are signs that there are moves toward a "*République plurielle*" but it is only very rarely that a version of multiculturalism will be openly embraced. The sociologist Alain Touraine is one example. Government policy, while it edges toward a more pragmatic response to such issues as the Muslim religion, remains in principle resolutely hostile to all communitarian claims, fearing social disintegration.

The question arises, therefore, whether, if French intellectuals retain a position of relative eminence, it is in part because they inhabit a society that continues not to perceive itself as being multicultural. Is it, for example, only an accident that such an ardent national-republican as Régis Debray should also be such a tireless advocate of the merits of the universal intellectual? I am inclined to think that there is a connection; and, moreover, to believe that, for as long as France's republican culture retains its vibrancy, intellectuals who speak out in the name of humanity and the universal will continue to have a privileged voice in public debate. How long that culture will survive in what looks to be an increasingly hostile environment is impossible to foretell, but this argument might indicate that the key question for the future is less likely to be "what does it mean to be an intellectual in France?" but rather, "can France's distinctive national political culture endure in a period of apparent increasing cultural and economic globalization?" If not, the French intellectual too might come to occupy the modest, if still critical, role of those intellectuals elsewhere who have long since been grounded. Given that such grounding does not necessarily denote either betrayal or the abandonment of a responsibility towards a broader public it might tell us also that the public intellectual need no longer be confined, in the words of Bruce Robbins, to "Parisian seating arrangements."[52]

## Notes

1 Todd Gitlin, *The Twilight of Common Dreams* (New York: Henry Holt, 1995).
2 Todd Gitlin, "The Renaissance of Anti-Intellectualism," *Chronicle of Higher Education*, December 8 (2000): B7–9 (quotations p. 9).
3 Michael Ignatieff "Where are They Now?" *Prospect* "Taster" issue (1997): 4–5.
4 Régis Debray, *Le pouvoir intellectuel en France* (Paris: Editions Ramsay, 1979), p. 97 (this and other translations from French are mine).
5 Régis Debray, *i.f. suite en fin* (Paris: Gallimard, 2000), section headings pp. 41–120.
6 Bernard-Henri Lévy, *Le Siècle de Sartre* (Paris: Grasset, 2000).
7 Pierre Nora, "Adieu aux intellectuels?" *Le Débat*, 110 (2000): 4–14. For an account of the history of *Le Débat* see B. Delorme-Montini "L'engagement démocratique," *Le Débat*, 110 (2000): 16–38.
8 Michel Winock, "A quoi servent (encore) les intellectuels?" *Le Débat*," 110 (2000): 39–44. Winock is referring specifically to Pierre Bourdieu's intervention in the debate about war in the Balkans; see P. Bourdieu, "Les intellectuels et la guerre," *L'Humanité*, May 18, 1999, p. 29.
9 *Esprit*, 262 and 263 (2000).
10 Jeremy Jennings, "1898–1998: From Zola's 'J'accuse' to the Death of the Intellectual," *The European Legacy*, 5 (2000): 829–44.
11 "Les intellectuels et nous," *Le Monde*, January 22, 2000, p. 14.

12  Pierre Bourdieu, *Contre-feux 2* (Paris: Raisons d'agir, 2001), pp. 7, 33–41.

13  *Contre-feux 2*, pp. 33–4.

14  Pierre Bourdieu, *Sur la télévision* (Paris: Liber, 1996).

15  Pierre Bourdieu, *Les Règles de l'art* (Paris: Seuil, 1998), p. 555. The attack upon the editors of *Esprit* is to be found in J. Duval et al. *Le "décembre" des intellectuels français* (Paris: Raisons d'agir, 1998). The response can be found in O. Mongin and J. Roman "Le populisme version Bourdieu ou la tentation du mépris," *Esprit*, 244 (1998): 158–75.

16  Bourdieu *Les Règles de l'art*, p. 545.

17  See especially Bourdieu, *Méditations pascaliennes* (Paris: Seuil, 1997); *Contre-feux 2*; "Les intellectuels et la guerre."

18  Jean-François Sirinelli, "Les enfants de l'éclipse," *Le Débat*, 103 (1999): 67–73; "Impressions soleil couchant?" *Le Débat*, 110 (2000): 45–52.

19  Bruce Robbins, *Intellectuals: Aesthetics, Politics, Academics* (Minneapolis: University of Minneapolis Press, 1990).

20  Russell Jacoby, *The Last Intellectuals: American Culture in the Age of Academe* (New York: Basic Books, 1987).

21  Richard Rorty, *Contingency, Irony and Solidarity* (Cambridge, UK: Cambridge University Press, 1989).

22  Russell Jacoby, *The End of Utopia: Politics and Culture in the Age of Apathy* (New York: Basic Books, 1999), pp. 33, 39, 66.

23  Gitlin, *The Twilight of Common Dreams*, pp. 29–33.

24  Jeffrey Goldfarb, *Civility and Subversion: The Intellectual in Democratic Society* (Cambridge, UK: Cambridge University Press, 1998), pp. 70, 74.

25  Thomas William Heyck, "Myths and Meanings of Intellectuals in Twentieth-Century British National Identity," *Journal of British Studies*, 37 (1998): 192–211.

26  See Jeremy Jennings, "L'anti-intellectualisme britannique et image de l'intellectuel français," *Mil neuf cent*, 15 (1997): 109–25.

27  Zadie Smith, *White Teeth* (London: Penguin, 2001), p. 132.

28  Stefan Collini, *Public Moralists: Political Thought and Intellectual Life in Britain, 1850–1930* (Oxford: Oxford University Press, 1991).

29  Julia Stapleton, "Political Thought, Elites and the State in Modern Britain," *The Historical Journal*, 42 (1999): 251–68 (quotation p. 251).

30  P. Anderson, "Components of the National Culture," *New Left Review*, 50 (1968): 1–57.

31  Heyck, "Myths and Meanings," p. 203; Bernice Rubens, *I, Dreyfus* (London: Little, Brown, 1999).

32  Stapleton "Political Thought," p. 252; "Cultural Conservatism and the Public Intellectual in Britain, 1930–1970," *The European Legacy*, 5 (2000): 795–814 (quotation p. 809).

33  Noel Annan, *The Dons: Mentors, Eccentrics and Geniuses* (London: HarperCollins, 1999), p. 12.

34  Richard English and Michael Kenny, "Public Intellectuals and the Question of British Decline," *British Journal of Politics and International Relations*, 3, 3 (2001): 259–83 (quotation p. 267).
35  Roger Scruton. *England: An Elegy* (London: Chatto and Windus, 2000).
36  See C. Hay, "The Invocation of External Economic Constraint: A Genealogy of the Concept of Globalization in the Political Economy of the British Labour Party, 1973–2000," *The European Legacy*, 6 (2001): 233–49.
37  English and Kenny, "Public Intellectuals," p. 267.
38  Stefan Collini, *English Pasts: Essays in History and Culture* (Oxford: Oxford University Press, 1999), p. 288.
39  Jean-Fabien Spitz, "Les trois misères de l'universitaire ordinaire," *Le Débat*, 103 (2000): 4–17 (quotation p. 17).
40  Antoine Compagnon, "Pourquoi la France n'a pas d'Université," *Critique*, LIV (1998): 16–38.
41  Jean-Luc Giribone and E. Vigne, "Le monde de l'édition et la création intellectuelle," *Esprit*, 262 (2000): 177–90 (quotation p. 185).
42  Jöel Roman, "La vie intellectuelle au regard de l' Université, de l'édition et des médias" *Esprit*, 262 (2000): 191–204 (quotation p. 193).
43  Areser, *Quelques diagnostics et remèdes urgents pour une université en péril* (Paris: Raisons d'agir, 1997), pp. 9–10. Areser stands for Association de réflexion sur les enseignements supérieurs et la recherche.
44  Mark Lilla, *New French Thought* (Princeton, NJ: Princeton University Press, 1994).
45  Jean-François Revel, *La Grande Parade: essai sur la survie de l'utopie socialiste* (Paris: Plon, 2000); Bourdieu *Contre-feux 2*, p. 36.
46  For an overview see B. Poulet, "A gauche de la gauche." *Le Débat*, 103 (1999): 39–59.
47  Pierre Rosanvallon, "L'esprit de 1995," *Débat*, 111 (2000): 118–20.
48  Bourdieu, *Contre-feux*, p. 30.
49  Bourdieu, *Méditations*, 145–51.
50  Viviane Forrester, *L'Horreur économique* (Paris: Fayard, 1996); *Une Etrange dictature* (Paris: Fayard 2000).
51  Bourdieu, *Contre-feux*, p. 12.
52  Bruce Robbins, *Secular Vocations: Intellectuals, Professionalism, Culture* (London: Verso, 1993), p. 6.

# Chapter 6

# New Art, Old Masters, and Masked Passions

## Linda S. Kauffman

The traditional function of the intellectual is critique, analysis, and explication, whether of politics or culture. In art and literature, the intellectual traditionally serves as gatekeeper of the canon, situating new works within a tradition. Hence the emphasis in my title on "new art and old masters." In an "ideal" world, the gatekeeper intellectual serves as arbiter of aesthetic merit and good taste. But ideal worlds are always gone. In reality, evaluating aesthetic merit is fraught with class values and ideological struggles.

Where can one find public intellectuals today? I spent the past decade researching, conducting interviews, and writing *Bad Girls and Sick Boys: Fantasies in Contemporary Art and Culture*[1] in order to answer that question. Today, they are behind the camera, writing novels, and performing in art spaces. The book is an ardent defense of artists who have been targets of censorship, ranging from performance artists like Bob Flanagan and Carolee Schneemann to writers like John Hawkes, Robert Coover, and Kathy Acker. I learned a great deal by interviewing writers like J.G. Ballard and filmmakers like David Cronenberg. All the artists I interviewed have seized innovations in science, medicine, and technology to radicalize artistic practices and challenge society's most cherished assumptions about the human body, subjectivity, and humanism.

What intrigued me is that despite working in different countries and in disparate media – fiction, film, and performance art – they had a shared objective: to describe *what is really happening* in our culture, at a moment when we are moving toward a radically different understanding of what "culture" might be. What does that mean, exactly? It means that the traditional dichotomies between critic and artist, theory and practice, have dissolved. The artist as intellectual reminds us, constantly, that culture is a domain of unconscious as well as conscious motivations and desires, and that what counts as the unconscious of culture is constantly under revision. It also means that the intellectual must read culture symptomatically, for, as J.G. Ballard observes below, artists must compete against an army of fiction-makers in advertising, politics, and entertainment. That awareness breeds a healthy skepticism about the possibility of transgression, for despite their audacious innovations, the artists are acutely aware that today's transgression is tomorrow's television commercial.

My essay focuses on events since *Bad Girls and Sick Boys* appeared. For example, when Bret Easton Ellis published *American Psycho* in 1991, he was universally reviled by gatekeeper intellectuals, in their self-professed capacity as arbiters of good taste, for his portrait of Patrick Bateman, a stockbroker/serial killer with yuppie – and cannibalistic – tastes. I defend Ellis in *Bad Girls and Sick Boys* by tracking the market forces that made the novel a casualty of corporate clashes, not conscience. What has happened since *Bad Girls and Sick Boys* premiered? Canadian filmmaker Mary Harron has adapted Ellis's novel to the screen.

Christian Bale (Fig. 6.1) stars as Patrick Bateman. He has all the best exercise equipment to get those abs and pecs into shape: he embodies *Playboy* magazine's motto, "Man at his best" – meaning, of course, the best that money can buy. In the scene illustrated, Bateman looks like he's setting up for the kill, complete with some sort of Freddy Kruger mask. But in fact, he is just giving himself a facial – showing how the cosmetics industry has zeroed in on the narcissism of a new target group – namely, men – to sell more commodities. Bateman is the truest true believer in the promises of Madison Avenue – he is the conspicuous consumer run amok.

Mary Harron is a feisty feminist whose previous credits include the 1996 bio-flick *I Shot Andy Warhol*, about Valerie Solanas, who wrote the SCUM (Society for Cutting Up Men) Manifesto. Like *American Psycho*, *I Shot Andy Warhol* focuses on an obsessive character who is fixated on the totemic power of celebrity. I spoke with Harron by telephone a month before the film's 2000 premiere. When I asked her what attracted her to Ellis's novel, she explained:

> The satire of the 1980s and Wall Street culture. But when we started writing the script in 1996, even four years ago, we viewed the phenomenon of massive consumption as well over. I saw the book as a period piece that had relevance today, but I thought of it as a bygone

Figure 6.1   Christian Bale as Patrick Bateman, *American Psycho*. © 1999 Lions Gate Films, Photo Kerry Hayes/Courtesy The Kobal Collection.

time – a kind of weird madness that was long over. It's odd how much has returned; the culture of spending that has come back is amazing. Society just seems to be awash in money.

Ironically, the idea of bringing *American Psycho* to the screen came to producer Edward R. Pressman when he read the novel while watching Los Angeles burning in the wake of the Rodney King riots in 1992. Pressman recalls, "on television were images of poor people looting and running through the streets. At the same time, I was reading this book about prosperity and people obsessed with objects. The contrast had a big impact on me."[2] It is an interesting moment in our culture when the producers and filmmakers are better readers than the literary critics, book reviewers, and gatekeeper intellectuals.

To appreciate *American Psycho's* satire, perhaps we had to wait for the dot-com billionaires and the tabloid reality-based television shows which now display a level of crassness devoid of parody. Harron's film slyly alludes to the historical amnesia of American society. Who now remembers that Ellis wrote the novel in the wake of the stock market crash of 1987? Who recalls the controversy over the Meese Commission on Pornography? Who now remembers the capitalist impresarios (men whom Bateman idolizes) like Ivan Boesky and Michael Milken? Ironically, in some ways the film is actually better than Ellis's book, because it translates Ellis's minute attention to social forms and surfaces into an extravagant visual banquet, conveying just how surrealistic Ellis meant his portrait of America to be. But the negative reaction to Ellis's novel created a climate so intimidating that numerous corporations would not even let their *products* be shown in the film – an ironic reversal of the growing trend toward cinematic product placement! Products not allowed in the film ranged from Rolex watches to Calvin Klein clothes. Even Huey Lewis withdrew approval for his 1980s hit, "Hip 2 Be Square" to be on the CD soundtrack. It is as if commodities have taken on a life of their own and can now be "guilty by association." The irony is especially rich since what really makes Bateman a psychopath is precisely that he buys everything he is told to buy and parrots everything he sees in popular culture.

When I suggested that censors seem to assume that audiences have precisely this monkey-see-monkey–do mentality, Harron agreed:

> There's a strange assumption now that if [as a filmmaker] you *show* bad actions, it is somehow an *endorsement* of those actions. If you really take that attitude to its logical conclusion, then you simply can't make any serious films at all. It's amazing how prevalent that's become – it's the current new hypocrisy.

Speaking of violence, Harron noted:

> I think if you refuse to have violence in the cinema, then you will be leaving out many of the greatest American movies: *The Godfather* 1 and 2; *Taxi Driver*; *Raging Bull*; even *Saving Private Ryan* . . . There is a complete frenzy over violence in entertainment, post-Columbine. There's not just more censorship, there's more self-censorship, and I think there will be more and more self-censoring.

Mary Harron braced herself for a controversial reaction to her film, but she was nevertheless astonished when a lawyer in Florida threatened a lawsuit while admitting that he had not read the book, the script, or seen the film. Eleanor Smeal, the president of the Feminist Majority Foundation, announced, "There are no redeeming qualities to a misogynist product like this" – without having seen it.

In reality, Harron's sly, devious film is indebted to 1930s screwball comedies, Sergio Leone's spaghetti Westerns, and to Luis Buñuel's *The Discreet Charm of the Bourgeoisie* – a work of surrealist fantasy. If the

Figure 6.2   David Cronenberg on location for *Crash*. © Columbia/Tri Star, Courtesy The Kobal Collection.

public, the critics, and the academy condemn what they have not read or seen, self-censorship will increasingly become the norm, and that is particularly pernicious because – by definition – it goes on unconsciously as well as consciously.

Since the publication of *Bad Girls and Sick Boys*, self-censoring has become pervasive in both publishing and in the film industry. With the merger of huge media conglomerates, fewer and fewer producers and publishers are willing to take a risk on edgy work, as André Schiffrin documents in *The Business of Books*.[3] For example, J.G. Ballard's novel, *Crash*, which he wrote in 1973, was adapted to screen by David Cronenberg in the Spring of 1997.

Figure 6.2 portrays Cronenberg on location while filming *Crash*, mugging for the camera between two smashed Mercedes, since the main character is obsessed with the fatal car crashes of James Dean, Jayne Mansfield, and other glamorous celebrities. But few film critics recognized that the film was an exploration of our deepest destructive drives and projections. Cronenberg's film was banned in several countries, attacked for displaying a morbid fascination with sex and death. The censors were literally afraid that the film might make people start *driving* badly! They argued that nobody in real life could possibly be

Figure 6.3  Diana's crashed Mercedes. © PA Photos.

so perversely fascinated with the intersections of death and destruction, fatality and glamour. What has happened since the film premiered?

The image (Fig. 6.3) of Princess Diana's fatal crash in the tunnel beneath the Alma Bridge in Paris on August 31, 1997, reveals just how accurate Ballard and Cronenberg were in capturing our obsessive fascination with celebrity and catastrophe. As if to drive home the point, immediately following Diana's fatal accident, the attorney in charge of licensing the images of James Dean and Jayne Mansfield urged Princess Diana's family to move swiftly to "copyright" her – just one of numerous examples of the myriad ways in which fiction has overwhelmed reality today.

The September 2000 issue of *Brill's Content*, a magazine devoted to analyzing the media, reported on a focus group's reaction to this and other catastrophes sensationalized by the media. Only two out of 20 people had a favorable view of the media, yet all 20 were frank in revealing their own hypocrisy, for while condemning the media for displaying such images, they admitted that they were *all* avid consumers of them. Rather than piously condemning sex and violence, the artists I'm discussing here investigate *why* sex and violence have such abiding and pervasive appeal, consciously and unconsciously. Moreover, as Ballard pointed out long ago, in the midst of the enormous media landscape, the novelist's function has changed dramatically:

> What can Saul Bellow or John Updike do that J. Walter Thompson, the world's largest advertising agency and its greatest producer of fiction, can't do better? . . . The social novel is reaching fewer and fewer readers, for the clear reason that social relationships are no longer as important as the individual's relationship with the technological landscape . . . The writer today . . . is now merely one of a huge army of people filling the environment with fictions of every kind. To survive, he must become far more analytic, approaching his subject matter like a scientist or engineer.[4]

In the summer of 1998, J.G. Ballard wrote me a letter from England, ruminating on all these matters. I quote it because it is so revealing about the public role of the intellectual – *at the very moment when events are unfolding.*

> Dear Linda
> Delighted to receive *Bad Girls and Sick Boys.* . . . We're living through a rather odd and unsettling time – I sympathize with the long pre-publication wait, which I've been through too many times myself, in both books and film (my latest effort, *Cocaine Nights*, a modest little fable, was turned down by more than a dozen New York City firms).

I find that confession amazing: here you have an author who has inspired generations of writers around the world. *Empire of the Sun*, his memoir about his boyhood internment in a Japanese camp during World War II, was made into a movie by Steven Spielberg. Yet even with such impeccable credentials, Ballard's work is considered too daring for New York publishers to risk publishing, in the current climate of censorship. Ballard's letter continues:

> A strange new kind of Puritanism is in the air, of which Cronenberg's *Crash* fell foul. Watching one of Clinton's erstwhile "friends," Joe

Lieberman . . . I wondered why the devious but likeable man [whom Lieberman] had once championed had forfeited all rights to his office. [I] wonder if Clinton isn't going to be the first important casualty of our Millennium-induced panic. Years ago, I wrote somewhere that our millennial decadence might take the form of an over-the-top Puritanism, and, having been through the year-long *Crash* panic over here – (an extraordinary storm whipped up in a million breakfast teacups for the anxious middle-class readers that the *Daily Mail* likes to keep on their edgy toes), I feel that poor Clinton, petty crook that he may be, is being stretched on the same rack. For a long time, I thought the fuss over Lewinsky was people's indirect way of punishing him for the Whitewater shenanigans that no one's been able to nail him for. Now, though, I think that his romps with the dizzy-eyed Monica are what so irk people . . . a curious kind of mass hysteria, as the stiff-lipped Brits showed a year ago when the nation mourned Diana. (What a 20th century death, by the way, dying, like Eurydice, glimpsed in the rearview mirror of her speeding Merc by the paparazzi-Orpheus who sang her fame – poor child.)

Ballard's letter, then, is a model for the public role of the intellectual today: in contrast to the glib, instantaneous analysis we get daily on television, he contextualizes current events; relates them to mythology and mythologies; and offers an acutely accurate roadmap of the cultural psyche – its symptoms and their significance. He simultaneously deflates the tabloid clichés of the *Daily Mail* and the sanctimoniousness of those grey eminences in the US Senate.

As we all know now, Joe Lieberman's so-called "courageous" condemnation of Clinton was rewarded with the invitation to be Al Gore's running mate. In retrospect, many Americans believe that Gore's repudiation of Clinton cost Gore the presidency. Ballard's allusions to Clinton serve as my transition to the next part of my essay, which is devoted to politics.

## The Body Politic

During the 2000 Presidential election, the assumption that America was suffering from a "decline in moral values" was woven into the narratives of the candidates, the media, the pollsters, and the focus groups, as Joan Didion notes, writing in *The New York Review of Books* on the eve of the election.[5] Paradoxically, both the Democrats and the Republicans subscribed to the same origin myth: that the populace must cast out its wicked allegiance to its disgraced leader and be saved before the final rapture (Didion, p. 76). She describes how Lieberman was repeatedly touted in the press as giving the Democratic ticket "moral authority" and for having "fearlessly spoken out to denounce both Clinton and popular culture." Hollywood, Lieberman asserted, "doesn't understand piety." Lieberman teamed with William J. Bennett, former drug czar and bully pulpit moralizer to decry "the rising tide of sex and violence in our popular culture." He teamed with Lynne Cheney, wife of Vice-President Dick Cheney, to denounce "political correctness" (Didion, p. 76), which was rumored to be endemic in American universities, particularly among feminists like myself.

If my first aim in *Bad Girls and Sick Boys* was to defend contemporary artists, filmmakers, and novelists, my second aim was to analyze the political climate over the past 40 years, for when we talk about the public role of intellectuals, we cannot ignore the fact that the Far Right has its intellectuals too. Ironically, a number of them began on the Left. Indeed, conservatives are especially fond of "conversion narratives" that led both leftists and feminists to see the errors of their ways and to embrace the conservative cause, like Carol Iannone, whose "Political Passages" describes her painful conversion from the leftist and feminist orthodoxies of the 1960s, as well as finding God.[6]

One significant player is Myron Magnet, whose book, *The Dream and the Nightmare*, was profiled in *Bad Girls and Sick Boys*.[7] Reading it is a topsy-turvy experience: Magnet blames Herbert Marcuse for the decline in family values; rock and roll for turning an impressionable generation on to crack cocaine. Magnet indicts "Elite institutions – the universities, the judiciary, the press, the great charitable foundations" for homelessness and poverty. In short, he blames the 1960s for every ill imaginable in contemporary society. What has Magnet been up to lately? With Marvin Olasky, he espouses the theory of "compassionate conservatism" that is the intellectual foundation of George W. Bush's presidency.

Marvin Olasky is another former leftist whose 1992 book, *The Tragedy of American Compassion* and the sequel, *Compassionate Conservatism* (2000)[8] describe "a specific and deeply radical experiment in social rearrangement" (Didion, p. 68). He rejects government funding for the arts and social programs, but claims not to turn his back on social needs. These ideals are modeled on nineteenth-century-style charity, but, as I said earlier, the problem with all idyllic epochs is that they are always gone. Didion, indeed, describes his thesis as being "reductive and rather spookily utilitarian" (p. 70). Citing biblical precedent, Olasky argues for the submission of women and the dominance of men as heads of family. He outlines his plans for transforming government by deploying an arsenal of "faith-based initiatives" that combine Twelve Step recovery programs for addictions with Bible study. Interestingly, just such a combination enabled George W. Bush to quit drinking: "The Personal is the Political" indeed! It was God who presumably led Bush to declare that Jesus Christ is the political philosopher whom he most admires. As Didion points out, however, genuine Twelve Step programs purposely espouse faith in an unspecified concept of a Higher Power, rather than a Christian God (Didion, p. 72).

Another notable figure on the Right is Paul Weyrich, who coined the term, "The Moral Majority" during Nixon's administration. He is the founder of America's Voice, the conservative cable television show, and is the leading crusader who has demonized popular culture in its entirety, saying, "We have to look at what we can do to separate ourselves from this hostile culture. What steps can we take to make sure that we and our children are not infected? We need some sort of quarantine."[9] The language of contamination is telling, because since its inception, America has envisioned itself as *besieged* by external and internal enemies capable of polluting its purity. As *Bad Girls and Sick Boys* documents, with the end of the Cold War abroad, the Right turned its attention to internal enemies at home, scapegoating the academy and the press, as well as liberals, leftists, feminists, homosexuals, and "minorities" (pp. 256–60).

All these groups and institutions paradoxically became tarred with the same brush, lumped together in the vague category of "elites." Frances Fitzgerald's stunning new book, *Way Out There in the Blue*, reveals that the demonization of so-called "elites" has a venerable history in America:

> Like most 19th century conspiracy theorists, the radical rightwingers of the fifties and early sixties were virulently anti-establishment and anti-intellectual. Though their economic program was far from egalitarian, they were engaged in a struggle against the cosmopolitan elite of the Eastern Seaboard, which, as they saw it, controlled Wall Street, the universities, and the federal government. In this sense they could be called populists.[10]

It was this rhetoric, of course, which George W. Bush shamelessly exploited in the recent campaign. How a Yale-educated son of a patrician family, who certainly knew his way around the White House as well as the Beltway, could succeed in presenting himself as a Washington *outsider* is difficult to fathom. What he's managed to do brilliantly, however, is to resurrect the same tropes of rhetoric Ronald Reagan used in his own cunning self-fashioning. As Fitzgerald explains:

> Reagan was Illinois come to California. He was the wholesome citizen-hero who inhabits our democratic imaginations . . . personified by [Frank Capra's] *Mr. Smith Goes to Washington* – in which homespun American virtue prevails over the wily and devious "special interests" that rule that nation's capital.[11]

Now that Bush is President, we're just beginning to see how many special interests, especially in the oil business, are really being rewarded. Vice-President Dick Cheney, after all, parlayed his Gulf War credits in the Middle East into a $45.5 million stake in the Halliburton Corporation (Didion, p. 75).

Weyrich saw the failure to convict Clinton of high crimes and misdemeanors as damning evidence that America has become completely immoral: He said, "I do not believe that a majority of Americans actually share our values. We have probably lost the culture war." But the culture war is never over, especially not now, since the leading poster girl for that war is Cheney's wife Lynne, who is an education specialist at the American Enterprise Institute, one of the two most prominent conservative think tanks in the USA. The Heritage Foundation (Olasky's institutional base) is the other one, considered more ideologically doctrinaire than the American Enterprise Institute, according to Dana Milbank of the *Washington Post*.[12]

When *Bad Girls and Sick Boys* debuted, I thought the argument that would get the most flack – despite the fact that it was well-documented – was my contention that today the major producer of porn is the US government itself (Chap. 9). What has happened since the book was published? Luckily for me, Kenneth Starr appeared on the scene, and made my case for me, as the letter from *Hustler* magazine's Larry Flynt in Fig. 6.4 makes clear.

Larry Flynt and much of the nation rebelled against the piety and sanctimoniousness Kenneth Starr embodied in his zealous pursuit of President Clinton. As Toni Morrison wrote in *The New Yorker* in October of 1998, in an eerily prophetic sentence, "This is Slaughtergate. A sustained, bloody, arrogant coup d'état. The Presidency is being stolen from us. And the people know it."[13]

September 22, 1998
The Honorable Judge Kenneth Starr
Office of Independent Counsel
1001 Pennsylvania Ave N.W.
Washington, D.C. 20004

Dear Judge Starr:

Let me take this opportunity to thank you on behalf of all the employees at Hustler magazine and LFP, Inc. for your tireless work in producing the Starr Report. I have been impressed by the salacious and voyeuristic materials in your work. The quality and quantity of material you have assembled in your report contains more pornographic references than those provided by Hustler Online services this month. I have included a chart in this letter that confirms this fact.

Given your exemplary work, I would like to enter into negotiations with you regarding full-time employment for Hustler magazine and related services offered by LFP, Inc. when you conclude your work at the Office of Independent Counsel.

You have broken historic ground in disseminating pornographic materials to a broader and more diverse community of Americans. In this context you have helped to shape and alter long held community standards regarding the acceptance of pornographic material. I congratulate you for having opened the doors of libraries and schools to pornographic literature. Those of us at Hustler need your assistance in extending the parameters of pornography to a wider community of adults. You have opened a new era in promoting explicit sexual materials. Your keen aptitude and relentless focus on disseminating pornographic materials is an inspiration to every employee at Hustler.

Please let me know when you or any of your representatives can sit down with me and discuss if you are interested in making a valuable contribution to promoting the First Amendment through Hustler magazine. As far as compensation and relocation issues are concerned, please do not be concerned. You are a valuable asset who needs to be well compensated.

Respectfully yours,
Larry Flynt

Figure 6.4   Larry Flynt's letter to Kenneth Starr.

I want to shift now to consider how these current events are already being represented in contemporary American fiction, specifically Philip Roth's recent novel, *The Human Stain*, for rituals of persecution and punishment are the motor that drive the narrative. Roth himself is a bundle of paradoxes: he has been described as a neoliberal, neoconservative, '60s-baiting, cranky curmudgeon. *The Human Stain* is set against the backdrop of the Clinton–Lewinsky scandal. Sounding uncannily like J.G. Ballard in the letter quoted above, Roth depicts America in the same summer of 1998 in the midst of an:

> enormous piety binge, a purity binge . . . America's oldest communal passion, historically perhaps its most treacherous and subversive plea-

sure: the ecstasy of sanctimony. In the Congress, in the press, and on the networks, the righteous grandstanding creeps, crazy to blame, deplore, and punish, were everywhere out moralizing to beat the band: all of them in a calculated frenzy with what Hawthorne . . . identified in the incipient country of long ago as "the persecuting spirit."[14]

The word "incipient" is telling here: Roth is engaged in an ideological exploration about the making of America. Here he pinpoints an unsavory aspect of the national character that remains to this day: the perpetuation of rituals of persecution and public humiliation.

Roth details the disgrace of Coleman Silk, an arrogant, ruthless, aging Classics Professor and Dean of the Faculty at "Athena College," a small New England liberal arts school. Dean Silk is dismissed for making an alleged racist remark. In Roth's acute critique of academic life, Silk is really being punished for lifting Athena College out of its complacent mediocrity. As Dean, he sacked the deadwood, hired a lot of young Turks, and pissed off nearly everyone. He's done in by what Roth calls "The Devil of the Little Place" – the gossip, the jealousy, the acrimony, the boredom, the lies. The pettiness in academe rivals that in government, for the Clinton scandal is a demonstration of Zeal in the Land of Busy.

In *The Human Stain*, Roth's alter ego, Nathan Zuckerman, befriends Coleman Silk, and discovers that – far from being remorseful – Silk is whiling away the hours of forced retirement by having a torrid affair with a woman half his age. After a lifetime of refusing to suffer fools gladly in the halls of academe, Coleman Silk has become a fool for love. Nathan finds Coleman Silk waxing eloquent about his new-found libido:

Nathan . . . I owe all of this . . . happiness to Viagra. . . . Without Viagra I would have the dignity of an elderly gentleman free from desire who behaves correctly. Without Viagra . . . I could continue to draw profound philosophical conclusions and have a steadying moral influence on the young, instead of having put myself back into the perpetual state of emergency that is sexual intoxication! (p. 32)

That is probably the first poetic send-up of a drug enhancing male potency *ever* to appear in fiction!

Since politics has become merely another branch of advertising, it makes sense that politicians themselves would eventually become the pitchmen for products. Figure 6.5 is one of only two images in my entire paper that strikes me as genuinely, grotesquely obscene. Do we

Figure 6.5    Bob Dole pitching Viagra.

really want to think about Senator Dole's erectile dysfunction while we eat dinner in front of the TV? Must we be forced to imagine him having sex with Elizabeth Dole, after popping his little pills? One can only imagine how much money Dole must have been paid for this performance. The craven commercialism of such product endorsements reminds us that however much Bible study he piously promotes, his real gods are Mammon – and, apparently, Priapus.

What Roth has in common with J. G. Ballard, Mary Harron, and David Cronenberg is a profound fascination with the dark, destructive side of the human psyche – the imp of the perverse. Here's how he expresses it in *American Pastoral*, another novel in the trilogy that concludes with *The Human Stain*, and which is similarly a sustained meditation on the hollowness of external images, materialism, and success:

> What was astonishing . . . was how people seemed to run out of their own being . . . and, drained of themselves, turn into the sort of people they would once have felt sorry for. It was as though while their lives were rich and full they were secretly sick of themselves and couldn't wait to dispose of their sanity and their health and all sense of proportion so as to get down to that other self, the *true* self, who was a wholly deluded fuckup.[15]

The title *The Human Stain*, therefore, reverberates to reflect not just Clinton, but the deeply embedded drive toward self-destruction.

Nathan Zuckerman eventually discovers that Silk is guilty of something far more egregious than a racist remark. What he discovers is that Coleman Silk himself is black, and he has been passing for white ever since he entered the Army. He utterly repudiated his birth family, and never told his wife and children the truth. *The Human Stain* thus refers to the pigment of our skin, and all the arbitrary divisions that alienate us from each other on the basis of color.

Speaking of the ways fictions of all kinds have overwhelmed reality, Roth's portrait is not just based on the real life of Clinton. Coleman Silk is a barely disguised portrait of Anatole Broyard, the literary critic for the *New York Times*, who died of prostate cancer in 1990. Like Coleman Silk, Broyard entered the Army as a white man, had an agile dancer's body, was a lifelong seducer of women, married a white woman, and was enormously erudite. In an elegant eulogy with a cleverly punned title, "The Passing of Anatole Broyard," Henry Louis Gates, Jr. calls Broyard "a Schzeherazade of racial imposture . . . his children would see the world in terms of authenticity; he himself saw the world in terms of self-creation."[16]

When we think of the public role of intellectuals today, we cannot ignore the role of race, for what writer has ever been accepted without recognition of his race? Broyard's successor at the *New York Times* was Brent Staples, another black critic and writer, who speaks of Broyard's passing for white indignantly:

Overall, it made me angry. Here was a guy who was, for a long period of time, probably one of the two or three most important critical voices on literature in the United States. How could you, actively or passively, have this fact hidden? (quoted in Gates, p. 208).

The final Sophoclean irony of Broyard's fate: his wife at last told their children the secret when Broyard was in the hospital, and he heard them discussing the revelation at length as he lay dying.

## The Sensation Show

That scene serves as my transition to the next section of my essay, which is devoted to visual art, for one of the sculptures in the *Sensation Show* at the Brooklyn Museum of Art in the Fall of 1999 was called *Dead Dad*. *Dead Dad* (Fig. 6.6) is an uncanny, lifelike sculpture by Ron Mueck, placed on the floor of the museum. *Dead Dad* suggests that the human stain of semen or skin color pales beside the pathos of death. On the one hand, it seems to evoke the Oedipal rivalry of the son who must slay the father; who must cut him down to size. (The sculpture

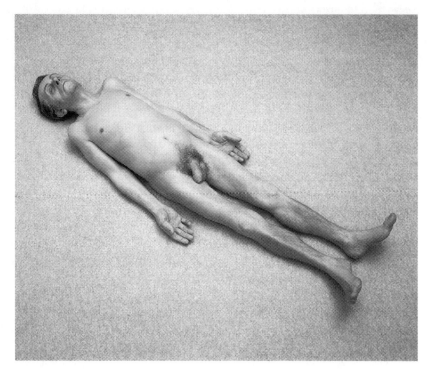

Figure 6.6   Ron Mueck, *Dead Dad*, 1996–7, silicone and acrylic. Courtesy Ron Mueck and the Saatchi Gallery, London.

is only three feet long.) On the other, it evokes the Grim Reaper, who cuts us all down.

A number of other artists found highly imaginative ways to confront us not just with mortality, but with the life and death of cultural stereotypes through the reproduction of cultural artifacts. In Damien Hirst's work *The Physical Impossibility of Death in the Mind of Someone Living* (a shark suspended in formaldehyde), the concept and its fulfillment hang in perfect balance, for one simultaneously imagines the shark's death and one's own in a confrontation with the shark. It is a work of eery and uncanny totemic power. This work has ancient analogues, as I discovered during a visit to the Museum of African and Oceanic Arts in Paris, where I saw a long carved bonita sculpture with a human skull embedded in the body. The totemic object from Melanesia was used in ancient rituals, marking the transition from life to death, and capturing the full range of human emotions that such metamorphoses entail.

Figure 6.7   Peter Davies, *Text Painting*, or *Art I Like*. Courtesy Peter Davies and the Saatchi Gallery, London.

Obviously, not every work in *Sensation* is of equal merit, and the debate about exhibiting the works overshadows critical attention to the works themselves. Indeed, one could argue that the New Labour Party has co-opted the Young British Artists into the context of Cool Britannia – a clever marketing ploy to enhance tourism.[17] Nevertheless, as an American, I see the real lesson of *Sensation* as being that Britain has more confidence in its young artists' merit than we in America have in ours. They take pains to nurture and promote their talent. This is doubly ironic, because the Brits are so clearly and pervasively influenced by American art and pop culture: Jeff Koons, Robert Rauschenberg, Jackson Pollock, Alex Katz, Andy Warhol. Indeed, Peter Davies' *Text Painting* (Fig. 6.7) memorializes these influences directly by recording all these names on the canvas.

But Davies also engages in a dialogue with them. For instance, some of his painted text reads:

> Bruce Nauman, all that aggressive white male rage stuff . . . John Currin now if I ever saw anyone turn a love of Metallica to their advantage . . . John Baldessari – that handpainting stuff and also that writing – he's like Bruce Springsteen – the Boss!

Besides American music, Davies mentions McDonald's, *Texas Chainsaw Massacre*, *Star Wars*, the Wicked Witch of the West, and Bugs Bunny. So, as I said earlier, today the artists themselves are incorporating actual criticism into their artworks, for Davies here *paints* a running commentary that is riveting and succinct art criticism. So in contrast to Myron Magnet and Paul Weyrich's paranoia about the menacing impact of pop culture, these saucy Brits pay homage to it everywhere in this show.

Similarly, Simon Patterson's *The Great Bear* (Fig. 6.8) seems at first merely to be a replica of the London subway map. Only upon close observation do you discover that it is an enormously clever and comprehensive genealogical chart of all the influences on artists through the ages – especially the "Underground" influences, a pun on the London tube's name. There is a Footballers' Line, a Comedians' Line, a Film Actors' Line, and a Musicians' Line, which of course only begins operation after noon. Many Americans are immortalized here, including entire families: Henry, Peter, and Jane Fonda; Walter, John, and Angelica Huston; Tony Curtis and Janet Leigh, and their daughter, Jamie Lee Curtis. As Peter Wollen notes,

> One of the things that interested me most about *Sensation* was that the thirty year old tension between Conceptualist avant-gardism and the global "Society of the Spectacle" was still bubbling away. Moreover, even though painting had certainly returned, it had come back, often enough, in the form of a kind of Conceptual painting – e.g. . . . Peter Davies' painted list of great painters and Simon Patterson's cultural underground map.[18]

One vital function of artists and intellectuals, obviously, is to provide a context in which to understand the origins and evolution of aesthetic concepts and movements. Another crucial role (a corollary of the first one) is to deflate those who demonize popular culture, for what these provocative Young British Artists are telling us is that – far from feeling *contaminated* by American pop culture – they have been enormously *energized* by it. It has become an indispensable component of their own psychic, creative processes and products.

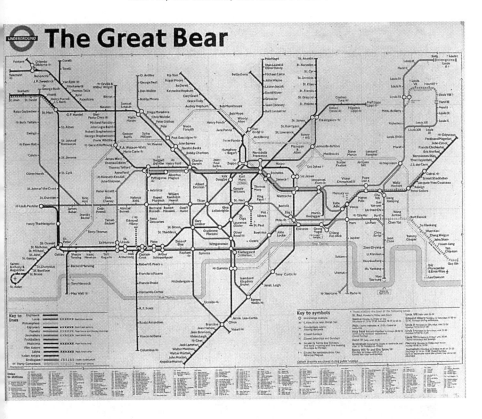

Figure 6.8   Simon Patterson, *The Great Bear*, 1992. Four color lithograph in anodized aluminium frame, edition of 50. Courtesy the Saatchi Gallery, London and Simon Patterson.

Was there anything genuinely obscene in *Sensation*? The answer is yes, but the most obscene work had nothing to do with sex *or* popular culture. Figure 6.9 depicts a three-dimensional sculpture exposing in graphic detail the atrocities of war. It should make the viewers think of Cambodia, Rwanda, Bosnia, and all other parts of the globe where man's inhumanity to man cannot be disavowed – particularly those atrocities carried out in the name of religious and ethnic differences. It is a sculpture about the heart of darkness – our deep destructiveness and barbarity. Yet even such a graphic display is merely a reworking of another old master: Goya's *The Disasters of War*.

Goya's work has become a symbol of the savagery of political tyranny in all epochs; his work still retains its own horrific, obscene

Figure 6.9  Jake and Dinos Chapman, *Great Deeds against the Dead*, 1994, mixed media with plinth. Courtesy Jake and Dinos Chapman and the Saatchi Gallery, London.

power. All the Chapman brothers have done is to transform Goya's vision into a three-dimensional sculpture. The Chapman brothers declare their immersion in theory in everything they write, while other artists have internalized theory without making it explicit in

Figure 6.10 Francisco de Goya, *Grand hazana! Con muertos!* (An Heroic Feat! with Dead Men!), 1863, etching. Lavis and drypoint, plate 5 from *Desastres de la guerra*. Courtesy National Gallery of Art, Washington, D.C., Rosenwald Collection.

their work.[19] The Chapmans have also done a series of 20 black and white etchings which are based on "Exquisite Corpse," a game involving several artists painting one work. Their fascination with Goya can also be seen in a series of etchings after Goya, entitled *The Disasters of War*; each has been delicately hand painted with watercolor and depicts mutilated bodies and full-frontal scenes of violence. The aim of both the old masters like Goya and the new artists I'm discussing here is to expose the deep irrationality of the human psyche – the intersections of sex and death, the anarchic impulses that erupt regardless of reason, and that we ignore at our peril.

Nowhere was that irrationality more in evidence than in the reception of the *Sensation* show itself. Mayor Giuliani tried to withhold funding from the Brooklyn Museum of Art if it went ahead and displayed these works, despite the fact that the US Supreme Court had recently ruled that the government cannot penalize cultural institutions or individual artists based on the viewpoints expressed in their art. In defiance of the Supreme Court (and therefore of the Constitution), both the House and the Senate adopted a non-binding resolution calling for the elimination of federal funds for the Brooklyn Museum if it did not cancel the *Sensation* show in the Fall of 1999.[20]

What has happened since the *Sensation* show? Mayor Giuliani has proposed a Decency Commission to determine what sort of art should be banned from New York museums. An odd proposal from a man who was noted for his own sexual escapades and who, as Gail Collins points out, "Has a wife in Gracie Mansion and a girlfriend . . . [who] is guarded by city police at taxpayer expense . . . The nation's supply of moral watchdogs is pretty well picked over right now . . . but Mr. Clinton might just be available.[21]

I've saved the most controversial work for last, to drive home the point that so many media spectacles deprive us of ever knowing what else was worth seeing: Chris Ofili's *The Holy Virgin Mary*. Unfortunately, I could not secure permission to reproduce this image, the corners of which are decorated with elephant dung. In light of the ensuing controversy, jaded New Yorkers quickly deflated the Mayor's sanctimoniousness by coining the memorable phrase, "Dung Happens." Given the examples I've been tracing, from Anatole Broyard to these remarkable Young British Artists, one has to wonder whether it was really the elephant dung that Giuliani found objectionable – or was it the image of a Virgin Mary who is *black*? Sadly, the controversy obscured the serious consideration this work deserved on its merits, for it is one of the most beautiful works in the show. It was, moreover, one of the few that seemed to have an organic logic and context. Ofili's parents are Nigerian and their first language is Yoruba. He himself is a practicing Catholic, and was much taken by his research visit to Zimbabwe, where he sought to represent connections between Mother Africa, Mother Earth, and the Virgin Mother. His painting is thus a work of sacred and magical power. Moreover, issues of representation become more complex in periods of colonialism, which was one of the things that interested Ofili, since his work in its entirety touches on the life and death of entire populations.

Today, the art museum is a sanctuary in both senses of the word: it is a repository for many of the great artifacts of religion through the ages, and it is a refuge from desecration and derision. Other artists have similarly seized on totemic objects for inspiration. The French performance artist, Orlan, for instance, stages the process by which religious icons are transformed through magic and ritual. This is not a natural

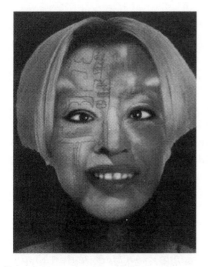

Figure 6.11   Digital image of Orlan, and pre-Columbian artifact she used as her model. Courtesy Orlan.

process; instead, it is a constructed one, fraught with political and ideological implications. To put it another way, in keeping with my central topic, *tradition* itself is an invention – sometimes a very recent one, as the images in this essay reveal. Orlan has long been interested in iconoclasms of all kinds – particularly the implicit eroticism in religious iconography, for one of her goals is to deconstruct icons of religion, beauty, and femininity through the ages.

As a public intellectual, Orlan declares, "I was of a generation of artists who were audaciously conceptual, bold, and fearless. At the age of seventeen, I was already on the street."[22] She is also a French art history professor who teaches her students that they must take the risk of being deviant and confrontational. She does not believe in coddling students or reinforcing their comfortable received ideas. Art, she tells them, is not mere decoration for your walls: it must be political, activist, and change consciousness.

When I interviewed Orlan in *Bad Girls and Sick Boys*, she was in the process of transforming her own face into a composite of the Mona Lisa and other paintings through actual plastic surgery. She wanted to demonstrate viscerally as well as visually that at the millennium, the body is a mere costume – one that can be rearranged at will. Indeed, her very name is an invention – invoking a synthetic fabric for a syn-

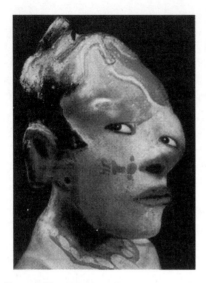

Figure 6.12   Orlan with prominent forehead, and pre-Columbian artifact she used as her model. Courtesy Orlan.


thetic identity. When her metamorphosis was completed, she planned to let an ad agency give her a new name to go with her new look. What has Orlan been up to since I first interviewed her?

We met again in Paris for a joint presentation on her work in January, 2000. She is now exploring mutant identities, and her show, *Self-Hybridations*, is based on extensive archival research she did into the Aztec, Olmec, and Mayan peoples of Mexico. She has abandoned plastic surgery and now uses digital imagery – with fantastically uncanny results. Transforming her own face into a composite of pre-Columbian standards of beauty, Orlan discovered that in those cultures, large noses were desirable because they signified force, elegance, and power. The deformation of the head was achieved by prolonged pressing on an infant's fontanelle. Crossed eyes were so highly coveted that parents created this "defect" artificially by putting a crucifix between the baby's eyes while the baby learned to focus. Orlan confesses that she learned a great deal about her own civilization through this research into Mexico and South America. In contrast to European concepts of identity, for example, the Mayans believed in multiple identities and celebrated multiple metamorphoses, constantly blurring the boundaries between the ancient and the contemporary.

Orlan remains fascinated by the idea of *monstrosity*, which, she discovered, can only be defined as the opposite of whatever is considered "normal." Her aim is thus to explore the life and death of cultural stereotypes and the aesthetic of beauty. She shows how each civilization fabricates its own concepts about the body. Each body then becomes determined by those laws. (One can see the Foucauldian implications of her research here.)

If the body is a mere costume, death indeed has no dominion if one approaches it as fearlessly as Orlan. I asked her what she envisions for the future. She replied cheerfully that she would like to be mummified in a museum, "kept company" by an interactive video. She envisions herself as someone who, with the aid of technology, is "impregnating" pre-Columbian civilization and testing her own image. The very notion of giving "birth" to an ancient civilization makes us rethink our very conception of old masters and new art. One thinks of Borges's elegant fable on that very topic – "Pierre Menard – Author of *Don Quixote*": Orlan translates Borgesian irony and ambition into the ephemeral realm of body art – with equally quixotic results.

## Conclusion

In fiction, film, and performance art, artists from widely diverse nations are exploring similar themes, theories, and objectives. J. G. Ballard's letter illustrates that the greatest challenge is to be a real part of one's time at the very moment when events are unfolding. It is not easy to describe *what is really happening* in our culture – while we are simultaneously moving toward a very different definition of "culture" itself. Yes fictions of all kinds have overwhelmed reality today. Yes, we are utterly immersed in popular culture. Yes, "New British Art" has become a brand name, but the work it encompasses is hardly one-dimensional, as David Burrows demonstrates.[23] The Heritage Foundation is well named, for neoconservatives define "culture" in terms of "heritage." However, as Peter Wollen points out, the rhetoric of modernization stands the traditional notion of culture on its head. We are in the process of exchanging a national for a global culture, epitomized by films, entertainment, books, telecommunications, computer games, and World Music. World Art cannot be far behind. In a global age, avant-gardes will be more cosmopolitan than ever, as one can see in the legacy of Surrealism, which has had a pervasive impact in Japan, the Arab world, the Caribbean, and later in the Fluxus art movement and Conceptual Art. The danger of such a trend lies in homogenization. But the virtue of globalization lies in crossover, nomadism, hybridity, enrichment, innovative new forms and approaches[24] – the very things I have been tracing here. In the fields of fiction, film, visual and performance art, the intellectual is very far from dead, and multiculturalism – far from signalling the demise of intellectualism – has revived it.

Nationalism obviously has its limits, as Homi K. Bhabha points out, for an idea of what constitutes a nation contradicts the cultural life of a nation.[25] National borders and boundaries themselves have become contested focal points: Canadian filmmakers like Cronenberg and Harron contribute a detached, mordantly satiric perspective on the USA; the *Sensation* artists brazenly borrow from American pop culture; Orlan reaccentuates the body modification rituals of ancient cultures from China to South America. By reproducing and repositioning cultural artifacts, these artists collectively demonstrate how what we define as "Beauty" is itself a projection of the desires and fantasies of others. The projection of fantasy and desire in rituals of persecution and purification unites many of the disparate works I've discussed here, ranging from Orlan to "The Holy Virgin Mary" to *The Human Stain*. The role of the artist and intellectual today is to highlight the complex processes of projection wherever they occur, in high culture and low, in popular media and arcane religious relics. It is also to highlight the dynamic, volatile processes of the unconscious of culture.

Finally, if *projection* is one key word, *iconoclasm* is the other, for all these artists are passionately devoted to smashing the icons of our most cherished images, assumptions, and beliefs. The role of artists and intellectuals is to expose the deep irrationality at the heart of psychic life. While politicians try to demonize popular culture in the name of "family values," their efforts are futile, for no one can legislate fantasy. The imp of the perverse will keep erupting, disrupting all pieties and proprieties – as Philip Roth demonstrates. If American politicians, censors, and other self-anointed Culture Police insist on fiction, film, and art that only consists of "positive images," what you will get is the equivalent of the kind of movies you see on airplanes: nothing too controversial, too sexy, or too disturbing. Airplane movies and airplane art – like Norman Rockwell's – feed us the images we already have of ourselves. They never make us uncomfortable, or challenge our most cherished conceptions. If we condemn things without reading, hearing, or seeing them, in the current climate of self-censorship, freedom of expression may disappear without a trace. In the immortal words of Dan Quayle, "We are on an *irreversible* course towards more freedom – but that could change."

## Notes

1   Linda S. Kauffman, *Bad Girls and Sick Boys: Fantasies in Contemporary Art and Culture*. (Berkeley: University of California Press, 1998).
2   Edward Pressman's remarks can be found in the production notes, Lions Gate Films, p. 7; my full interview with Mary Harron can be found in Linda S. Kauffman, "Review of *American Psycho*," *Film Quarterly* 54, 2 (Winter 2000–1):41–5.
3   André Schiffrin, *The Business of Books: How International Conglomerates Took over Publishing and Changed the Way We Read* (London, New York: Verso, 2000).
4   V. Vale and Andrea Juno (eds.), *J. G. Ballard* (San Francisco: Re/Search Books, 1984; rpt. 1989), p. 99.
5   Joan Didion, "God's Country," *New York Review of Books*, November 2, 2000, pp. 68–76, hereinafter cited parenthetically in the text.
6   Carol Iannone is discussed in Kauffman, *Bad Girls and Sick Boys*, pp. 256–7.
7   Myron Magnet, *The Dream and the Nightmare: The Sixties' Legacy to the Underclass* (New York: William Morrow, 1993); discussed in *Bad Girls and Sick Boys*, p. 257.
8   Marvin Olasky, *The Tragedy of American Compassion* (Washington, D.C.: Regenery Gateway, 1992); *Compassionate Conservatism: What it is, What it Does, and How it Can Transform America* (New York: Free Press, 2000).
9   Richard L. Berke, "The Far Right Sees the Dawn of the Moral Minority," *New York Times*, February 21, 1999, p. A3.
10  Frances Fitzgerald, *Way Out There in the Blue: Reagan, Star Wars, and the End of the Cold War* (New York: Simon and Schuster, 2000), p. 33.
11  Ibid, p. 28.
12  *Washington Post*, December 8, 2000, p. A39.
13  Toni Morrison, *The New Yorker*, October 5, 1998, pp. 31–4.
14  Philip Roth, *The Human Stain* (New York: Houghton Mifflin, 2000), p. 2, hereinafter cited parenthetically in the text.
15  Philip Roth, *American Pastoral* (New York: Random House, 1997), p. 329.
16  Henry Louis Gates, Jr., "The Passing of Anatole Broyard," *Thirteen Ways of Looking at a Black Man* (New York: Random House, 1997), p. 200, hereinafter cited parenthetically in the text.
17  Henry Rogers, "Introduction," *Making a Scene*, ed. Henry Rogers and David Burrows (Birmingham, UK: ARTicle Press, 2001), pp. 8–9.
18  Peter Wollen, "London Swings," in David Burrows (ed.), *Who's Afraid of Red White & Blue?* (Birmingham, UK: ARTicle Press, 1998), pp. 21–7.

19  Patricia Bickers, "Mind the Gap: The Concept of Critical Distance in Relation to Contemporary Art in Britain," in *Who's Afraid of Red White & Blue?*, pp. 10–20.
20  *New York Times*, October 5, 1999, A25:2.
21  Gail Collins, "The Art of Rudy," *New York Times*, February 28, 2001, p. A27.
22  All quotes from Orlan are from the Symposium on her work, Stanford Abroad Program, Paris, January 29, 2000.
23  Burrows, *Who's Afraid of Red White & Blue?*, p. 6.
24  Wollen, "London Swings," pp. 25–7.
25  Cited in Burrows, "Introduction," p. 4.

# Chapter 7

# Apathy and Accountability: The Challenge of South Africa's Truth and Reconciliation Commission to the Intellectual in the Modern World[1]

## Jacqueline Rose

Another man will never be able to know the degree of my suffering, because he is another and not me, and besides a man is rarely willing to acknowledge someone else as a sufferer.[2]

In perhaps one of the strangest moments in the extraordinary document that makes up the report of the Truth and Reconciliation Commission of South Africa, an application for amnesty, described as "intriguing," is recorded from an unnamed Indian woman applying for amnesty for what she described as her "apathy." The application stated that those appealing for amnesty on these grounds recognized that they:

> as individuals can and should be held accountable by history for our lack of necessary action in times of crisis . . . in exercising apathy rather than commitment we allow(ed) others to sacrifice their lives for the sake of our freedom and an increase in our standard of living.[3]

In this case amnesty was not granted. Although the applicants argued that apathy fell within the brief of the Commission as an act of omission, the Commissioners decided that it did "not disclose an action or omission which amounts to an offence or a delict in respect of which amnesty can be granted." Amnesty – the most controversial, the last added, and legally challenged clause of the Mandate of the Commission – could only be granted for acts whose motivation was political, which occurred between the Sharpeville massacre of 1960 and the inauguration of Mandela as President in 1994, on the basis of full disclosure of relevant information, and if the rubric of proportionality – ends to means – was observed. A declaration or confession of apathy falls at the first of these conditions. No political organization asked for it. Apathy receives no official sanction. Indeed only rarely and reluctantly – hence the strangeness of this moment – do people admit to it, although they are very ready to diagnose it in others (it has in fact become one of the favourite recent political diagnoses of the West).

But if apathy does not come on political instruction, one could nonetheless argue that the system of apartheid, and not only of apartheid, relied on it, or something close: that inhuman political structures depend, for as long as they last, not just on the power of the oppressors and the silent complicity of the beneficiaries, but also on numbers of the oppressed being struck with an inability to connect, or give themselves, to their own cause. It depends as well on those beneficiaries who may have hated the system but did not – by their own repeated account in the Report – do enough: "At the very time when we should have continued to speak out clearly for the truth and against injustice," the spokesperson for the Stellenbosch Presbytery of the Dutch Reformed Church submitted at the human rights violations hearing in Paarl, "we grew tired and gave up protesting" (5, p. 384). History, the precise formula insists, will hold individuals accountable for "a lack of necessary action in time of crisis." For apathy, since the Commission did not recognize the offence, history is the only court.

In fact the charge falls before the conditions for amnesty on more than the first count. What is the time of apathy? How would you date it? What are the means and what the end? Is it in fact an intention at all? And what could count as full disclosure? Is apathy something communicable, is it something we have a language for talking about? Or does it, more like a disease or shameful secret, rely on doing its work invisibly in the dark? How can you fully disclose something whose chief property is deficiency, to be in some sense absent from history and missing to yourself? In today's political climate, in Great Britain at least, apathy tends to be talked about as something that has been done to civic and political responsibility ("18 years of Conservative rule"). As if you could only be *made* apathetic – a kind of double passive, an act of grammatical bad faith which mimics or repeats the problem it is claiming to diagnose. But the idea of apathy as purely passive should make us suspicious – as Freud once famously commented, it requires a great deal of activity to achieve a passive aim.

For anyone reading the Report of the Commission, it is hard not to be "overwhelmed," to use the word of the Commissioners, not by apathy but by the opposite, that is, by what people are actively capable of. The Commissioners were "almost overwhelmed," the chapter on Recommendations in the last volume, begins, "by the capacity of individuals to damage and destroy each other" (5, p. 306). As we look back on the last century, this has become the recurrent and chilling refrain. To use a recent formula of the historian Eric Hobsbawm, we are faced with the paradox that the twentieth century "has killed more people than any other century, but at its close, there are more people living and living better."[4] We are faced, that is, with the fact that, in the second half of the century we have barely taken leave of, the human capacity for destruction and the human capacity for improvement have – arm in arm as it were – reached new heights. It must then be one of the roles of the modern intellectual to try to understand this paradoxical fact of modern times, one half of which must be to try to understand what makes it possible for people to act in this way (it was part of the mandate of the Commission – part of its aim of "restorative justice" – to understand the "motives and perspectives" of the perpetrators, 1, p. 130). At what has become a famous moment in the Hearings, former Security Branch officer, Jeffrey Benzien, demonstrated wet bag suffocation on a dummy in front of the court and when asked by former victim, Tony Yengeni, what kind of man could do this, replied: "I, Jeff Benzien, have asked that question to such an extent that I voluntarily – and it is not easy for me to say this in a full court with a lot of people who do not know me – approached psychiatrists to have myself evaluated, to find out what type of person am I" (5, p. 370).

Some of the students on a course I teach on South African literature saw this as the supreme moment of fraudulence in the proceedings, whereas – despite the "pride" Benzien also expressed in his method ("Mr Yengeni, with my absolutely unorthodox methods and by removing your weaponry from you, I am wholly convinced that I prevented you and your colleagues . . . I may have prevented you from being branded a murderer nowadays," 5, p. 263) – I am more inclined to take this question at its word. Not least because it brings us close to one of the defining features of atrocity in the modern world. Something akin to disbelief. In which part of your mind are these testimonies to be stored? How can these narratives be held in the mind at all? – questions which seem to me to go way beyond the issue of remembrance or forgetting. In his extraordinary book on Rwanda – to move for a moment to a very different part of Africa – Phillip Gourevitch writes: "All at once, as it seemed, something we could only have imagined was upon us – and we could still only imagine it. This is what fascinates me most in existence: the peculiar necessity of imagining what is, in fact, real."[5]

Amongst many other things, the Truth and Reconciliation Commission will take up its place historically for its relentless charting of the horrors of our age. Early in the report we are however given a warning: "This focus on the outrageous has drawn the nation's attention away from the more commonplace violations," producing a failure on the part of ordinary South Africans to recognize, "the 'little perpetrator' in each one of us" (1, p. 133). The implication is not only, as the paragraph continues, that "only by recognising the potential for evil in each one of us [can we] take full responsibility for ensuring that such evil will never be repeated," but also that the hearings themselves, the explicit dwelling on atrocity, have let huge swathes of the white population off the hook, those who in Njabulo Ndebele's words dwell in "the interstice between power and indifferent and supportive agency": "Yes, they [the bleeding-heart liberal English-speaking South Africans] have a story to tell [. . .] In that interstice the English-speaking South African has conducted the business of his life."[6]

But what this unnamed Indian woman is talking about is something rather different. She is suggesting, in a way that was clearly baffling to the Commissioners, that what you don't do as a political subject can have effects – might be as important in the transformations of the world – as what you do. To read the Report of the Commission is to be confronted on almost every page with how difficult it is to speak of atrocity, whether as victim or perpetrator of the act, although the difficulty is radically different for each. It has been at the center of the Commission and the source of its greatest difficulty that language – in the words of Antjie Krog, the Afrikaans poet commissioned by the South Africa Broadcasting Association to report on the hearings – does not easily "bed" the truth.[7] But we are presented here with the strange suggestion that the ways in which we do not implicate ourselves in the burdens of history might be something which it is even harder to talk about. Intellectuals are of course always accused of talking too much, not acting enough – hence also the relevance of the Commission Report which presents the problem of speech, and its relation to acting, and failure to act, in such uniquely focused terms.

Although Hobsbawm places most of Africa outside the reach of Western modernity and democratization – there are, he states boldly, no democracies in Africa – no country perhaps has enacted the paradox he describes as fully as South Africa: the very existence of the Commission is testimony to the violent gestation of a democracy which puts the Western world to shame. Hobsbawm contrasts the mile-long queues of the 1994 election in South Africa with the dwindling numbers of voters in the democracies of the West, and takes this fact to be one of the clearest signs of failure in the polity ("at the cost of the integrity of the political process"[8]; 34–8 percent of the electorate voted in the last US election). The Chairman of the Commission, Archbishop Desmond Tutu, makes a similar point. "In normal [his word] countries," he comments on the second page of his own book on the Commission, trying to convey the exhilaration of April 1994, "the concern was usually about voter apathy."[9] "What's normal?" we might ask. True to the spirit of one strand of modern intellectual life, Tutu has given to abnormality a positive, celebratory, political gloss.

The Indian woman's testimony is given at the end of the report of the Special Hearing for Women which came about when a workshop on gender pressured the Commission to acknowledge that it might be "missing some of the truth through lack of sensitivity to gender issues" (4, p. 282). This may at a superficial glance seem surprising, for there is a sense in which the Truth and Reconciliation Commission was dominated by the voices of women. It is they who predominantly speak. But they mostly testify as the often sole surviving relatives and dependents of the mainly males who had suffered violations of human rights. The aim of the special hearing, then, was to create a space in which women might talk of the violations they had undergone, might therefore speak for themselves. The Indian woman appears at the very end of this section of the report concluding the fourth volume – concluding in a sense the whole report, since the fifth and final volume gives the Findings – under a section entitled "Women as Perpetrators." Barely five pages long, it is perhaps the most depleted section of the Report (the Report runs to nearly 3,000 pages overall). Of the 7,128 applications for amnesty received by the Commission only 56 were known to come from women. Under apartheid, the message seems to be, there is very little women were guilty of.

It is in this blurred and almost empty context – like a frame with no painting – at a moment of the hearings which might, but for pressure from below, have not even existed, that a woman steps forward and claims for apathy a fully political status, presenting the Commission with something which it had by its own account neglected (it lists apathy as a feature under the "Neglected Factor" of "Secrecy and silence": "much of the country's population went silent through fear, apathy, indifference or genuine lack of information," 5, pp. 250, 299), something intriguing, unexpected, disturbing perhaps, certainly bizarre. What – her appearance dramatically focuses – are the limits of accountability? How far does it spread? If the idea of apathy is so disquieting in this context, it is because it brings the issue of accountability, for the last person who might seem to be accountable, home to roost. It seems to me that it is not a coincidence – nor the first or last time – that a woman, tucked away almost in the back-pages of history, speaks – if not *the* – certainly *a* truth. One of the things her testimony forces us to acknowledge is that we cannot claim apathy as the exclusive political property of the West.

I always start the course I take on South African literature by asking the students to say, as economically as possible – a word, image, character – what, when they think of South Africa, comes into their minds. It gives us a sense before we begin of an engagement which is going to be, for most people in the room, partial, tentative, and refracted in space and time. In one year, the course almost didn't get going when a white student, in response to this query, said "guilt." She was challenged by another white student who claimed, outraged, that in relation to South Africa, whites in Britain had nothing whatsoever to feel guilty about. Should this happen again, I will refer the students to the Truth and Reconciliation Report which, in the spirit of fullest reconciliation (hence of course the title), nonetheless does not mince words when it comes to naming the British. In addition to providing a full historical account for each region whose stories of human rights violations it tells, the Report opens, after the Chairman's foreword, with a chapter on History which regresses accountability for apartheid into South Africa's British-dominated past. This is just one example from the very first pages of the report:

> It is important to remember that the 1960 Sharpeville massacre (with which the mandate of the Commission begins) was simply the latest in

a long line of similar killings of civilian protesters in South African history. In was, for example, not a National Party administration but the South African party government, made up primarily of English-speaking South Africans, that in July 1913 crushed a series of miners' strikes on the Reef – sending in the army and killing just over one hundred strikers and onlookers. Thrice in 1921 and 1922, this same governing party let loose its troops and planes [. . .]

Thus, when the South African Defence Force (SADF) killed just over 600 men, women and children, combatant and non-combatant, at Kassinga in Angola in 1978, and when the South African Police (SAP) shot several hundred black protesters in the weeks following the June 16 events at Soweto, they were operating in terms of a well-established tradition of excessive or unjustifiable use of force against government opponents. (1, p. 26)

A simple act of historical recollection which contains a gentle rebuff to the temporal mandate of the TRC (Sharpeville, the start date, was not the start). And while South Africa entered a permanent winter with the Native Land Act of 1913 – "There is winter in the Native Land Act [. . .] the trees are stripped and leafless" – this too is not the beginning:

But if this was an act of wholesale dispossession and discrimination, so too was the 1909 South Africa Act which was passed, not by a South African legislature, but by the British Parliament. (1, p. 28)

In relation to British accountability, the TRC report – from its very opening pages – chooses to jog the mind. To use the words of Gerrie Hugo, former intelligence officer of the South African Defence Force and torturer (the interview in *Index on Censorship*'s special issue on Truth Commissions and War Tribunals is entitled "Confession of a Torturer"): "Accountability doesn't stop" (he is in fact talking about de Klerk).[10]

But it is not as simple as this (you might think that there is nothing easier for the white liberal intellectual in Britain than to point to historical accountability in this sense). For in fact the Report of the Truth and Reconciliation Commission can also be read for the immense difficulty with which it surrounds the issue of accountability – historical and political, collective and individual – in the modern world. The Indian woman's appeal gives one particularly bold, or striking, instance of this. Accountability, the Commission itself and the controversies it has generated clearly demonstrate, is not just a matter of answering the question: who? It is not just a matter of burrowing into corners to find responsibility, or indeed guilt, lurking in the dark – even apathetic – night of the soul. On this issue, although it takes up a strong position, the Commission is not so much judge (it was not of course a criminal hearing) as the active, troubled, sometimes uncertain, not always unified participant in the changing face and climate of what it describes. Hence the "challenge" of my subtitle for this essay. I read the TRC Report as a document which testifies not only to the horrors of the modern world but to a problem integral to the very recognition of such horror, a recognition which it has perhaps done more than any other modern process to achieve (this was the only Truth commission of our time to have held its hearings in public, no other hearing has managed to combine truth-seeking with quasi-judicial power, 1, p. 54). How do you at once recognize the fullness and extent of historical accountability and draw boundaries around it, how do you let it flow (in the words of Roelf Meyer of the National Party: "wrongs [. . .] flowed from apartheid," 5, p. 403), while also keeping it in, if not its proper, then at least a definable, precisely *accountable*, place?

To take perhaps the most important and controversial decision of the Commission on this topic: it is only recently in international law that non-state actors have been indictable for gross violations of human rights (1, p. 69). Drawing on decisions of the International Criminal Tribunal in relation to the former Yugoslavia as recent as 1997, the Report states: "The Act establishing the Commission adopted this more modern position. In other words it did not make a finding of a gross violation of human rights conditional on a finding of state action" (1, p. 70). If this was crucial to pull in all the abuses committed between the release of Mandela and his election in 1994, when "the great majority of human rights violations were being carried out by persons who were not bound to a political authority" (2, p. 5), it also means that all human rights violations, regardless of their provenance, whether carried out by resistance movements or by the apartheid state, become not ethically, but effectively, equal: "A gross violation is a gross violation, whoever commits it and for whatever reason" (1, p. 12). What matters is the nature of the act. Justification, the central plank of legal accountability, is therefore set aside:

> the position adopted by the Commission was that any killing, abduction, torture or severe ill-treatment which met the other requirements of the definition, amounted to a gross violation of human rights, regardless of whether or not the perpetrator could be held accountable for the conduct . . . There is legal equivalence between all perpetrators. (1, pp. 72, 12)

The Commission therefore holds to the distinction, older in international law, between the justice of the means and the justice of the cause of war: "The Commission concurred with the international consensus that those who were fighting for a just cause were under an obligation to employ just means in the conduct of this fight" (1, p. 69). On the justice of the cause, the Report is of course unequivocal: apartheid was a crime against humanity, and the struggle against it a just war.

Within these terms, confusing as it may seem, and for some critics unjust, the ANC – in the finding that almost stopped the publication of the Report – becomes wholly accountable. Not legally – legal accountability has been set aside (the Commission is not a court, it is a hearing) – but something more like answerable. And ironically, all the more so because, unlike those at the summit of former power, specifically de Klerk, the ANC accepted responsibility for the action of its members:

> The Commission takes note that the political leadership of the ANC and the command structure of MK have accepted political and moral responsibility for all the actions of its members in the period 1960–1994 and therefore finds that the leadership of the ANC and MK must take responsibility and be accountable for all gross violations of human rights perpetrated by its membership and cadres in the mandate period. (2, p. 685)

(All the findings of the Commission are presented in small bold capital letters which makes them look on the page like an inscription on a tomb.)

A great deal of attention has been paid to this finding of the Commission; it is, depending on from where you are looking, the finding on which the ethical viability of the Commission either falls or rests. But there has been less focus on what it says about the issue of accountability, the fraught and fine distinctions, in and out of law, on which it is based. For one set of critics, which includes the present Minister for Education, from the moment the Commission chose to define violations of human rights in terms of individual acts, it ceased – politically and historically – to be viable: "There is," write Kader and Louise Asmal and Ronald Suresh Roberts, in a follow-up article to their book on the Commission, "simply no proportionality between the two sides of the struggle, a fact that is lost in the Commission's decision to individualise its definition of a gross human rights abuse ..." (interestingly in view of this all individual explanations of atrocity are rejected in the chapter on "Causes and Motives" in favor of an analysis in terms of the group). They continue: "this is a failure deriving from a lack of political and ethical understanding".[11]

How can everyone be equally answerable when the means available to the opponents, given in advance, are so unequal? How can you hold in the same measure – consider both as perpetrators – an illegal state and the combatants of a just war? For Asmal et al., in response to apartheid and as its appropriate legacy for international human rights law, the distinction between just cause and means of war has become – or rather, it *should* become – redundant: "Given the convention-dependent nature of the morality of war, and apartheid's wholesale breach of those conventions, the question of *jus ad bellum* cannot be arbitrarily separated from the latter question of justice in the conduct of the cause, *jus in bello*."[12] Ironically, however, if this path had been followed, the Truth and Reconciliation Commission might never have started. Although called into being to effect the transition to democracy (without the possibility of amnesty in some form, the transition could not have been peacably guaranteed), it nonetheless had its germ in the decision by the ANC itself to investigate its own human rights abuses. In fact it was Kader Asmal who mooted the idea, on behalf of the ANC, on his installation as Professor of Human Rights Law at the University of the Western Cape on May 25, 1992.

Spread accountability too wide by flattening out the differences between the state and its opponents, then oddly, symmetrically, it will also start to shrink, as the crimes of apartheid become more and more the acts of individuals, less and less the machinery of the unjust, and illegal apartheid state ("the violence of the law" in the Report's own words – pushed over the legal edge, 1, p. 40). Once it has been individualized, the act stands out in bold, plucked out of its context. In fact the more inhuman and outrageous the act – remember the Commission's own self-critique for its stress on the "outrageous" – the more drastically it curtails the Commission. The Report acknowledges as one of its failings its inability to bring under its sway the basic daily humiliations, inequalities, and fundamental social injustice – mostly still unredeemed – of the apartheid state: "our mandate was not the policies of apartheid" (5, p. 48).[13] When Commissioner Dr. Ramashala, referring to those who fall outside the Commission's mandate, especially the orphaned children of the struggle, tells Roelf Meyer of the National Party: "I really have never heard any discussions from the political parties about these children and our future, because these are our future South Africa," Meyer replies: "if we can't find an answer to the very question that you have put, then the work of the Commission, with all respect, is not going to be in the long term worth anything" (5, p. 403).

A similar point was made by Lewis Nkosi when Judge Albie Sachs, also central in the founding of the Commission, came to Queen Mary College at the invitation of the Law Department in 1998 to lecture on the history and justification for the Commission (a lecture he has given worldwide). Nkosi simply asked him what the present government was planning to do about redistribution of land (the issue which has of course emerged so explosively in Zimbabwe in the past year).

So what comes first? Which form of transformation – psychic and subjective, or material and redistributive – will provide the real, sure, foundation for the other? For you could of course argue – as the rationale for the whole Commission and as Asmal himself argued when putting his original proposal for the Commission in 1995 – that a nation aiming to build a new future for its people, whatever concrete measures it enacts, without a reckoning with its own past violence will be building the whole edifice on sand:

> We must take the past seriously as it holds the key to the future. The issues of structural violence, of unjust and inequitable economic social arrangements, of balanced development in the future, cannot be properly dealt with unless there is a conscious understanding of the past.

(His words are cited on the first pages of the Mandate chapter in volume 1 of the Report, p. 49).

Accountability as an issue is therefore inseparable from that of justice. Justice, of course in the most familiar sense, was set aside by the Act establishing the Commission. "There would have been no negotiated settlement and so no new democratic South Africa," Tutu writes, "had the negotiators on one side insisted that all the perpetrators be brought to trial. While the Allies could pack up and go home after Nuremberg, we in South Africa had to live with one another." (This chapter of his book is called "Nuremberg or national amnesia? A third way.")[14] No trials also because they would simply have been too long and too costly, and because with the burden of absolute proof – "beyond all reasonable doubt" – falling on the investigators, too many of the guilty would have escaped the net (although the Commission itself was enormously hampered by the Corbett decision, which stipulated that anyone against whom a detrimental finding was being contemplated should be given forewarning and a reasonable opportunity to respond). "We discovered in the course of the Commission's investigations", Tutu observes as part of this case, "that the supporters of apartheid were ready to lie at the drop of a hat [...] They lied as if it were going out of fashion, brazenly and with very considerable conviction."[15] He doesn't however pause to ask whether his comment casts the whole basis of a Truth Commission into doubt.

But if justice, as in full-scale criminal proceedings, is set aside, it reappears as redistributive justice all the more forcefully through the Commission's back door. I have already given one example in the exchange between Ramashala and Roelf Meyer. This is from the Minister of Justice, cited in a section called "Amnesty and Social Justice" in the chapter on Concepts and Principles from Volume 1 of the Report:

> We have a nation of victims, and if we are unable to provide complete justice on an individual basis [...] it is possible for us ... to ensure that there is historical and collective justice for the people of our country. If we achieve that, if we achieve social justice and move in that direction [...] at that level we will be able to say *that justice has been done*. (1, p. 124, emphasis original)

And on this matter, there is, as it were, a faultline running through the Commission more or less by its own account. For if the Commission, or rather its associated amnesty hearings, has the quasi-judicial power to grant amnesty, on reparation and rehabilitation it has solely the power to recommend. It was one of the chief principles of the Commission to restore the dignity of victims (the discussion of whether indeed they should be called "victims" turned on this concern): "restoring the human and civil *dignity* of [such] victims by granting them an opportunity to relate their own accounts of the violations of which they are the victims" (1, p. 55). Dignity in the act of speech – this the Commission could enact, in this sense the Commission is one of the great performatives of modern times; dignity of a continuing life is something else: "and by recommending reparation measures in respect of them", "the individual reparation grant provides resources to victims in an effort to restore their *dignity*" (5, p. 184, emphasis mine).[16]

One of these forms of dignity is measurable, calculable; one is not. The strength and uniqueness of the Commission is to have thrown itself into the realm of the incalculable, speech upon speech for victims for whom speech – pained, sometimes reluctant, by no means always healing – was the only thing left to say. But you could say that these two forms of dignity – of speech and of daily life – are not so much incommensurable as critically reliant on, or even subtractable from, each other; that the speech of the victim, the speech to which at one level the whole of the hearings was devoted, cannot reach its destination, unless economic equality, social justice is achieved (the minority, dissenting Commissioner, Wynand Malan, even argues that liberal rights can act as an obstruction to social rights – the granting of social rights by a previously elite minority costs, as in hurts, more). The last paragraph of Findings and Conclusions states:

> Ultimately, however, because the work of the Commission includes reconciliation, it needs to unleash a process that contributes to economic developments that redress past wrongs as a basis for promoting lasting reconciliation. This requires *all those who benefited* from apartheid, not only those whom the Act defines as perpetrators, to commit themselves to the reconciliation process. (5, p. 258)

The differential of accountability, lost in one sense in the body of the Report, returns therefore on the issue of redistributive justice; as does its infinite, one might say, interminable extensibility: "all *those who benefited*" is in italics.

Wole Soyinka – in a wonderfully theatrical moment in an already theatrical speech on "Reparations, Truth, and Reconciliation" – gives the comic – black comic – version:

> Just to let one's fantasy roam a little – what really would be preposterous or ethically inadmissable in imposing a general levy on South Africa's white population? This is not intended as a concrete proposal, but as an exercise in pure speculation [. . .] such an offer could originate from the beneficiaries of Apartheid themselves, in a voluntary gesture of atonement – it need not be a project of the state. Is such a genesis – from within the indicted group itself – truly beyond conception? [. . .] [should] some external prodding prove necessary, the initiative could be taken up by someone of the non-establishment stature of Archbishop Desmond Tutu. The respected cleric and mediator mounts his pulpit one day and addresses his compatriots on that very theme: "White brothers and sisters in the Lord, you have sinned, but we are willing to forgive. The scriptures warn us that the wages of sin are death but, in your case, they seem to be wealth. If therefore you chose to shed a little of that sinful wealth as a first step towards atonement . . . etc. etc."[17]

The suggestion that perpetrators should make a financial contribution to the families of victims is also made by Cynthia Ngewu, mother of one of the Gugulethu Seven at the forum on Reconciliation, Reconstruction and Economic Justice in Cape Town in March 1997 ("the best way to demonstrate a truthful commitment to peace and a truthful commitment to repentance," 5, p. 402). But it says something that outside that context, Soyinka can only conjure up the possibility of such material accountability on the part of the white community as fantasy.

There is therefore, by its own account, a hiatus in the Commission, a double deal on either side of the truth in which one justice is exchanged for another, neither of which is exactly there: justice, as in criminal proceedings, set aside for the Commission to do its work; justice as in social justice suspended beyond its remit into an unknowable future. In the middle sits "restorative justice", the foundation of the Commission's daily work, but only "if the emerging truth unleashes a social dynamic that includes redressing the suffering of victims will it meet the ideal of restorative justice" (1, p. 131). If the Commission presents us more starkly than any other modern document with the difficult relationship between truth and language it also forces a no less crucial and fraught connection between the registers of justice and truth. As Wole Soyinka puts the question: "is knowledge on its own of lasting effect?"[18]

It is not then, quite, that making accountability a matter of individual acts fails to discriminate appropriately, veiling the state behind its agents; if anything it is the opposite, as each individual act described, along with all the acts which surrounded it and made it possible – the "interstice between power and indifferent or supportive agency" – are, in a still unredeemed future, held to indefinite account. To read the Report is to watch accountability contract and expand, pulsing under the pressure of a set of crucial but barely sustainable distinctions. "Accountability doesn't stop." There is no upper limit – hence the devastating effect on the Commissioners of the denials and fudges of de Klerk; there is no outer limit – the interstice between "power and indifferent or supportive agency" is very very wide; not before, not after – the Commission makes its recommendations, half way between a pledge and a plea.

To end, therefore, by bringing these matters a little closer to home, to the University back door, "The Commission should" – this from a final section on the Commission's shortcomings – "for example, have investigated [. . .] educational institutions (in particular universities).

. . ." (5, p. 207, also p. 434). Universities are named as one of the institutions of civil society into which the Commission did not reach: they did not appear at any of the Institutional and Special Hearings which included Business and Labor, the Faith and Legal Communities, the Health Sector, Media and Prisons. The University was then, one could almost say, the only institution that escaped.

It cannot, I think, be wholly coincidental that J.M. Coetzee situates, or at least opens, his much acclaimed and much critiqued novel, *Disgrace*[19] in the setting of a University, and that he chose, to the objections of many critics, to write this novel, at this particular moment in South Africa's slow emergence from the night of apartheid, about someone who could be taken for himself (Susan Barton in Coetzee's *Foe* couldn't be, nor Magda in *The Heart of the Country*, nor the old lady in *Age of Iron*, nor even, although this one doesn't require a gender leap of the same order, *Michael K.*).

I read *Disgrace* as Coetzee's response to the Truth and Reconciliation Commission. David Lurie, a semi-depressed university professor, sexually harasses a young female student, is charged, refuses to justify himself, refuses to speak. Disgraced, he goes to live with his daughter Lucy on a white farm where they are subjected to a violent assault by a group of black youths; she is raped, he is severely beaten. The novel then charts the psychic trajectory of both of them, as she decides to keep the baby who will result from the abuse and to accept the marriage proposal of her black co-manager into whose hands the farm, the baby, and herself will then fall; while he takes up work at a clinic where he devotes himself – with a humanity which neither he nor the reader can at first imagine him capable of – to the comfort of a succession of stray, sick, and finally condemned dogs. In "the interstice between power and indifferent agency", Lurie lives outside the mainstream of a history which gradually engulfs him. Opening his novel at the University, Coetzee brings his character closer than any other to his own world (Lurie is a University Professor of Literature). At the same time – while Lurie does acquire the partial status of trauma victim, and he is, or at least it could be argued that he is, partially redeemed at the end of the novel – in this novel, Coetzee seems to have gone out of his way to create a character with whom it is almost impossible for his reader to sympathize or identify. Lurie is repellent – simply, literally, people withdraw from him – incapable of intimacy with the women he sexually approaches, and repellent to himself.

Lurie is someone who cannot feel, even before he is the subject of an assault which robs him of all feeling. This is perhaps the only moment, in a novel which in fact constantly forces unexpected and unwelcome moments of identification between its protagonists, when we are drawn into something like empathy for what Lurie has experienced. It is after the assault:

> Aimlessly he roams about the garden. A grey mood is settling on him. It is not just that he does not know what to do with himself. The events of yesterday have shocked him to the depths. The trembling, the weakness are only the first and most superficial signs of that shock. He has a sense that, inside him, a vital organ has been bruised, abused – perhaps even his heart. For the first time he has a taste of what it will be like to be an old man, tired to the bone, without hopes, without desires, indifferent to the future. Slumped on a plastic chair amid the stench of chicken feathers and rotting apples, he feels his interest in the world draining from him drop by drop.[20]

He is already disconnected before the assault, which his daughter will take on as the burden of atonement for the past wrongs of South Africa, drains him of all connection to the world. "Indifferent", his interest in the world "draining from him drop by drop" – the terms embedded in this passage hover between diagnosis and accusation. As the effect of trauma, Lurie enters a state of mind – indifference, lack of interest, failure to connect – for which, in terms of the history of his country to which he has paid such scant regard, he could also be held accountable. In *Disgrace*, the psychic consequences of trauma are also being offered as their own cause.

In *The Lives of Animals*, Coetzee's last publication before *Disgrace* consisting of his Tanner lectures, which he chose to write in fictional form, Elizabeth Costello, feminist fiction writer and campaigning vegetarian, uses the occasion of two public lectures (not unlike the Tanner lectures) to make the case against the slaughter of animals: "There is no limit to which we can think ourselves into the being of another."[21] In the discussion papers which followed (also included in the book), by literary critic Marjorie Garber, ethical and religious philosophers Peter Singer and Wendy Doniger, and anthropologist Barbara Smuts, South Africa is not mentioned once, despite this moment from Elizabeth Costello in which she is, surely, making the link:

> To me, a philosopher who says that the distinction between human and nonhuman depends on whether you have a white or a black skin, and a philosopher who says that the distinction between human and non-

human depends on whether or not you know the difference between a subject and a predicate, are more alike than they are unlike.[22]

And yet it does seem to me that these two texts by Coetzee share a question. How do you get from dissociation, a consciously or unconsciously willed refusal to connect to the horrors going on around you, a drastic failure of historical imagination as we might call it, to empathy with – being able to think yourself into the being of – a dog? (An aside, or perhaps not an aside: Marlene Van Niekerk's prize-winning Afrikaans novel *triomf*,[23] which centers on another group which falls out of the remit of the Truth Commission, South Africa's white trash, not only, like the UK edition of *Disgrace*, has a dog on its cover, not only opens with a chapter called "Dogs," not only at a key point signals its catastrophically dysfunctional family's humanity through their telepathic awareness of the death of their dog, but also at several points is written from the point of view of a dog.). "They just buried him like a dog" (5, p. 152). Accountability halts at the barrier of identification. As does atrocity. All the evidence suggests that people do not kill if they can imagine themselves in the other person's shoes. "The horror," Costello states in a deliberately shocking analogy between animal slaughter and the Nazi death camps, "is that the killers refused to think themselves into the place of their victims, as did everyone else."[24] Another way of putting this would be to say that we should never under-estimate people's ability – internal as well as external – to ward off bad news (a victim is of course someone for whom this has ceased to be an option). There are exceptions: "I thought," said the Afrikaans Johan Smit talking of the death of his eight-year-old son in a bomb blast in 1985: "I thought that if I placed myself in the other person's shoes, how would I have felt about it [. . .] I realised I would not have liked it [. . .] I realised how it must have felt for them" (5, p. 377). After he had spoken, Tutu stopped the proceedings to express his appreciation.

One of the things for which the Truth Commission has become famous is the concept of *"ubuntu,"* a traditional Zulu term which is placed by the Commission at the basis of restorative justice: *"Ubuntu*, generally translated as 'humaneness', expresses itself metaphoricaly in *umuntu ngumuntu ngabantu* – 'people are people through other people' " (1, p. 127). "A person," Tutu expanded at his inauguration as Archbishop of Cape Town in 1986, "is a person because he recognizes others as persons."[25] As Mark Sanders argues, the term involves more than a call to collective solidarity, and more than a recognition from a safe place; for such a recognition to occur, you have fundamentally to lose or disappropriate yourself. Sanders retranslates: "a human being is a human being through human beings," "a human being is realised through his or her being (human) through human beings."[26] Perhaps, however, even this does not go far enough. Perhaps, Coetzee is suggesting in *The Lives of Animals*, the human is the block. So how about animals? Or, even, a corpse. Pushing her analogy and her audience to the limit, Elizabeth Costello announces in the middle of her lecture: "For instants at a time, I know what it is like to be a corpse."[27]

The original meaning of the word "apathy" was to be without "pathos," insensibility to suffering, the highest virtue for the Stoics, only gradually degrading itself to listless, stolid indifference. It could be, however, that in the setting of South Africa, apathy includes something of the earlier meaning, in which suffering – actively – is held at bay. A state of mind racing away from itself. Apathy in the modern sense would then contain, working away inside it, the germ of its own undoing, a kind of internal dissent. The implication would be that, for anyone struck with apathy in a situation of historic injustice, there is a partial recognition, not just of the suffering of others, but of what it would do to you, just how far you might have to go, to make the link. If making those links is, as I see it, one of the tasks of modern intellectual life, one of the things South Africa's Truth and Reconciliation Commission teaches me is that it has never been more important or harder to do so.

## Notes

1  Many people have contributed to my engagement with South African politics and literature, but the person whose writings have most consistently inspired and informed my understanding is Gillian Slovo. My special thanks to her.

2  Fyodor Dostoyevsky, *The Brothers Karamazov* (London, New York: Quartet, 1990), p. 237.

3  *Truth and Reconciliation Commission of South Africa Report*, 5 volumes (London: Macmillan, 1998, 1999), 4, p. 313. Hereinafter cited parenthetically in the text.

4  Eric Hobsbawn with Antonio Pollio, *The New Century*, Allan Cameron trans. (London, New York: Little Brown, 2000), p. 86.

5  Phillip Gourevitch, *We Wish to Inform you that Tomorrow we will be Killed with our Families – Stories from Rwanda* (London: Picador, 1999), p. 7.

6 Njabulo Ndebele, "Memory, Metaphor and the Triumph of Narrative," in Sarah Nuttall and Carli Coetzee (eds.) *Negotiating the Past – the Making of Memory in South Africa* (Cape Town: Oxford University Press, 1998), pp. 19–28, quote p. 26.

7 Antjie Krog, *Country of My Skull* (Johannesberg, Random House, 1998), p. 36. I discuss Krog and the question of representation and language in relation to the Truth Commission more fully in "Aux marges du littéraire: justice, vérité, reconciliation," in *Ou en est la théorie littéraire?*, Julia Kristeva and Evelyne Grossman, eds., Actes du Colloque organisé a l'Université Paris 7, May 1999, *Textuel*, 37, (2000): 99–108.

8 Hobsbawm, *New Century*, p. 115.

9 Desmond Tutu, *No Future Without Forgiveness* (London: Rider, 1999), p. 2.

10 Gerry Hugo, "Confession of a Torturer," *Wounded Nations, Broken Lives – Truth Commissions and War Tribunals, Index on Censorship*, 5 (1996): 61–6, quote p. 66.

11 Kader Asmal, Louise Asmal, and Ronald Suresh Roberts, "When the Assassin Cries Foul: Modern Just War Doctrines," in Charles Villa-Vicencio and Wilhelm Verwoerd (eds.), *Looking Back, Reaching Forward – Reflections on the Truth and Reconciliation Commission of South Africa* (Cape Town: University of Cape Town Press/London: Zed Books, 2000), p. 93; see also *Reconciliation Through Truth – A Reckoning of Apartheid's Criminal Governance* (Cape Town: David Philip, 1997). Compare Neville Alexander: "The fundamental flaw in the conceptualisation of the TRC as a mechanism for 'dealing with the past' lies in the fact that the question of moral debt (Habermas) is fudged by both trying to 'share' it between victim and perpetrator and by individualising it, ie, removing it from systemic embedment" ("The Politics of Reconciliation," unpublished mimeo of chapter of book forthcoming from University of Natal Press. My thanks to Benita Parry for making this available to me.)

12 Asmal et al., "When the Assassin Cries Foul," p. 92.

13 For fuller discussion, see Alexander, "The Politics of Reconciliation," and Deborah Posel, *1948–1961, The Making of Apartheid: Conflict and Compromise* (Oxford: Clarendon, 1991).

14 Tutu, *No Future*, p. 25.

15 Ibid., p. 28.

16 See Arthur Chaskalson, "Human Dignity as a Foundational Value of our Constitutional Order," Third Bram Fischer lecture. My thanks to Stephen Clingman for making this text available to me.

17 Wole Soyinka, *The Burden of Memory; The Muse of Forgiveness* (New York: Oxford University Press, 1999), pp. 25–6.

18 Ibid., p. 9. See Janet Cherry, "Historical Truth: Something to Fight for," in Villa-Vicencio and Verwoerd (eds.), *Looking Back*, pp. 134–43. For me the best critique of the Commission in relation to the category of truth is contained in Gillian Slovo's extraordinary latest novel, *Red Dust* (London:

Virago, 2000). I do not, however, agree with those critiques of the Commission which see it as "an officially instituted memory-loss" (Benita Parry, "Reconciliation and Remembrance," *Pretexts*, 5, 1–2, (1995): 84–96) or which suggest, as Alexander does at points in his chapter on the Commission, that the truth offered by the Commission was simply unexamined truth, or rather that this was a problem of which the Commissioners were unaware. See for example this statement by Professor Simpson, a psychiatrist specialising in post-traumatic stress disorder, cited in the final volume chapter on Reconciliation: "Truth is one essential component of the needed social antiseptic which could cleanse the social fabric of the systematised habit of disregard for human rights, but it needs to be an *examined truth; it needs to be considered, thought about, debated and digested and metabolised by individuals and society*" (5, p. 356, my emphasis); and the statement from Bishop David Beetge at the follow-up hearing workshop in Reiger Park: "We retell our painful stories so that we shall remember . . ." (5, p. 350).

19   For a summary of these critiques see Anthony Sampson, "The Gloom and the Glory," *Prospect*, April 2000, p. 58.
20   J.M. Coetzee, *Disgrace* (London: Secker and Warburg, 1999), pp. 106–7.
21   J.M. Coetzee, *The Lives of Animals* (Princeton, NJ: Princeton University Press, 1999), p. 35.
22   Ibid., p. 66.
23   Marlene Van Niekerk, *triomf*, Leon de Kock, trans. (London, New York: Little Brown, 1999) (first published in Afrikaans, Quellerie, 1994).
24   Coetzee, *The Lives of Animals*, p. 34.
25   Cited in Mark Sanders, reviewing the *TRC Report* and Thomas Keenan, *Fables of Responsibility, Diacritics* (fall, 1999): 3–20, quote p. 12.
26   Ibid., p. 13.
27   Coetzee, *The Lives of Animals*, p. 32.

# Chapter 8

# The Sweatshop Sublime

## Bruce Robbins

There is a passage in David Lodge's 1988 novel *Nice Work* in which the heroine, a Marxist-feminist critic who teaches English literature, looks out the window of an airplane and sees the division of labor.[1]

> Factories, shops, offices, schools, beginning the working day. People crammed into rush-hour buses and trains, or sitting at the wheels of their cars in traffic jams, or washing up breakfast things in the kitchens of pebble-dashed semis. All inhabiting their own little worlds, oblivious of how they fitted into the total picture. The housewife, switching on her electric kettle to make another cup of tea, gave no thought to the immense complex of operations that made that simple action possible: the building and maintenance of the power station that produced the electricity, the mining of coal or pumping of oil to fuel the generators, the laying of miles of cable to carry the current to her house, the digging and smelting and milling of ore or bauxite into sheets of steel or aluminium, the cutting and pressing and welding of the metal into the kettle's shell, spout and handle, the assembling of these parts with scores of other components–coils, screws, nuts, bolts, washers, rivets, wires, springs, rubber insulation, plastic trimmings; then the packaging of the kettle, the advertising of the kettle, the marketing of the kettle, to wholesale and retail outlets, the transportation of the kettle to warehouses and shops, the calculation of its price, and the distribution of its added value between all the myriad people and agencies concerned in its production and circulation. The housewife gave no thought to all this as she switched on her kettle.

To contemplate one's kettle and suddenly realize, first, that one is the beneficiary of an unimaginably vast and complex social whole; and second (a point further emphasized elsewhere in the novel) that this means benefiting from the daily labor of kettle- and electricity-producing workers, much of it unpleasant and under-remunerated – neither of these realizations is entirely outside the domain of everyday experience. What seems special about this passage is a third realization: that this moment of consciousness will not be converted into action. The passage concludes:

> What to do with the thought was another question. It was difficult to decide whether the system that produced the kettle was a miracle of human ingenuity and co-operation or a colossal waste of resources, human and natural. Would we all be better off boiling our own water in a pot hung over an open fire? Or was it the facility to do such things at the touch of a button that freed men, and more particularly women, from servile labour and made it possible for them to become literary critics? [. . .] She gave up on the conundrum, and accepted another cup of coffee from the stewardess.[2]

Let me now juxtapose this passage with a *New Yorker* cartoon by Roz Chast. Its protagonist, "you," is an unshaven man in pyjamas. He or "you" combines Lodge's tea-drinking housewife with his airborne intellectual; your feet are firmly on the ground, indeed you are not yet out of your own door, yet you do "give a thought" to the system that provides you with goods and services. And it is this thought that we follow. At the top of the cartoon are the words "One morning, while getting dressed." From that common point, lines branch off toward boxes containing different possible outcomes. One morning, while getting dressed, you either do or do not examine the label of your shirt. If you do, you either do or do not realize the conditions of life under which this shirt was, or perhaps was not, produced: the pitifully inadequate wages, not to speak of the locked fire exits, the arbitrary harassments and firings, the refusal of genuine union representation, and so on. But whether your thoughts linger or not, whether the shirt turns out to have been made in Mexico or Thailand or the USA, the result is the same, the same as if you had not examined the label. All lines converge in the end on the same box: you put on the shirt and forget about it.

In both cases, there is a moment of insight accompanied by a surge of power. In thought, at least, you are launched on a one-click leap from the tender, drowsy privacy of early morning at home – the shirt not yet on your back, the first cup of tea just finished – to the outer reaches of a world economic system of notoriously inconceivable magnitude and interdependence, a system that brings goods from the ends

Figure 8.1   Cartoon "One morning, while getting dressed," by Roz Chast, *New Yorker*, November 29, 1999. © The New Yorker Collection 1999 Roz Chast from cartoonbank.com. All Rights Reserved.

of the earth (as Baudelaire put it, with an accuracy that you suddenly recognize) in order to satisfy your slightest desire.[3] Yet at the same time this insight is also strangely powerless. Your sudden, heady access to the global scale is not access to a commensurate power of action *upon* the global scale. You have a cup of tea, or coffee. You get dressed. Just as suddenly, just as shockingly, you are returned to yourself in all your everyday smallness.

"That in comparison with which everything else is small" is one of Kant's descriptions of the sublime, also defined as "a feeling of the inadequacy of [the] imagination for presenting the ideas of a whole, wherein the imagination reaches its maximum, and, in striving to surpass it, sinks back into itself, by which, however, a kind of emotional satisfaction is produced."[4] Considering how Lodge and Chast play up and down the scales of the immensely large and infinitesimally small, how they combine pleasure with pain in contemplating the obscure infinity of the social whole, and above all the paradox by which they make us sense that we possess transcendent powers (albeit powers exercised on our behalf and in this case without our active will) and yet finally let us "sink back into ourselves," failing to express those powers in any potentially risky, disobedient action, I would suggest that we provisionally call this trope, with a certain inevitable discomfort, the sweatshop sublime.[5]

The sublime may not seem like the most obviously useful way to pose the question of our responsibilities as citizens faced with the reality of sweatshop labor. A certain usefulness will, I hope, become more apparent as I proceed. But the pairing of sweatshops and sublimity is also intended to raise issues of politics and aesthetics, scholarship and commitment, that have become irritatingly familiar of late to progressives working in and around the humanities. Rather than rehearse those issues here, let me simply assert, by way of setting an agenda, two propositions that the notion of a sweatshop sublime is meant to suggest. First, that literary critics in allegorical airplanes, looking down from above on putatively unconscious housewives – let's say, intellectuals contemplating non-intellectuals – are subject to the same dilemma of concern and confusion, action and apathy. To recognize that this *is* a dilemma means that we should not expect any simple solution to it. And to recognize that it is a *shared* dilemma, rather than a dilemma resulting from the uniqueness of our work, ought to help us calibrate more accurately the responsibilities that do and do not attach to that work.

At the same time (this is my second point), the idea that intellectuals do not escape this dilemma is not merely an argument in favor of modestly retracting some of the political expectations we attach to our work. It's also a factor of wider political importance. This is especially true for those of us searching (perhaps immodestly) for political answers that would operate on the same global or international scale as the causes of our ethical and political problems. If internationalism in the desirable sense is ever going to come into existence, if we are ever going to see some organized impulse toward the equalization of life chances between those who make shirts and those who wear them, this will clearly not happen by means of a sudden mass exercise of Kantian ethics. It is going to happen as an outgrowth of habitual desires, fears, and anxieties, embarrassed perceptions and guilty pleasures, that, though pervaded by thought, do not belong on that level of rigorous conceptual rationality that Kant elsewhere demanded. An example is the childhood experience of being told to eat unappetizing food because children elsewhere are starving. The experience of sweatshop sublimity is another item in this illogical but peremptory series. Unpropitious as it may seem, this limited moment of ethically inspired consumer consciousness is just the sort of raw or semi-processed phenomenological material in which private and public, domestic and international, are fused, and it is out of such materials that an internationalist anti-globalization politics on a mass scale will have to emerge, if indeed it ever does emerge. To put this in other terms, this moment of awareness is a rough analogue to what Gramsci called the "national-popular": an imperfect and historically determined version of common sense, perhaps only emergent but significant enough to be worth tracking, that links the thoughts and feelings of ordinary people to the fate of others within a larger collectivity. To Gramsci this collectivity was the nation. But I see no reason why the process of collectivity-formation should somehow stop at the nation's borders, as if fellow-feeling found its natural and inevitable *telos* in nationality. The gradually increasing reservoir of everyday tropes and images that connect our sense of ourselves and our fate with the fates of those who are not our fellow citizens can thus be thought of, I propose, as the *international*-popular.

It is to be expected that the international-popular will fall well short of any ideal action-oriented solidarity. But it is also to be expected that, under present global conditions, solidarity and even action itself will fall similarly short, will be subject to the same sorts of quasi-sensory, all-too-human interference that we have come to associate with the aesthetic – the illegitimate but seemingly irremediable tyranny of the close over the distant, the analogous perspectivisms of the other senses, the vulnerability to shapeliness, decibel level, boredom, and so on. Thus sweatshop sublimity offers grounds for anyone interested in defending the significance to society at large of work performed in the domain of the aesthetic – a kind of case that can never rely on the language of the aesthetic alone, must always step outside that language in order to anchor itself in other interests and concerns.

\*　　\*　　\*

Now there are, of course, things to be done about sweatshops. The literature of groups like the National Labor Committee, the Campaign for Labor Rights, and United Students Against Sweatshops abounds in invitations to sudden perception more or less like the cartoon's. For example: "When you purchase a shirt in Wal-Mart, do you ever imagine young women in Bangladesh forced to work from 7:30 a.m. to 8:00 p.m., seven days a week, paid just 9 cents to 20 cents an hour ...?" But this literature always follows with a section called something like "What We Can Do," urging readers to write to Wal-Mart with specific and entirely reasonable demands. And it has real grounds to claim, as it does: "We do have an impact. We do have a voice."[6] It has helped rally supporters, and it has won a number of small but significant victories. The celebrity of American television personality Kathie Lee Gifford was successfully used against her, and against the brands she endorses, to publicize sweatshop abuses in Honduras; many American universities have agreed to new standards concerning how school sweatshirts and other paraphernalia are to be manufactured. If little progress has been made on the crucial questions of wages and the right to unionize, where corporations have been most resistant, it is nonetheless a genuine accomplishment to have brought the beginnings of transparency, monitoring, and accountability to the murky domain of anonymous sub-contracting in which the brand-name multinationals have so profitably been hiding out. The anti-sweatshop movement, increasingly active on US campuses, was one of the most powerful constituents of the volatile anti-WTO protest mixture in Seattle and since. Moves toward alliance between students and labor unions, and between unions and the environmental groups, are two of the most promising features of recent international activism aimed against no-holds-barred globalization.

In short, to discover that the sales price of one Disney Pocahontas T-shirt, sold at Wal-Mart for $10.97, amounts to five days wages for the women who sewed that shirt, is not necessarily to be struck down by paralysis and inertia, though it helps if some available mode of action is specified. Even the Roz Chast cartoon, which offers a description of lethargy, might also be interpreted as a provocation intended to shock us out of lethargy. Literary analogues are not hard to find in which economic epiphany leads toward, rather than away from, action. Consider the passage toward the end of George Eliot's *Middlemarch* in which Dorothea, who has just spent a miserable and sleepless night after finding Will in a compromising position with Rosamund, gets up at dawn and asks herself, "What should I do – how should I act now, this very day, if I could clutch my own pain, and compel it to silence, and think of those three?" (the third being Lydgate, the husband Rosamund seems in danger of betraying):

> It had taken long for her to come to that question, and there was light piercing into the room. She opened her curtains, and looked out towards the bit of road that lay in view, with fields beyond, outside the entrance-gates. On the road there was a man with a bundle on his back and a woman carrying her baby; in the field she could see figures moving – perhaps the shepherd with his dog. Far off in the bending sky was the pearly light; and she felt the largeness of the world and the manifold wakings of men to labour and endurance. She was a part of that involuntary, palpitating life, and could neither look out on it from her luxurious shelter as a mere spectator, nor hide her eyes in selfish complaining.
>
> What she would resolve to do that day did not yet seem quite clear, but something that she could achieve stirred her as with an approaching murmur which would soon gather distinctness.[7]

Dorothea follows through on her resolution to act. And though the sphere of her action is quite limited – it does not include for example the people she sees out her window or the system that sends them into the fields at that hour – it is rewarded with visible results. Like the anti-sweatshop movement, she feels with a jolt her place in the "involuntary, palpitating" world of labor around her, resolves to do something, and does. And with such an example in mind, it's tempting to conclude that the later texts by Lodge and Chast represent a moral step backwards, a sophisticated evasion of the responsibility for action.

But the sweatshop sublime is not, I think, a simple or easily avoidable error. And error or not, I would argue that, appearances to the contrary, it is precisely the mode in which Eliot herself is writing. Dorothea's early-morning revelation, in which everyone else who is awake is going off to work and only she remains behind in her "luxurious shelter," has been anticipated some chapters earlier by what is surely the novel's most direct reference to the sublime, and perhaps also its most sublime moment. "If we had a keen vision and feeling of all ordinary human life," Eliot writes in a famous sentence, "it would be like hearing the grass grow and the squirrel's heart beat, and we should die of that roar which lies on the other side of silence."[8]

In the later scene, Dorothea is hearing the grass grow. She suddenly takes in the daily "labor and endurance" that put the bread on her table, but that do not ordinarily attract any notice. And she draws from that extraordinary perception stern, not to say self-punishing, conclusions. The problem is the self-punishment, which is just what is predicted by the metaphor of "hearing the grass grow." Going to see Rosamund is action, but action that displays an altruistic self-effacement so radical as to leave behind almost no self, or no self-interest. To hear the "roar which lies on the other side of silence" is indeed, from the point of view of an ordinary self, to die. The purely disinterested, selfless self that remains to Dorothea is only too well suited to the metaphor, for it is incapable of forceful action that would change the rules or terms of ordinariness, and forceful, extraordinary action of this sort is just what is rendered irrelevant, if not precluded, by the notion of "hearing the grass grow." Asking us to hear the grass grow is not asking us to interfere with it. The only imperative here is to be conscious of what is already happening, to respect what exists. And respect for what exists is a better argument against change than for it. If the division of labor in the early morning passage is like the grass in the "hearing the grass grow" passage, and I think it is, then the same moral applies: the only scandal is unconsciousness of the division of labor, not failure to change the division of labor. As Steven Marcus puts it in an essay on George Eliot's social theory, "Society, however errant and unfair some of its arrangements may be, is never a scandal in this way of conceiving things. To say so would be tantamount to saying that human existence itself is a scandal."[9]

The larger story in which Dorothea is obliged to abandon her heroic St. Theresa-like ideal of action, to which this hesitation belongs, can perhaps be explained in part by Eliot's intermittent attraction to the values of the landholding gentry, which owned a good deal of grassland and had famously mixed feelings about plans for modernizing interference with it. It is most neatly described in Raymond Williams's account of Eliot's organic view of social interdependence:

> Her favorite metaphor for society is a network: a "tangled skein"; a "tangled web" . . . "One fears," she remarked, "to pull the wrong thread, in the tangled scheme of things." The caution is reasonable, but the total effect of the image false. For in fact every element in the complicated system is active: the relationships are changing, constantly, and any action – even abstention . . . – affects, even if only slightly . . . the very nature of the complication.

Eliot fails in her depiction of working people, Williams concludes, because to her "there seems 'no right thread to pull.' Almost any kind of social action is ruled out."[10]

David Lodge's moment of sublimity produces more or less the same effect. In the name of realism, he too chastises and paralyzes his would-be activist heroine, Robyn Penrose. For both novelists, to glimpse even for a moment the unimaginable face of society-as-a-whole is to go through a near-death experience in which the activist self dissolves. Forced to ask "Are My Hands Clean?" – to quote a sweatshop poem by the African-American writer Bernice Johnson Reagon – each loses the moral leverage that has helped her challenge the status quo and thus sinks back into the private.[11] Sublimity is not the end of action itself – Robyn, like Dorothea, is successful in her personal mission – but to repeat Williams's judgement, "any kind of social action is ruled out."

Yet "social action" sets a very high standard, both for the novel and for academic discourse like our own. To say that Eliot rules it out is to imply that it would otherwise be available. Is it available even to so severe a critic of Eliot as Williams himself – available, that is, while he is in the act of writing criticism? Francis Mulhern, in a book entitled *Culture/Metaculture*, suggests that Williams's judgement of Eliot can be extended to most if not all of the "Culture and Society" tradition Williams so influentially assembled, a tradition that has joined Marxists with romantic reactionaries on the common ground of visions like those of Eliot and Lodge, visions of "organic interdependence."[12] For Mulhern, Williams's identification of culture as ordinary, which inaugurates the era of Cultural Studies, has much the same effect as Eliot's "hear-the-grass-grow" openness to the ordinary. In Williams's own words, "The arguments which can be grouped under [the heading of culture] do not point to any inevitable action or affiliation."[13] Williams stands at the juncture between the older Kulturkritik tradition of Thomas Mann, T.S. Eliot, F.R. Leavis, and company, for which culture was extraordinary, a standard cutting against "mass society," and Cultural Studies, for which culture is ordinary, hence not readily separable from the status quo. But this is less of a break than it appears, Mulhern suggests, for *both* senses of culture are anti-political. The Cultural Studies formula "everything is political" leaves nothing political in a usefully specifiable sense, and thus has the same practical effect as Mann's explicit ideal of the "unpolitical man," inspired by culture to reject with disgust both mass democracy and political instrumentality as such. In other words, Dorothea looking out her window

187

in the morning, hearing the grass grow, sensing the organic interde-
pendency of the division of labor, is a figure for the academic study of
culture *tout court*, whether in the older or the present generation. Both
versions of literary criticism represent the individual's relation to an
obscure, infinite whole that is at once politically compelling and yet
seemingly deterred by its premises from resulting in a proper political
subject or proper political action.[14]

I will not pursue this parallel here, though there is more to be said,
for example, about how Dorothea is eventually rewarded for her visit
to Rosamund (with the news that Will does love her after all), and we
humanists too are rewarded for our apparent altruism, with employment that is not very high-paying but relatively stable, unusually
autonomous, and unusually gratifying – desirable enough, in short, to
make others wonder whether we are quite as disinterested as we
pretend. For us too, an apparent exteriority to the division of labor
helps secure a place within the division of labor. And for this reason,
inaction should not be seen as a lapse that humanists tumble into in
a moment of moral inattention and that can thus be corrected by res-
onant calls to stand up and grasp once again our designated responsibilities. Inaction, or hesitation when action seems called for, is built
into the conceptual structure we inhabit. And so too, therefore, are
calls to responsibility, which must be perpetually repeated and must
remain perpetually unanswered. One of the strangest things about
words like "action" and "activism," at least as they are currently used
in the humanities, is their functional equivalence to apparently distant
words like "culture," "intellectual," and "art," each of which is accorded the privilege of transcending the division of labor. Even when
what is meant is not revolutionary action, action is the latest in a series
of terms that, for reasons that go back to our own disciplinary formation or deformation, we have asked to stand for the magical resolution of social contradictions, the ideal unities, the antidotes to the state
of division, fragmentation, reification, and so on that we imagine
reigning outside, thereby justifying our disciplinary existence. But if
we actually look outside, it is immediately clear that action is no such
thing, possesses no such impossible powers, has less to do with art than
with politics, politics in the de-idealized, messy sense.

Mulhern accuses the Kulturkritik tradition of covert nationalism,
and he accuses Cultural Studies of incoherent populism. Both charges
are reasonable and important, but neither charge can be pinned to the
concept of culture. For the anti-sweatshop movement, which does not
share our academic dependence on that concept, is saturated with both

nationalism and populism. How could it not be, given the movement's need to juggle or reconcile the interests of constituencies as different as organized labor, with its history of protectionism, and the ethical universalism of the so-called "constituencies of conscience"? This is what politics does. It brings groups together in a common action that will not, cannot, perfectly represent the interests of any of them, that will oppose an antagonist each of them will find scandalous for a slightly different reason – will oppose, in effect, a slightly different antagonist.

*    *    *

At the bottom of the *New Yorker* cartoon, three boxes offer three possible facts about the people who made your shirt. In the middle there is an exaggerated clarity: they "earned three cents an hour." To the left, however, there is ambiguity: they "probably have dysentery or diphtheria or worse." This could be another sign of their misery but could also be a reason for our anxiety and disgust (yuck, germs on my shirt!). And to the right is more ambiguity: they "hate your stupid Yankee guts." To which the likely American response is, "In that case, too bad for them." In one box we have fear of foreign infection in the AIDS or Ebola style; in the other we have a national circling of the wagons in the presence of hostility judged (*"stupid* Yankee guts") to be childish. In other words, two of the three confirm the strong hint of American nationalism that was already suggested above when the cartoon assumes, or assumes its readers will assume, against all the evidence, that a label reading "Made in USA" guarantees union wages and decent working conditions – in effect, that there are no sweatshops in the USA (which gets no illustration). Pushing these nationalist buttons no doubt helps Chast prepare for her anti-anti-sweatshop climax. But they are not just *her* buttons. They are also the anti-sweatshop movement's buttons.

The history of checking for a "Made in USA" label has recently been recounted in Dana Frank's book *Buy American: The Untold Story of Economic Nationalism.* Frank opens the book by describing what she calls an "import panic attack": "Ms Consumer's epiphany" that "all the goods she had examined" at the local mall "were made in China, Japan, or Korea . . . she peered at label after label and discovered to her horror that she couldn't find a TV or a VCR or a toaster made in the U.S.A." What follows is the conclusion that "because people like herself were buying imports, American workers were losing their jobs"[15] The power of the "epiphany," in Frank's analysis, is in direct proportion to the weakness of the logic, or rather its failure to impose an appropriate conclusion, either about the causes of this phenomenon or what to do about it. The general reaction in the USA has been to want to "buy American,' and anti-immigrant racism has never been far away. Epiphanies like these have often led to action, in other words, but action of a sublimely confused and nationalist kind, including bashing a Toyota with a sledgehammer and the (in my opinion) no less confused act of lobbying the US Congress to deny normal trade relations to China, thereby claiming a presumptive national virtue for the United States government in the very act of refusing it to another government.[16] Once you are attuned to the motif of nationalism, examples are all too easy to come by. Randy Shaw, activist and historian of activism, entitles his account of the anti-sweatshop movement *Reclaiming America: Nike, Clean Air, and the New National Activism.* The America Shaw sees the movement trying to reclaim is one that, as recently as the 1970s, was supposedly "moving toward the equitable society envisioned in the ideals of its founders."[17] If you can believe that, then you will have no trouble referring, with ambiguous restrictiveness, to the "new *national* activism."

Yet if we drop the requirement that this activism be genuinely internationalist, then Shaw's patriotism has a certain specifically political astuteness. A Disney spokesman, responding to accusations about conditions in a Haitian factory that produces Disney clothes, turned the question back at the newspaper reporter: "'With the newsprint you use, do you have any idea of the labor conditions involved to produce it?'"[18] I have little sympathy for Disney or its spokesmen, but the point, however disingenuous, is not irrelevant or uninteresting. How special a case *are* foreign sweatshops? When David Lodge omits the international dimension, talking about the kettle but saying nothing about the tea and treating bauxite as if it were a product of the Home Counties, is he making a significant omission? What precisely is added by the realization that those who work and suffer on Asian tea plantations and in Mexican maquiladoras are not fellow nationals? If the foreignness of the Disney factory in Haiti offers political leverage that is not offered by the production of newsprint, it's in part because of national shame. And there is no national shame without national pride. Can national pride be turned into an ally of internationalism?

Many others have suggested before me that it can and must, and more generally that global commitments can only emerge in a more or less organic and continuous way from local, personal, familial commitments. This is a point where agreement is suspiciously easy, yet getting to the next step of the argument – agreeing, say, on a tipping point where continuity will switch over into opposition – is much more challenging. Consider, for example, the somewhat risky role in anti-sweatshop discourse of disease and disgust. People are not worried about the "moral losses" occasioned by their reliance on paid household help, Barbara Ehrenreich speculates in one of her undercover essays on menial labor, because "Almost everything we buy, after all, is the product of some other person's suffering and miserably underpaid labor. I clean my own house . . . but I can hardly claim purity in any other area of consumption. I buy my jeans at The Gap, which is reputed to subcontract to sweatshops."[19]

> We can try to minimize the pain that goes into feeding, clothing, and otherwise provisioning ourselves – by observing boycotts, checking for a union label, etc. – but there is no way to avoid it altogether without living in the wilderness on berries. Why should housework, among all the goods and services we consume, arouse any special angst?

But paying for other people to clean one's home does arouse angst, she says, and the reason is that one's home is felt to be different: "Someone who has no qualms about purchasing rugs woven by child slaves in India or coffee picked by impoverished peasants in Guatemala might still hesitate to tell dinner guests that, surprisingly enough, his or her lovely home doubles as a sweatshop during the day."[20] It is not the simple existence of sweatshops, but seeing your *home* as a sweatshop that offers a political hold. The Orwellian disgust that makes something seem actionably political in the household is akin to the disgust that makes us squeamish about something foreign suffusing our shirts, our breakfasts, our most intimate space. Fine if I know it's happening, just so long as it's not happening *right here*. This is the slogan of the NIMBY movements: not in my back yard. Once you think about it, the disgust is itself a bit disgusting. And yet one asks oneself whether there can be any politics without it, in other words without provisionally reinforcing borders and hierarchies, privileges and property lines, that we know to be more or less illegitimate.

The "moral challenge," Ehrenreich concludes,

> is to make work visible again: not only the scrubbing and vacuuming but all the hoeing, stacking, hammering, drilling, bending, and lifting that goes into creating and maintaining a livable habitat. In an ever more

economically unequal culture, where so many of the affluent devote their lives to such ghostly pursuits as stock-trading, image-making, and opinion-polling, real work – in the old-fashioned sense of labor that engages the hand as well as the eye, that tires the body and directly alters the physical world – tends to vanish from sight.[21]

Hoeing, stacking, and hammering, like Lodge's list of labors in *Nice Work*, belong to the argument that a "livable habitat" depends on a great many kinds of work that are normally invisible. But as the culmination of an argument about who cleans the toilets and mops the floors at home, the seemingly innocuous demand to make work visible also makes a riskier suggestion, a suggestion that might paradoxically work against this perception of interdependence. To refuse the division of labor at a point of intimacy is to flirt with refusing the division of labor as such. When Ehrenreich contrasts "real" work at home with such "ghostly" sorts of non-manual labor as "opinion-polling," it seems to me she is inadvertently doing just what the ideology of the work ethic does: assuming a criterion of individual self-reliance and self-sufficiency. If it is disgusting to have someone do manual labor in your house, if within our own four walls at least we should be sturdily independent of the work of others, then how can we keep the desire for sturdy independence from spilling over and generalizing itself? Are we prepared to deny our dependence, for example, on such "ghostly" forms of non-manual labor as the planning of rational traffic patterns, or collecting opinions on behalf of national health care, or teaching at public universities? The work ethic protects and legitimates the system of individual rewards: it suggests to people, falsely, that they've earned what they receive, that they receive what they receive because of their individual labors. In other words, it blots out the existence of society and the interdependence without which no individual effort could lead to any results, let alone any reward. Whatever else it does, the sweatshop sublime rightly forces upon us this knowledge of social interdependence. Ehrenreich, perhaps because she feels the pain of this knowledge more acutely than most, tries to escape it by imagining the home as an enclave of hard-working self-sufficiency. If the home is a pattern – and the essay's arc from housework to manual labor as such suggests exactly that – then the appreciation of "real" work can easily become (as it so often has in recent public discourse) an argument against the hard-won sense of interdependence, and the ethical conclusions drawn from that interdependence, that have made possible voter support for the little we have left of the social welfare state.

In other words, disgust with dependence on the work of other people in the home risks passing over into disgust with dependence on the work of other people in general – a disgust with being part of a highly elaborated division of labor. Yet learning to be part of a highly elaborated division of labor seems a precondition for almost any progressive politics, both nationally and internationally. And it would seem to demand – on the as yet counterfactual and very urgent condition, of course, that everyone would receive proper wages and benefits – that we *un*learn our desire that other people get out of our most intimate space: our shirt, our morning coffee. The social division of labor serves to naturalize and disguise social inequality. But that is not all it does. It was not so long ago that poverty was seen as an individual moral failing. Still more recently, it seemed unnatural and unethical for mothers who had any choice in the matter to put their children in the paid care of state-sponsored day care centers. To the extent that this is no longer true, and to the extent to which our society has begun to act on the welfare state's "no fault poverty" assumption, it's because we have taken some deep ethical lessons from the division of labor. It's at least worth speculating that ceasing to be scandalized by paid work in our homes may eventually have to be one of those lessons.

What exactly *is* the scandal about sweatshops? Naomi Klein, author of the best-selling book on the anti-sweatshop movement *No Logo: Taking Aim at the Brand Bullies,* argues that the key to contemporary injustice is brand names: "The astronomical growth in the wealth and cultural influence of multinational corporations over the last fifteen years can arguably be traced back to a single, seemingly innocuous idea developed by management theorists in the mid-1980s: that successful corporations must primarily produce brands, as opposed to products."[22] It is this not unfamiliar but really quite questionable premise that allows her to intensify the sense of scandal around the all-too-substantial sweatshop labor that goes into these after all so strangely insubstantial commodities. And this intensity has of course been a major political resource of the movement; the "outrage" against transnational corporations is special when they can be presented as a "global logo web," when there is "high name-brand recognition."[23] Note what assumptions this argument involves. Capitalists are "abandoning," Klein writes, "their traditional role as direct, secure employers to pursue their branding dreams."[24] "Direct, secure employers"? It would be news to workers laid off or fearing lay-offs long before the logo take-off of the 1980s that the "traditional role" of capitalists was to offer security of employment. It's as if what Engels found in Manchester in 1844 was the Good Old Days. Klein's insistence that the real problem is brands means she has to overvalue the "old-fashioned idea that a manufacturer is responsible for its own workforce."[25]

This is indeed a very old-fashioned idea. It is old enough to reproduce that "organic conception, stressing interrelation and interdependence," whose opposition to crude laissez-faire Raymond Williams termed "one of the most important facts about English social thinking in the nineteenth century."[26] It's a bit surprising to find something so close to George Eliot's ethic of service and top-down solicitude, to the forthright paternalism of Gaskell's *North and South* (Lodge's model in *Nice Work*), reappearing now in the most up-to-date anti-sweatshop discourse. But it is not, I think, an absolute mistake. "As frustrating and irrational as it is," Randy Shaw writes, "the stance that 'all corporations are evil so there's nothing to be done' has been a remarkably effective rationalization for inaction in the face of injustice."[27] This is the commonsense version of "everything is political," and it too leaves people thinking, "in that case, *nothing* is political, and so why bother?" In other words, a relative, compromised criterion will have to be posited according to which some corporations are less evil than others, or else inaction will triumph. The willingness to accept, for rhetorical purposes, the somewhat mythic figure of the responsible employer offering secure employment makes sense as a way of opening up the landscape to action.

This is a backhanded case for the continued political relevance of the "Culture and Society" tradition, which turns up unexpectedly in the very middle of today's timeliest discourse of political action. It is also a case to understand action itself in a less theological sense, a sense that is not irreconcilable with the humble acknowledgment that (as novelists like Lodge and Eliot have suggested) those who want to understand the world are not thereby privileged to stand outside and against the division of labor. If action is just as politically confused and promiscuous as Mulhern says culture is, then action cannot serve scholars and critics of culture as a repository and arbiter of virtue. And the attempt to make it so serve is politically counterproductive for academics in that it can only appear to potential allies as a claim to moral superiority. To call on ourselves to aim our work at "action" or "activism" is to imply that we can have the singular good fortune to live, even potentially, a fusion of high moral principles with the universal need to make a living, a fusion that ordinary people could hardly dare to dream of. Listening in on this call to responsibility, the general population is likely to hear only another form of elitism. And when we need allies – and we *do* need allies, for example in order to defend the dignity of our work against its reduction to the logic of the bottom line – we will thus have reason to expect more resentment than solidarity. If action is what we want, then "action!" is not the motto we want.

I have been arguing against the sort of self-aggrandizement that often hides out in calls to activist responsibility. I hope it's clear that I'm not arguing against responsibility itself. In pointing out that moments of insight like ours into the distant workings of the world are more ordinary than we like to think, and that the weight of confusions, ambiguities, and other responsibilities that keeps ordinary people from acting on such moments is more characteristic of *us* than we like to think, I've been trying to give a more modest and more accurate sense of what our responsibilities are, but not a less binding one. The fact that even action against sweatshops must take place in a muddled zone where it's difficult at best to distinguish principled internationalism from scary nationalism can stand as one piece of evidence, among others, of the need for scholars and critics not to step out of character, but on the contrary to take up our responsibilities in the workplace, to exercise our most rigorous academically trained powers of analytic discrimination. And as far as action is concerned, there is always the imperative to do some institutional housecleaning – that is, to do what we can to ensure that we do not work in universities, libraries, museums and other cultural institutions that for many of our colleagues will function, as they are under more and more pressure to do, like intellectual sweatshops.[28]

*     *     *

I began this essay by speaking about the division of labor and suggesting that the effort to perceive one's place in it offers a contemporary experience of the sublime. The critic who is most associated with this suggestion is Fredric Jameson. Indeed, Jameson is criticized on just this point by Gayatri Chakravorty Spivak in her *A Critique of Postcolonial Reason*. "It should . . . be clear," Spivak says," that Jameson's fable about unrepresentable technology leading to a (generally unsatisfactory) paranoid social practice, a (satisfactory if correctly understood) schizophrenic aesthetic practice, and cognitive (not 'moral') political practice, is not a complete rupture with Kant's Analytic of the Sublime."[29] To put this more crudely: in the face of global capital,

Jameson fails to imagine any satisfactory politics and offers instead the compensatory satisfactions, such as they are, of cognitive and above all aesthetic practice.

If this is true, there are extenuating circumstances. Among them is the difficulty of arriving at anything like a satisfactory politics under present global conditions – a shared difficulty. When heavy industry moves from Manchester and Milwaukee to Mexico and Malaysia, the map of political possibilities becomes more complicated for Mexicans and Malaysians as well. The complications are different, of course, but they share the challenge of seeing, speaking, and acting transnationally. And it is at this point that expertise in cognitive and aesthetic practice can properly claim to be of use, and even of significance.

In the final chapter of *Postmodernism, or, The Cultural Logic of Late Capitalism*, Jameson concedes that the word "reification," understood as "the transformation of social relations into things," "probably directs attention in the wrong direction for us today." He sees more relevance, however, in a second definition of the word,

> "the effacement of the traces of production" from the object itself, from the commodity thereby produced. This sees the matter from the standpoint of the consumer: it suggests the kind of guilt people are freed from if they are able not to remember the work that went into their toys and furnishings. Indeed, the point of having your own object world, and walls and muffled distance or relative silence all around you, is to forget about all those innumerable others for a while; you don't want to have to think about Third World women every time you pull yourself up to your word processor, or all the other lower-class people with their lower-class lives when you decide to use or consume your other luxury products: it would be like having voices inside your head.[30]

The paragraph that immediately follows, however, makes the opposite point, and makes it about art: "The reification of culture itself is evidently a somewhat different matter, since those products are 'signed'; nor, in consuming culture, do we particularly want, let alone need, to forget the human producer." This frank admission changes everything. If in the case of art we don't need to forget the human producer, if we actively desire to *remember* the human producer, if we want to see traces of production, indeed will pay good money in order to have those voices echoing in our heads, then why mightn't we go on to want the same thing with other products as well, products that are not classified as art? The Lodge and Chast texts I've been discussing, taken together with the successes of anti-sweatshop campaigns based unapologetically in the psychology and ethics of the consumer, offer evidence that consumers don't come in two entirely distinct types, one artistic and the other unartistic – that there exists, in other words, a certain desire to live with voices inside our heads, not just among intellectuals, and not just when contemplating works of art. This desire seems to mark a certain political possibility in the humanities. There are certainly less feasible and less consequential goals for humanistic education than the cultivating, augmenting, and channeling of the desire for voices inside our heads. There are also worse ways of thinking about political action in the narrow sense.

Curiously, sublimity and sweatshops turn up together again on the back cover of Spivak's *A Critique of Postcolonial Reason*. The cover tells us that the book "ranges from Kant's analytic of the sublime to child labor in Bangladesh." Yet this is not quite so wide a range as Harvard University Press appears to think, for both the discussion of the sublime in chapter one and the discussion of child labor in the conclusion are versions of the same argument. Questioning the "interested use of 'child labor' as a way of blocking export from developing countries," Spivak accuses anti-sweatshop activists who call for boycotts against the Bangladesh garment industry of blindly helping to protect Northern jobs and markets. "The transnationally illiterate benevolent feminist of the North supports this wholeheartedly, with 'ignorant goodwill'."[31] The ignorant goodwill of Northern progressives is also the theme of the "philosophy" chapter, which treats the figure of the Aboriginal in Kant. So-called "New Hollanders" and "inhabitants of Tierra del Fuego . . . bubble up in the cauldron of Kant's contempt," as Spivak nicely puts it, because Kant needs examples of "man in the raw," man lacking in culture and therefore unable to appreciate the sublime. Only those lacking in culture will allow him to define the process by which culture is capable of manufacturing a rational subject, which offers in turn "a justification for Europe to be the global legislator." Kant's "global project for the subject . . . of reason" is "the project of transforming [the New Hollander and the Fuegan] from the raw to the philosophical."[32]

According to Spivak, Kant's analytic of the sublime does precisely the same thing that Western human rights discourse does when addressed to Bangladeshi sweatshops: it flattens out the complexity and difference of Third World society to suit a First World standard of ethical rationality. But it is unclear that Kant was always and everywhere committed to that standard. He turns to the aesthetic in his *Critique of Judgment,* as I suggested hastily above, not because he wants to defend rationality but precisely because he can see that the rational community he desires will never come about by means of submission to rationality. People must be induced or cajoled by other means to bind themselves together. They are more likely to do so, he speculated, by means of their uncoerced and individual yet also universalizing act of appreciating the beautiful than by means of their rational obedience to the good. In other words, Kant's aesthetics can be read as his political theory, a theory rendered necessary by the political insufficiencies of Reason. According to this view, Kant would be saying that political action has to take on the limits and confusions of the aesthetic. For if it does not, if it attempts to embody and enact Reason itself, it risks producing effects which are rationally and ethically undesirable.

But what this alternative account of Kantian sublimity seeks to accomplish is to support Spivak's own argument concerning political action against Asian sweatshops, and to do so by showing how broadly she agrees with Jameson. What Spivak complains about, in Northern anti-sweatshop campaigns, is the simplification of action whereby "the only imperative – 'What You Can Do in India' – is boycotts and sanctions." In calling for resistance to sweatshops that would be accompanied by long-term "infrastructural followup,"[33] Spivak is trying, one might say, to theorize a politics in which Northerners would have to forgo the illusory satisfactions of immediate action in a domain of ostensible political transparency and ethical universality. Like Jameson, she writes in or near the mode of the Kantian sublime. She insists that constraints, obscurities, hesitations, and self-questionings, the inevitable by-products of capitalism in its global mode, must be factored back into the tempting simplicity of action, a simplicity that, as she points out, has not become less treacherous in the epoch of humanitarian intervention and human rights. For this "sinking back into ourselves" is what politics itself requires, even and especially at a global scale. Of course, this sinking back also serves to confirm the "emotional satisfaction" we derive from intellectual work in all its lonely specificity, the slow and patient labor of filling in the steps, both analytically and politically, between the perceptual and emotional jolt and the outlet in action that may or may not be found to suit it. But if the public intellectual is to pursue something higher than publicity, this continuing communion with privacy is an inescapable part of her task.

## Notes

1  David Lodge, *Nice Work* (London: Secker and Warburg, 1988), pp. 192–3.

2  Ibid., p. 193.

3  I owe the Baudelaire reference (from "L'Invitation au Voyage") to Philip Fisher, *Hard Facts: Setting and Form in the American Novel* (Oxford, New York: Oxford University Press, 1987), p. 133.

4  Immanuel Kant, *Critique of Judgment*, J.H. Bernard, trans. (London: Collier Macmillan, 1951), pp. 88, 91.

5  See Gary Shapiro, "From the Sublime to the Political: Some Historical Notes," *New Literary History* 16:2 (Winter 1985): 213–35. Apropos of this "sinking back," Shapiro finds in both the Burkean and the Kantian sublime "a dual structure of communication and the possibility of withdrawal which constitute society" (p. 219). See also Jonathan Arac, "The Media of Sublimity: Johnson and Lamb on *King Lear*," *Studies in Romanticism*, 26 (Summer 1987): 209–20. Arac argues that this valued moment when our usual categories break down and we find ourselves suddenly defenseless in the face of the new is also about the paradoxical comforts of non-realization.

6  "Wal-Mart's Shirts of Misery," a report by the National Labor Committee (New York: National Labor Committee, July 1999).

7  George Eliot, *Middlemarch* (New York: Norton, [1871–72] 1977), p. 544. Dorothea's direct dependence on these people is not really clarified by this passage, which does not capture them in the moment of productive labor, nor state, like the Lodge passage, that but for that labor she would not enjoy good food, clothing, or shelter. On the sublime in *Middlemarch*, see Neil Hertz, *The End of the Line: Essays on Psychoanalysis and the Sublime* (New York: Columbia University Press, 1985). ch. 5.

8  *Middlemarch*, p. 135.

9  Steven Marcus, "Literature and Social Theory: Starting in with George Eliot," in *Representations: Essays on Literature and Society* (New York: Columbia University Press, 1975, 1990), pp. 183–213, (quote, p. 204). As a female member of the landed gentry, Dorothea is neither expected nor permitted to work for a living; she lives purely in the domain of consumption. This passage can thus also be construed as her revolt against her exclusion from the domain of production.

10  Raymond Williams, *Culture and Society, 1780–1950* (London: Chatto and Windus, 1958), pp. 108–9.

11  "Are My Hands Clean?" *Sweet Honey and the Rock*; lyrics and music by Bernice Johnson Reagon, Songtalk Publishing Co., 1985:

I wear garments touched by hands from all over the world
35% cotton, 65% polyester, the journey begins in Central America
In the cotton fields of El Salvador

In a province soaked in blood, pesticide-sprayed workers toil in a
  broiling sun
Pulling cotton for two dollars a day
[. . . .]
Far from the Port-au-Prince palace
Third World women toil doing piece work to Sears specifications
For three dollars a day my sisters make my blouse
It leaves the Third World for the last time
Coming back into the sea to be sealed in plastic for me
This third world sister
And I go to the Sears department store where I buy my blouse
On sale for 20% discount.

12  Francis Mulhern *Culture/Metaculture* (London: Routledge, 2000).
13  Quoted in Mulhern, p. 66.
14  It is perhaps worth noting here that the division of labor, while responsible of course for the disguising of systematic economic inequality, is also responsible for the beginnings of a positive attitude toward social difference:

> Different kinds of different human beings appeared to be able to live harmoniously with each other. Indeed, it became possible to *define* a society as the harmonious interplay of very different kinds of human beings living very different kinds of lives without the social whole dissolving into chaos. It takes something like a leap of the imagination to grasp the difference between the old view and the new. The new view meant that differences between men were socially integrative. The old view that a society was better the more its members were the same was simply overturned. J.S. McClelland, *A History of Western Political Thought* (London, New York: Routledge, 1996), p. 433.

Durkheim, who looked more favorably on the division of labor than the "Culture and Society" tradition, nevertheless joined with it in defining the role of the intellectual in relation to the division of labor. As Frank Parkin writes, "Durkheim placed a lot of faith in people's willingness to bear burdens provided they could see themselves as part of some meaningful and just design. His entire theory of the division of labour as the basis of solidarity depended upon the general readiness to make such a connection. If individuals saw their daily toil in isolation, rather than as one important element in a purposeful whole, social solidarity would be sabotaged by the division of labour," Frank Parkin, *Durkheim* (New York: Oxford University Press, 1992) pp. 64–5. We are rescued from fragmentation only by consciousness of the whole, and it is intellectuals who specialize in providing this consciousness.

15 Dana Frank, *Buy American: The Untold Story of Economic Nationalism* (Boston: Beacon Press, 1999) p. ix.

16 As Kim Moody notes: "the campaign against PNTR status for China [was] really about the fear of rising, ever-cheaper imports, not human rights." And he goes on:

> There is also more than a little hypocrisy in singling out China's labor rights record with its implication that labor rights in the United States – or Mexico, or South Korea – are some sort of model ... Finally, there is the fact that focusing exclusively on China brings out the jingo and the cold warrior still under the skin of many labor leaders. This was exemplified by Teamster President Jimmy Hoffa, who invited Pat Buchanan to speak at a Teamster rally on April 12. (Kim Moody, "Global Capitalism and Economic Nationalism, 1: Protectionism or Solidarity?", *Against the Current*, 15,3 [July/August 2000]): 34–98 (quote, pp. 35–6); see also Kim Moody, "Global Capital and Economic Nationalism, 2: Finding Protection in the Crowd", *Against the Current*, 15, 4 (September/October 2000): 26–30.

17 Randy Shaw, *Reclaiming America: Nike, Clean Air, and the New National Activism* (Berkeley: University of California Press, 1999), p. 1.

18 Naomi Klein, *No Logo: Taking Aim at the Brand Bullies* (New York: Picador USA, 1999), p. 198.

19 Barbara Ehrenreich, "Maid to Order," *Harper's* (April 2000), pp. 59–70, quote p. 69. See also Ehrenreich's *Nickel and Dimed: On (Not) Getting By in America* (New York: Metropolitan Books, 2001). Ehrenreich's insistence on the working, cleaning body can be balanced by Ann Cvetkovich's analysis of sweatshop rhetoric in *Capital*. Cvetkovich sees Marx using the sensationalism of the suffering body even as his analysis demonstrates that the suffering body is *not* the key to capital's working. Ann Cvetkovich, *Mixed Feelings: Feminism, Mass Culture, and Victorian Sensationalism* (New Brunswick, NJ: Rutgers University Press, 1992), pp. 165–97.

20 Ehrenreich is writing about corporate housecleaning agencies that systematically overwork and underpay their employees. It is to be assumed that a private individual who chooses to pay good wages for housecleaning, however uncomfortable the exchange might be, would at least avoid the sweatshop charge.

21 Ehrenreich, "Maid to Order," p. 70.

22 Klein, *No Logo*, p. 3.

23 Ibid., p. xviii.

24 Ibid., p. 441.

25 Ibid., p. 197.

26 Williams, *Culture and Society*, p. 140.

27 Shaw, *Reclaiming America*, p. 21.

28  This will mean after-hours work; it can't be the content of our teaching and writing.
29  Gayatri Chakravorty Spivak, *A Critique of Postcolonial Reason: Toward a History of the Vanishing Present* (Cambridge MA: Harvard University Press, 1999), p. 325.
30  Fredric Jameson, *Postmodernism, or, The Cultural Logic of Late Capitalism* (Durham, NC: Duke University Press, 1991), pp. 314–15. The passage continues: "indeed, it 'violates' the intimate space of your privacy and your extended body. For a society that wants to forget about class, therefore, reification in this consumer-packaging sense is very functional indeed."
31  Spivak, *A Critique*, pp. 415–16. Spivak seems to think the sort of subject represented by contemporary feminists, and the sort of subject contemporary feminists seek to produce, resembles Jane Eyre in the sense that she has a missionary zeal to act, even when action involves the objectification of the Third World woman. For better or worse, I don't think this is accurate. The teaching of culture can certainly politicize, but the sort of consciousness it produces is more likely to be unhappy. If we collectively can be said to teach commitment, we also teach hesitation.
32  Spivak, *A Critique*, pp. 26, 28n., 32–3, 36.
33  Ibid., pp. 418n., 420.

# Chapter 9

# "Every Fruit-juice Drinker, Nudist, Sandal-wearer . . .": Intellectuals as Other People[1]

## Stefan Collini

I

When in 1937 Victor Gollancz published George Orwell's *The Road to Wigan Pier* as part of the Left Book Club, he felt obliged to write a Foreword which attempted to disarm some of Orwell's more stinging criticisms of the Left. In the course of this uncomfortable exercise, Gollancz tried to explain away some of Orwell's more intemperate remarks by saying "the truth is that he is at one and the same time an extreme intellectual and a violent anti-intellectual."[2] When Orwell eventually read this Foreword (after the book had been published while he was in Spain), he wrote to Gollancz to say that "I could have answered some of the criticisms you made."[3] It is not hard to imagine some of the answers Orwell might have given – about, for example, his descriptions of working-class life – but it is more difficult to see how he might have responded to this particular observation. The tension between being (in Gollancz's formula) "an extreme intellectual and a violent anti-intellectual" repeatedly surfaces in Orwell's writing, to the point, in fact, of becoming one of its tonally structuring characteristics, and this is not the least of the reasons for taking him as my point of departure.

There has probably been no major writer in English who used the terms "intellectuals" and "intelligentsia" as frequently as George Orwell. Anyone who has read extensively in his essays and journalism will recognize the tendency to flog his hobby-horses unmercifully, and on few subjects was he as finger-jabbingly insistent as on the alleged failings of "the intelligentsia," more especially "the Left intelligentsia." Although, as will soon become clear, this essay is not going to be *about* Orwell, there are at least two reasons for beginning with him. First, Orwell probably did more than any other single writer in the middle of the twentieth century to shape and harden attitudes towards intellectuals in Britain. His iconic status both as courageous truth-teller and as champion of the individual in the face of the totalitarian tendencies of modern states has meant that his writings helped to shape a particular semantic field, in which freedom, honesty, and plain speech are contrasted with tyranny, ideological fashion, and pretension, and in which the term "intellectuals" is strongly associated with the latter of these two poles. But, beyond this, Orwell also provides a notable example of a larger pattern or problem, namely the fact that nearly all extended attacks on intellectuals as a category are by those who, in at least some senses of the term, would have to be classified as other intellectuals. This always raises, or should raise, the question of where such critics situate themselves and on what grounds they claim exemption from the strictures directed against their fellow-intellectuals.

This question poses itself most pressingly in considering that section of *Wigan Pier* in which Orwell purports to be explaining why the "normal" (his unblinkingly coercive term) middle-class person was put off by socialism. The nub of Orwell's argument here was that "as with the Christian religion, the worst advertisement for socialism is its adherents." At this point, clearly, the authorial voice is not locating itself among those "adherents," and this sense of distance increases as he warms to his theme. Having more or less explicitly equated socialists and intellectuals, he went on: "There is the horrible – the really disquieting – prevalence of cranks wherever Socialists are gathered together," and then, notoriously, "One sometimes gets the impression that the mere words 'Socialism' and 'Communism' draw towards them with magnetic force every fruit-juice drinker, nudist, sandal-wearer, sex-maniac, Quaker, 'Nature Cure' quack, pacifist and feminist in England."[4]

Now, of course, the use of such incantatory hyperbole is one of the polemicist's time-honored weapons, but a characteristic limitation of Orwell's writing becomes evident if we juxtapose this passage to, say, one of Nietzsche's wonderful tirades about how the man who has become truly free "spurns the contemptible sort of well-being dreamed of by shop-keepers, Christians, cows, women, Englishmen, and other democrats".[5] Both lists want their flagrant outrageousness to be at once registered and forgiven, but Nietzsche's list was genuinely provocative precisely because it ran so counter to received sensibilities. Its offhand inclusiveness could be shocking because it suggested that, beneath the exaggeration, a wholly new moral perspective was being hinted at which cut across established categories. By contrast, Orwell's list, for all its deliberate comic or rhetorical effect, is in fact a compendium of widely accepted middle-brow prejudices. Indeed, the conventional status of his list is underlined by the fact that when he tries to repeat the effect in subsequent paragraphs, he simply rounds off an abbreviated version with "etc."

In attempting to ridicule middle-class supporters of socialism, Orwell emphatically endorses the popular notion of the "crank." A "crank," he went on to spell out, is by definition "a person out of touch with common humanity." By implication, the vantage-point from which he is writing is that of someone who is more in touch with "common humanity" than are most socialists and intellectuals, someone who is definitely not a "crank." But in fact, of course, he was at the time engaging in precisely the same activities as were the "cranks," attending ILP branch meetings, lecturing at Adelphi summer schools, and so on.[6] And so just as his prose never offers itself as expressing what "we cranks" are like, so he never seems to be speaking from the point of view of "we intellectuals." Orwell's writing in general made inauthenticity or bad faith the fundamental fault of the intellectuals, but that writing was itself shot through with a systematic inauthenticity of its own in so consistently positioning him outside the group to which, by the very fact of his writing, he so clearly belonged.

For all the directness of Orwell's attacks on intellectuals, one is nonetheless left, as so often when encountering exaggerated, obsessive behavior, with the feeling that there must be more than meets the eye here, that the purported object of criticism cannot quite be the real one. In some ways, this sense of displaced hostility or anxiety is a recurrent feature of the more or less continuous criticisms made of writers and journalists, especially those of radical leanings, stretching from (to go no further back) the conservative Romantics' denunciations of "mere opinion" right up to contemporary dismissals of "the chattering classes." This repetitive litany expresses a distaste for, even a weariness at, the unending circulation of "views," "comment," "ideas," "theories," "opinions," and so on. Reading these laments, one detects – it is particularly marked in Orwell, but not of course in Orwell alone – a deep yearning for a state of affairs that is quiet, settled, solid, genuine. In all this, the contemporary world is clearly figured as being marked by the opposite of these qualities. What has to be recognized, therefore, is that intellectuals – the noise they make, the discord they express, the attention they attract – are taken to be one striking embodiment of the distressingly open-ended nature of modernity, just as they are at the same time expressive of what is presumed to be the increasing removal of life from its anchoring in the natural and material world.

This helps explain why there is no place for such parasitic, opinionated creatures in that archaic ideal commonwealth, the half-memory of which always lurks behind the political criticism of Orwell the antique moralist. In this kind of dream of an English Eden there is never either need or room for those who only stand and carp. In so far as Orwell indulged this strain in himself – and it was, of course, partially offset by other, less culpable strains – he encouraged an undiscriminating hostility to intellectuals as such, and he was then surely guilty of that most unlovely and least defensible of inner contradictions, the anti-intellectualism of the intellectual.

I begin with Orwell because, in addition to supplying me with my title, he provides a strategically important example of what is a common feature of writing (by intellectuals) about (other) intellectuals, and the theme I want to pursue in this essay is precisely the way in which the literature on this topic is bedevilled by the tendency always to represent intellectuals as Other People – sometimes as idealized, romanticized others, more often perhaps as derided or derogated others, and very commonly as only really flourishing elsewhere, either in the past or in other societies. And I want to suggest that there is a dialectical relationship between these different forms of distancing, which is expressive of tensions within the concept of the intellectual itself (in one of the main senses of that protean term which I'll clarify in a moment), and that it represents an uncomfortableness with, and at the extremes an incapacity to acknowledge, the sheer ordinariness of the role of the intellectual. Many of the statements about intellectuals one hears from scholars and writers – including, I have to say, from one or two contributors to this volume – seem to me to be over-heated and self-dramatizing; many of the views one encounters in the press and society more generally fall, on the other hand, into being too easily hostile and dismissive. Identifying and diagnosing these patterns may be one useful step towards accurately representing the diverse, ordinary activities of intellectuals in the here and now, and thus a way of resisting the related urges to glamourize and to disdain.

## II

Reading extensively in the literature on any topic, one will, inevitably, encounter a certain amount of repetition and overlap, but the sheer predictability of so much of the writing on intellectuals is truly awful to behold. I have sometimes thought that I could earn a steady income by marketing a software package which, used correctly, would guarantee the production of a whole series of publishable 1,200-word articles on the subject, so limited does the collection of journalistic tropes appear to be – real intellectuals are only found elsewhere, in other countries, in the past, or in the mind; intellectuals aren't speaking out when they should be; intellectuals should keep quiet for once; once upon a time intellectuals were important; only intellectuals have ever thought intellectuals were important; happy is the land which has no intellectuals; why does Britain, uniquely, have no intellectuals; and, most commonly, some variant on what one might call "the 3-D version" – the decline, disappearance, or death of the intellectual. And there is a similarly limited repertoire of concluding flourishes: "pygmies in the shadow of giants," "being awkward is what they're for," "Socrates as role model, hemlock and all," "speak out or sell out," and so on. If the term "ivory tower" does not appear somewhere, then it is just possible that a little genuine thinking may be going on.[7]

Some of this is, of course, the necessary condition of journalism: as print is increasingly challenged by other media as the source of *news*, so the need for a thousand words of more or less readable *opinion* grows: turning out a piece on the theme of "intellectuals" might almost seem the would-be columnist's equivalent of passing the driving test. Some of it reflects the inescapable guilty conscience of journalists – the sense that serious or sustained thinking is being done elsewhere on the topics about which they hold forth so readily – and bad conscience usually results in obsession and aggression, directed outwards as well as in. Some of it reflects the plasticity of the term itself, the range of not usually carefully discriminated meanings it embraces, a semantic playground where everyone can have at least one ride. Some of it is the local form taken by meditations on national identity, the intractable task of attempting to sift a distinctive reality out of the historical detritus of image and cliché. And some of it, finally, is surely a sign that there is a genuinely important subject here: it is, ultimately, nothing less than the question of whether thought, enquiry, imagination, pursued to the highest level, issue in any wisdom about how we ought to live. Very often, the term "intellectuals" marks a space in which needs and anxieties are expressed about the relation between the daily round and the ends of life, and about what it might mean for there to be some source of cultural authority on such matters.

Although academic writing on the topic usually manages, as it should, to be less merely topical and (somewhat) less parochial, it is, in its own way, almost equally repetitive – the rise of a new class, the comparison with France, the decline of an old class, the comparison with France, the level of social integration of elites, the comparison with France, the impact of European emigrés, the comparison with France, the failure to be a true intelligentsia. . . . In Britain, the Victorian sages (Carlyle, Mill, Arnold, and Ruskin), will receive honorable mention, and then attention will be focused on the failings of the usual suspects – the Utilitarians, the Fabians, Bloomsbury, the Auden generation, the Angry Young Men. . . . And, with a show of rigor, the same narrow band of idealizing definitions will be trotted out by way of contrast: intellectuals are/ought to be critical, dissident, oppositional, independent, outspoken, tellers of unpopular truths. . . .

And in both the journalistic and the academic literature one figure will almost always make an appearance, causing one to wonder whether the inclusion of such a cameo role might not be some kind of requirement insisted upon by the actors' union, Equity. At some point, a short, bespectacled, wall-eyed Frenchman will come on stage, climb up on a piece of antique furniture labeled "barricades," and proceed to demonstrate the correct way to unite intellect and politics, while a voice-over laments that his like is not to be found in our time. Scholars may demonstrate time and again how poorly he in fact played this role, or how exaggerated is his reputation, or how pernicious his example or unrepresentative his status; but no amount of historical analysis, it seems, can do much to sever the now established association between the mention of the noun "intellectual" and the appearance of the little wall-eyed chap.

The term "intellectuals" itself is part of the problem here, since in Britain, in particular, the word triggers some very deep cultural reflexes. At its appearance, people immediately sense pretentiousness, arrogance: on most of its outings, "so-called" travels with it like a bodyguard, never far away, even if not immediately in view. Those who accept the label can seem rather too self-conscious about their role, a little too intent on parading a conviction of their own seriousness. As a result, in Britain the term is always having to cope with the resistance its presence engenders, making it difficult for it to move unselfconsciously in the society of other words.

But meanwhile, it is assumed (enviously or smugly according to taste), that, somewhere else, intellectuals do as they do: they go about speaking for the oppressed, vindicating human dignity, articulating national identity, outfacing absolutism. And by what means do they encompass these great ends? By writing, meeting, writing, signing, writing, talking, writing, demonstrating, writing, transgressing, writing . . . , calling up the heavily armored units of treatises and monographs to support the first wave of articles, yomping from issue to issue, planting phrases in public places; adepts of saturation journalism, commandos of the word, crack essayists, optimists of the pen, the Samurai of the keyboard.

It may help to lower the temperature a little just to register that there are at least three senses of the noun "intellectuals" used and confused in current usage. First, there is what might be called the sociological sense, referring to a whole range of socio-occupational categories, extending, in large advanced societies, into millions. Secondly, there is what may be called the subjective sense, where the focus is upon an individual's level of interest in or attitude toward ideas, regardless of their occupation or social role. And third, there is what has now become the dominant sense, which we may call the cultural, where the term designates those figures who, on the basis of some recognized standing in a creative, scholarly, or other non-instrumental activity, are also accorded the opportunity to address a wider audience on matters of general concern. Not only do these senses co-exist, but any given usage of the term may be something of a hybrid, the resonances of one or more of the basic senses becoming attached to what is at bottom a different sense. Thus, where "intellectuals" is being used (as it now most frequently is) in the third, cultural sense, there can be a certain confusion in talking of "the public role of the intellectual": insofar as individuals occupy the role of the intellectual, they are *by definition* playing a "public role," since it is precisely the movement between their initial specialized or creative activity on the one hand and addressing the wider audience on the other that constitutes the activity of the intellectual. In this sense, to speak of "the public role of intellectuals" risks being as pleonastic as speaking of, say, "the military role of soldiers." Moreover, writers who attempt to speak out to such a wider audience are *thereby* acting as intellectuals, so that, in this context at least, we cannot strictly speak of "writers *and* intellectuals"; we would at best have to say "writers and other

209

intellectuals." But these hybrid usages are no doubt too well-established to be dislodged simply by clearer analysis. Similarly, the term
'the public intellectual," which has established itself in American usage
in the past couple of decades and is now being used with increasing
frequency in Britain as well, indicates a continuing unsteadiness in the
use of the noun alone. "Public intellectual" tends to be used in the
United States of someone who, from an academic or creative base,
addresses a non-specialist public on matters of general concern, often
(though by no means always) policy matters. This reflects the tradition, more widely established in the United States than in Europe, of
using "intellectual" to refer primarily to "college professors." As this
category has hugely expanded in the late twentieth century, consti-
tuting a kind of "academic public sphere" of its own, the term "public
intellectual" has come into play to identify those who step outside this
sphere.[8] "Public intellectual," therefore, is increasingly the term that is
used to refer to "intellectuals" in the third, cultural sense.

## III

I want now briefly to indicate some of the forms taken by the
tendency to represent intellectuals as Other People, where they are
either far more full of themselves than we are, or far more wonderful
than we are: where they are either foreigners or dead. Certainly in
Britain for most of the twentieth century, the noun "intellectual" has
remained five syllables in search of an owner, consistently *dis*owned
as a form of self-description. Let me here just offer three very brief
examples.

Many foreign observers would probably have identified Bertrand
Russell as the best-known intellectual in Britain in the first two-thirds
of the twentieth century. But any reader of the repetitive and under-
researched literature on intellectuals in Britain would almost certainly
have encountered the following comment by Russell himself: "I have
never called myself an intellectual, and nobody has ever dared to call
me one in my presence. I think an intellectual may be defined as a
person who pretends to have more intellect than he has, and I hope
this definition does not fit me." It is a characteristically perverse remark
which has now served several tours of duty as an illustration of the
negative connotations of the term in English, though without any
source ever being given.

Only if one happens to light upon the correspondence columns of *Encounter* in June 1955 can a point of origin be traced, and it reveals incidentally that Russell never actually "said" or "published" this remark. Referring to the article in *Encounter* earlier that year on intellectuals in Britain by Edward Shils, H.O. Alexander wrote in to report that, "four years ago," he had written to several "prominent British intellectuals" specifically asking them "whether they agreed with this description [of themselves], and inviting them to volunteer some general observations." The oft-quoted passage was Russell's reply to this enquiry, an enquiry which was surely always likely to provoke the countersuggestible Russell into such deliberate mischief, and his reply was then quoted in Alexander's letter on this later occasion.[9] The fact is that when, at other moments during his exceptionally long writing career, Russell was not being provoked by such acts of labeling by others, he did not feel the need to issue such noisy denials, although even then his attitude to the term was at best equivocal.

Someone who certainly regarded Russell as an intellectual supplies my second example. The historian G.M. Trevelyan expressed a brisk impatience with "those who think of themselves as intellectuals," and in an address delivered in 1944 in honor of his friend John Buchan, Trevelyan made it clear that he admired Buchan because the latter "despised literary coteries," and avoided "the squabbles and narrowness to which 'intellectuals' of all periods are too prone." And more generally, as he wrote to his daughter in 1942: "As to 'intellectuals,' . . . one of the greatest disappointments of my life has been the decadence of that class (if you can call it a class) of which I first became aware when Lytton Strachey came up to Cambridge."[10] The characteristics Trevelyan ascribed to Strachey could also have doubled as a kind of check-list of all that the hard-working, hard-walking Englishman of his generation found disagreeable about "intellectuals." What makes Trevelyan a particularly instructive figure in this instance, it seems to me, is the way in which he helped to sustain a particular idiom of "manliness" at the heart of historical accounts of English national identity deep into the middle of the twentieth century, firmly attaching to "intellectuals" the opprobrium of being cliquey, feline, unmanly, untrustworthy, and unhealthy: in a word, foreign.

My third example comes from another historian, though R.H. Tawney was at least as well known in his lifetime as a social critic and radical political activist, one who deliberately linked his scholarship to a fundamental moral critique of contemporary society. But listen to

Tawney in a lecture in 1949, as he warmed to one of his most cherished themes: the need for large, simple truths to be stated in large, simple terms. His topics on this occasion were History and Literature, and at one point he observed with mild sarcasm:

> Both offer ample opportunities for finished exhibitions of the great art of complicating the simple and obscuring the obvious by which the authentic intellectual proves his title to that proud name. I observe these gymnastics with admiration and awe; but a consciousness that the stratosphere is not my spiritual home deters me from imitating them.[11]

This is the classic topos of scorn disguised as false humility, a kind of back-handed compliment to one's own down-to-earth style; the sardonic use of "intellectual" is here readily available for the purpose of disparaging such heady abstractions, and it allows a sense of complacent collusion between Tawney and his listeners.

A description could, of course, be given of each of these three figures in which they are, rightly, represented as among the leading British intellectuals of their time, even as their denials illustrate the tenacious power of a certain discursive tradition. Obviously, much more could be said about the tone and force of each of these passages, but the pattern of consistent self-distancing is striking, and could of course be illustrated with numerous other examples.

Let me now turn to what I regard as the obverse of this form of distancing, namely the tendency to romanticize or dramatize the role of the intellectual. I can be briefer here since the evidence of this tendency is, as I have already suggested, all around us. One of the most common failings of this literature is that of stipulative definition, where a commentator attempts to build certain idealized features into the very meaning of the term itself. I take, almost at random, the following sequence of sentences from a recent work on the topic where the noun "the intellectual" is the subject, followed by the verb "to be," followed by a whole host of not obviously compatible predicates: the intellectual is someone who "tells the truth"; the intellectual is "the voice of the voiceless"; the intellectual is in "permanent opposition to the status quo"; the intellectual is the real or symbolic "exile"; the intellectual is someone who is both "modest" and "effective," and so on.[12] Or take the recent dictum by another well-known commentator on the subject that "the intellectual should live in truth."[13] One might as well say that the intellectual should live in Basingstoke: intellectuals have no monopoly of truth, nor are all other roles in society functionally committed to error and deceit.

Similarly, it should also be clear that it is not part of the *concept* of "the intellectual" that persons so described should be "dissident," "oppositional," "marginal," and so on. There are good historical reasons why these characteristics are often associated with the use of the term, but they are precisely *associated* with it, they are not intrinsic to it. It is, of course, true that, insofar as intellectuals address a particular issue from a more general perspective, there is a sense in which they will always be engaged in something which may be described as "criticism." The very act of "placing" an issue, of taking a more analytical or comparative perspective on it, is in effect a form of distancing and a corrective to more limited or one-eyed views, and to this extent all redescription has a critical edge. But it is the tiredest cliché of the radical ideologue's trade to equate criticism in this generic sense with being "oppositional" or "marginal." Still less plausible is the old claim that the intellectual stands "outside" society, wherever that is or could be: a piece of pure romanticization, often implicitly involving self-romanticization.

A similar elision between social realities and political idealizations seems to me present in the claim that "genuine" intellectuals must be "unattached." This usage was at one point relatively common within the confines of sociological theory, especially that developed in the United States out of German sources. The most notable instance here was Karl Mannheim, who took over from Alfred Weber the term *"freischwebende Intelligenz,'* glossed by him in the English translation of *Ideology and Utopia* as 'the socially unattached intelligentsia," an "unanchored, *relatively* classless stratum."[14] But more often assertions about "the independent intellectual" do not presuppose this, or any other, general sociological theory. At the heart of all such claims is the idea of "independence," of being free to be critical because not in the pay of or dependent upon the good favor of a patron or constraining institution (being "critical" or "oppositional" is here again assumed to be built into the definition).

But the truth surely is that no one can escape "attachment" in this sense: freedom from one kind of dependence (on a patron or a government) is only achieved by another kind of dependence (on a public or a family). Still, the ideal of the freelance or "independent" intellectual retains a certain glamour which clouds further analysis. Nowadays, this notion is most frequently wheeled out by way of contrast with the situation of those intellectual figures who hold posts in universities, nearly always in disparagement of the supposed conformism or caution of the latter. But, other problems with this description aside,

213

it is never clear why being, for example, shackled to the relentless rhythms of journalism and the need to cater to the tastes of a particular readership (or at least to those tastes as interpreted by an editor or proprietor) should furnish more "independence" than the relative security and freedom enjoyed by the tenured academic. Moreover, since the claim about the superiority of being "unattached" is, like most other writing about intellectuals nowadays, most often put forward by those who themselves work in universities, it also figures as part of the familiar mix of nostalgia and bad faith that I have already identified. Everyone recognizes that they themselves are "attached" in multiple ways, but somehow the fantasy lingers on that someone else, somewhere else, can escape such mundane circumstances and rise to the heights of being a "true" intellectual.

I trust it is clear that I am not denying that it may be desirable for intellectuals of various kinds to live up to high standards of various kinds; rather, I am arguing, first, that we should not build the successful achievement of such values into the very definition of the term, and, second, that we should not speak as though intellectuals were somehow the only people who have a primary concern with such matters. And there is, it seems to me, an obvious dialectical relationship between these various romantic idealizations of the intellectual and the corresponding sneering: the more the positive claims are jacked up, the more they invite the knocking response.

## IV

I want now to turn to the other main way in which intellectuals, "real" intellectuals, are figured as Other, namely the reflex of assuming that they are only really to be found in other societies or other ages, never here and now. Let me, to begin with, confine my discussion to Britain, or rather to England, since for many people, the very phrase "English intellectuals" may appear to be an oxymoron.[15] The following passage may stand in here for countless others to the same effect:

> Is there such a thing as an English intellectual? It is as well to pose the question from the start, since anyone acquainted with the habits and social position of intellectuals on the continent of Europe must have serious doubts as to whether the same word can reasonably be applied to English conditions.[16]

The sentiment is almost wearyingly familiar; this particular expression of it comes from an interesting "condition-of-England' rumination published in 1963 entitled *A State of England*, by the author and journalist Anthony Hartley. The fact that the frequently encountered claim that there are no intellectuals in England is generally advanced by those who, were they living in other societies, would unhesitatingly be recognized as intellectuals should in itself suggest that we are here dealing with something requiring explanation. It may even suggest that we are dealing with a claim which serves, in the strictest sense of the term, an ideological function – that is, that its systematic misrepresentation of reality furthers a certain collective interest. But denial in a psychological as well as sociological sense is involved here, too. When an individual insists, repeatedly and emphatically, that something is not true of them, it is hard not to speculate, even without resorting to psychoanalytic theory, about the source of the need to issue such frequent denials. Moreover, common speech has appropriated the phrase "in denial" to refer to a state of willful blindness or a condition of being unwilling to recognize the truth of bad news. But why should having certain of one's compatriots described as "intellectuals" be either bad or news?

The traditional argument about the absence of intellectuals in Britain takes many forms, but one may separate out analytically at least the following five claims (bearing in mind that each of the following claims may be made in either a critical or a complacent manner).

1.   There are no intellectuals in Britain.
2.   Intellectuals in Britain, such as they may be, do not form an intelligentsia.
3.   Intellectuals in Britain, such as they may be, are not dissident and oppositional.
4.   Intellectuals in Britain, such as they may be, are of no account, since hardly anyone pays attention to them.
5.   There used to be major intellectuals in Britain, but now they have disappeared.

When several of these claims occur in sequence, as in discussion of this topic they tend to do, they seem irresistibly reminiscent of the old joke about official responses to the allegations of the existence of labor camps in Soviet Russia, which came in the form of three propositions:

first, such camps do not exist; second, they will soon be abolished; and third, they are a good and necessary part of true Socialism.

It is a topic that invariably seems to excite stronger feelings than the historiographical issue in itself might seem to warrant. In part, this is obviously because it forms part of a long-standing national self-definition: the roots of this view can be traced back at least as far as the nineteenth-century sense of Whiggish self-congratulation on England's fortunate political history. Some of those who have wished to continue to uphold some such interpretation of British history in the twentieth century have found in the "absence thesis" one explanation of the continuing virtues of British political culture. Those who have wished to challenge this identity have, in turn, also identified this as one crucial explanatory element, and have correspondingly lamented it. In both cases the claim about the absence of intellectuals has been largely propounded *by* intellectuals, and in each case it has served their interests and constitutes an undeniable element of self-promotion. Particularly, among those who represent themselves as deploring this alleged feature of the native culture, there is also a kind of nostalgia, a yearning for a more exciting state that they have never known. Wading through the laments that in Britain the aristocracy was too adaptable, or the church was too tolerant, or the military was too apolitical, or the bourgeoisie was too reformist, to produce the need for a properly "oppositional" intelligentsia, one has to conclude that many British writers on this subject are suffering from a condition one can only call "Dreyfus-envy."

Moreover, it is assumed that this situation expresses a broader anti-intellectualism which is *peculiarly* strong in Britain. One cannot read very far in this literature without encountering the following quotation: "No people has ever distrusted and despised the intellect and intellectuals more than the British." This sentence, the crisp brutality of its conclusiveness being not the least of its charms, clearly entered the recycling chain as a result of being quoted in Richard Hofstadter's widely used *Anti-Intellectualism in American Life,* where it is credited to Leonard Woolf. In the paragraph in which the quotation occurs, Hofstadter is giving an even-handed consideration of whether anti-intellectualism is more marked in American society than elsewhere: his graceful prose allows him at one moment to appear to endorse American exceptionalism – "Perhaps Mr Woolf had not given sufficient thought to the claims of the Americans to supremacy in this respect" – and at another to appear to question it – "Although the situation of American intellectuals poses problems of special urgency and poignancy, many of their woes are the common experiences of intellectuals elsewhere."[17]

Actually, if one tracks the Woolf remark to its source, one finds that he, too, is balancing contrasting emphases. In an article which appeared in *Encounter* in 1959, the 79-year old Woolf was recalling the brilliant figures whom he knew at Trinity College, Cambridge at the turn of the century, singling out the philosophers, A.N. Whitehead, Bertrand Russell, and G.E. Moore, for the last of whom the article is a kind of obituary tribute. Woolf then goes on: "It is a remarkable fact – a superb example of our inflexible irrationality and inconsistency – that, although no people has ever despised and distrusted the intellect and intellectuals more than the British, these three philosophers were each awarded the highest and rarest of honours, the Order of Merit."[18] That does indeed appear to be a singular way of expressing scorn and distrust, though it would be entirely consonant with the case I am making here to find that a tradition of self-satisfied hostility to the *idea* of "intellectuals" has co-existed with the kind of respect for intellectual activity which is assumed to be characteristic of other societies.

Both the smug (and in political terms largely right-wing) and the complaining (and largely left-wing) each have a great deal invested in assumptions about the unique or "deviant" nature of English history, not least in the matter of intellectuals, whereas my starting-point is that we need to get away from such implicitly binary classifications, and instead attempt to identify both the common features and the specific characteristics of the activities of intellectuals in various societies. For, the truth is that each of the major societies is "exceptional" in its own terms. Familiar claims about "the peculiarity of the English" can easily be matched by comparable claims about *"der deutsche Sonderweg"* or about "American exceptionalism" or about *"la singularité française,"* and so on. Britain is indeed unique – and so is every other country. The question, of course, is whether, when viewed from a series of analytical historical perspectives, Britain emerges as consistently deviant from what can be identified as a broadly common pattern elsewhere. Discussion of the question of intellectuals has been dogged by superficial or lazy invocations of a presumed European "norm" against which the British case is to be contrasted. I would argue, though I cannot support the case here, that there turns out on closer analysis to be *no* such common pattern elsewhere: almost invariably the implicit content of the contrast is provided by a stereotyped account of the situation in just one country – France. But this, too, helps us to

217

see how the roots of this question are to be found in the dominant nineteenth-century story of British political good fortune. Even now, discussion of the issue of intellectuals in Britain is conducted in the shadow of alleged "truisms" that can in fact be traced back to the writings of figures like Burke and Tocqueville.

If one were looking for a statement to stand as a concise summary of these views, the following would seem to propose itself as an ideal candidate:

> In a country where, very significantly, the usage of the noun "intellectual" is far from being current ... intellectuals display very little sense of group identity ... and evince a long-standing disposition to remain outside political debate ... except when acting in the role of experts. ... The prestige attached to ideas and the taste for abstraction found in France is largely absent, ... and political life is characterized above all by its pragmatism. ... As a result, there is even today very little historiography on the role of intellectuals.

Nearly all the elements are present here in miniature: the unsteadiness in the use of the term itself, the absence of a sense of collective identity, the aloofness from political *engagement*, the contrast with France, the empiricist or pragmatist tradition, the corresponding lack of a historiography about intellectuals. All this may seem to underline, once again, a version of the "peculiarities of the English" in this matter.

In fact, the passage comes from an essay on the situation of intellectuals in ... *Belgium*. What is more, the collection of case-studies in which the essay appeared is full of similar remarks about the relative weakness or absence of "intellectuals" in other European countries. The essay on Germany, for example, begins: "There is practically no bibliography on intellectuals in Germany in the strict sense of the French conception of the term, despite the existence of a particularly rich actual history of intellectuals in the country." The contribution on Switzerland notes "the relatively weak public presence of intellectuals in Switzerland," and argues that "in effect, the intellectual does not figure in conceptions of Swiss society." The essay on the intellectual in Denmark concludes: "Their statements are not considered as oracles. They have a far less privileged status than their French counterparts." In fact, so common are such remarks in this collection, that one contributor very pertinently wonders "whether it is not the French model of the intellectual, listened to and respected in the world, that is the exception, while the more representative figure is the intellectual as the object of scorn or distrust."[19]

Even this brief medley of quotations suggests that the "absence thesis" may look very different indeed when seen from a comparative European perspective. In fact, as I have already argued, the bundle of assumptions and claims that go to make up the "absence thesis" are themselves already implicitly comparative, but precisely by being implicit they attempt to profit from comparison without laying themselves open to counterevidence and correction. Obviously, I cannot here attempt to analyze the *actual* position of intellectuals in different societies, but let me just give one more example of the *perceived* superiority of elsewhere by briefly considering the case of a European country that might be assumed to stand at the opposite pole in these matters from England. Italy has been particularly susceptible to French cultural influence in the modern period, and British commentators, remarking the extraordinary imperium exercised by figures such as Croce or Eco, tend to see it as a country in which intellectuals are prominent, well-treated, and effective. This is hardly the picture that emerges, however, from one well-informed recent summary of what its author refers to as "Italy's exceptionalism":

> Unlike intellectuals in other Western countries, Italian intellectuals never were sufficiently prestigious to achieve legitimation independently [sc. of their connection with power, especially political parties]. There have rarely been intellectuals in Italy as famous as their counterparts in France, where the history of the country is dotted with the names of the great representatives of culture. Nor does the academic world have the moral and scientific authority which characterizes British universities. And journalists, to choose another example, lack the power conferred on them in the USA.

The historical narrative offered in support of this analysis, by Carla Pasquinelli, also emphasizes the peculiarly unfavorable conditions in which Italian intellectuals have operated. The 1980s saw "the beginning of the end of Italian exceptionalism," but even now, she argues, "the Italian professional market does not offer intellectuals the same possibilities and benefits found in the United States and in the majority of Western countries."[20] Obviously, Pasquinelli's claims are disputable, but they provide a striking example of the transposition of themes familiar from the English case, not just to a quite different setting, but to one normally assumed to offer the strongest contrast where the position of intellectuals is concerned. Reading it, one begins to wonder – at least one should begin to wonder – whether the doubts and exhortations expressed here, wholly familiar as they are in their tone as well as assumptions, should not be seen at least as much as expressive of a more general logic as of a peculiarly Italian situation. And this, it seems to me, is borne out in the present case by Pasquinelli's emphasis on the contrast between the role of the intellectual and that of "the expert" and on the need to transcend the limitations of "specialization." These are, it turns out, the terms in which every society phrases its laments about how *its* intellectuals fall short of some flourishing condition presumed to be enjoyed by intellectuals elsewhere. The very similarity of the laments surely indicates a shared structural logic rather than a uniquely national condition.

One final comparative perspective, and one with special relevance to this volume, is provided by the traditional perception of the place of intellectuals in the United States. For my, relatively limited, purposes, the place to start may be with the long-standing American tradition of simultaneously lamenting the marginal or despised status of intellectuals in the United States and envying their (supposed) position in England. As with the corresponding English tradition, these attitudes have deep roots, going back long before the term "intellectuals" established itself in American English. The representation of American society upon which such attitudes depended was, in essence, that made almost commonplace by foreign commentators such as Tocqueville, Arnold, and their successors: America as the first "new," wholly created society, lacking tradition, aristocracy, culture, and so on. "Democratic" was a key term in Tocqueville's profound analysis, "philistinism" a recurring term in Arnold's much more off-hand and opportunistic remarks. The native tradition of commentary domesticated these accounts in various ways, now emphasizing the dominance of the business ethic, now the appeal of populism; at times worrying over the low level of the political class, at others taking pride in the practical bent of the growing number of educational institutions; sometimes celebrating the unparalleled regional and ethnic diversity, sometimes deploring the lack of a dominant capital in which political, social, and cultural elites overlapped. For much of the nineteenth century, what Santayana was later to label "the genteel tradition" cultivated its ties to old England while increasingly acknowledging that their own ever-growing country was less and less inclined to let its cultural style be entirely dictated by the upper class of New England. All this meant that subsequent writing on these topics in America was to be at least as deeply imbued as the corresponding literature in England with a sense of the distinctiveness of the country's history and cultural situation, one that was supposed to be *uniquely* inhospitable to those whom the twentieth century was increasingly to term "intellectuals."

However simplistic or partial these views were (and each element was subsequently to generate a revisionist industry of its own), they colored the perception of the comparative position of thinkers and men of letters in nineteenth-century America compared to their counterparts in Victorian Britain. And this contrast long survived the period in which it was first formulated:

> To an American looking backward, the English intellectual of the Victorian era appears as *the* intellectual, one who could lay claim to the title and estate by what might almost be regarded as the principle of legitimacy – the unimpeachable right of descent. . . . The English intellectual had, until very recently, that additional mark of legitimacy which stamped a career that was at the same time dignified, remunerative, and socially influential – a unique combination of virtues to which Herr Professor, the feuilletoniste, and the American college teacher could never aspire.[21]

This comes from the middle of the twentieth century, and again, I leave aside the question of the accuracy or persuasiveness of this view in order simply to point out how the three types singled out by Himmelfarb for the purposes of making national contrasts differ from the three cited earlier from Pasquinelli's article about Italy. Here, the influential and well-connected English intellectual is contrasted with the *less* exalted condition of the German professor, the French essayist or journalist, and the American academic; in Pasquinelli's case, the relatively low status of the politically dependent Italian intellectual is contrasted with "the great representatives of culture" in France, "the moral and scientific authority" of academics in Britain, and the "powerful" journalists in the United States. As so often, the outcome of comparisons turns on the choice of what to compare, and that choice in turn reflects one's pre-existing sense of the contrasts. For, the truth, surely, is that Parnassus is always elsewhere, and that even when one finally arrives on its slopes, one finds that the gods have always already gone. But perhaps where intellectuals are concerned, the mistake lies in thinking of them as gods in the first place.

## V

Many years ago Raymond Williams wrote an influential essay entitled "Culture is ordinary." Perhaps it's time that someone wrote an essay entitled "Intellectuals are ordinary." "Ordinary" in the sense that they are indeed part of the cultural landscape of all complex societies; ordinary in the sense that it is neither unthinkable nor shocking to recognize that the noun 'intellectual" might regularly be applied to some of one's friends or one's colleagues or even, in some circumstances, oneself; and, above all, ordinary in the sense that carrying on the activities characteristic of intellectuals should not be seen as exceptionally heroic or exceptionally difficult or exceptionally glamorous or – and I realize that here I particularly lay myself open to misunderstanding – even exceptionally important. Important, yes, but not exceptionally important.

So, perhaps it's time to stop thinking of intellectuals as Other People, and to try not to fall so easily into the related tabloid habits of demonizing and pedestalling. Some intellectuals are PLUs (People Like Us), some aren't. But isn't that precisely what we should expect, once we get away from the stereotypes? Speaking for myself, I would frankly acknowledge that I drink a certain amount of fruit juice, I'm undeniably a sex maniac, if running counts as a "nature cure" then I'm a quack, and if it didn't risk being presumptuous I'd be pleased to be described as a feminist. It's true that I'm not much of a nudist, sandal-wearer, Quaker, or pacifist, but, hey, no one's perfect. And *that*, I have been suggesting, is true of other intellectuals as well.

## Notes

1  This essay, it will be clear, was initially written for oral delivery; apart from adding references for quotations, I have here retained this original form. The essay is thus provocative by design and brief by necessity: the issues touched upon will be discussed at greater length in a forthcoming book, *The Question of Intellectuals* (Penguin Press).

2  Gollancz's "Foreword" is reprinted as an appendix to *The Road to Wigan Pier* in Peter Davison (ed.), *The Complete Works of George Orwell*, 20 vols (London: Secker, 1998), V, quotation p. 221. Hereafter references to this magnificent edition will be by volume and page number.

3  Orwell to Gollancz, 9 May 1937; XI, pp. 22–3.

4  *Wigan Pier*, V, p. 161.

5  Friedrich Nietzsche, *Twilight of the Idols* (1889), R.J. Hollingdale, trans. (Harmondsworth, UK: Penguin, 1968), p. 92.

6  *Wigan Pier*, V, p. 162; cf. editorial note, X, p. 493.

7  It is unnecessary to provide references for such a familiar and widespread cultural pattern, but just to indicate how little danger there is, alas, of its

coming to an end one may refer to the most recent soufflé of journalistic cliché and half-truth on the subject, Andrew Anthony, "What are We Thinking of?," *The Observer*, Review (July 8, 2001), pp. 1–2.

8   For a fuller statement of this argument, see Stefan Collini, "Before Another Tribunal: The Idea of the 'Non-specialist Public'," in *English Pasts: Essays in History and Culture* (Oxford: Oxford University Press, 1999), pp. 305–25.

9   "Communications: The British Intellectuals," *Encounter*, 4 (1955): 68–72.

10   Both quotations from David Cannadine, *G.M. Trevelyan: A Life in History* (London: HarperCollins, 1992), pp. 44, 45.

11   R.H. Tawney, "Social History and Literature," in *The Radical Tradition: Twelve Essays on Politics, Education, and Literature*, Rita Hinden, ed. (London: Allen and Unwin, 1964), pp. 183–209, quotation p. 184.

12   Edward W. Said, *Representations of the Intellectual: The 1993 Reith Lectures* (New York: Pantheon, 1994).

13   Timothy Garton Ash, see Perry Anderson, "A Ripple of the Polonaise," *London Review of Books*, 21/23 (November 25, 1999): 3–10 (quotation p. 8).

14   Karl Mannheim, *Ideology and Utopia* (London: Routledge, [1936] 1960), pp. 9–10.

15   There are, of course, relevant cultural and political differences among the countries that make up "Britain," but on this as on other topics usage slides between making such discriminations on some occasions and using "Britain" and "England" more or less interchangeably on others.

16   Anthony Hartley, *A State of England* (London: Hutchinson, 1963), p. 25.

17   Richard Hofstadter, *Anti-Intellectualism in American Life* (New York: Vintage, 1963), pp. 19–20.

18   Leonard Woolf, "G.E. Moore," *Encounter*, 12 (1959): 68–9.

19   Philippe Bradfer, "Quelques remarques sur les intellectuels en Belgique," in Marie-Christine Granjon, Nicole Racine, and Michel Trebitsch (eds.), *Histoire comparée des intellectuels* (Paris: IHTP, 1997), pp. 19–22; other quotations pp. 31, 37, 107 (my translation).

20   Carla Pasquinelli, "From Organic to Neo-corporatist Intellectuals: The Changing Relations between Italian Intellectuals and Political Power," *Media, Culture and Society*, 17 (1995): 413–25, quotations pp. 418, 414.

21   Gertrude Himmelfarb, "Mr Stephen and Mr Ramsay: The Victorian as Intellectual," *The Twentieth Century*, 152 (1952): 513–25, quotations pp. 514–15.

# Index

Index

# Index

# Index

# Index

# Index